Language Functions Revisited

Theoretical and empirical bases for
language construct definition across
the ability range

Also in this series:

Criterial Features in L2 English
John A Hawkins and Luna Filipović

Language Functions Revisited

Theoretical and empirical bases for language construct definition across the ability range

Anthony Green
University of Bedfordshire

with contributions from
John L M Trim
and Roger Hawkey

CAMBRIDGE
UNIVERSITY PRESS

CAMBRIDGE UNIVERSITY PRESS
Cambridge, New York, Melbourne, Madrid, Cape Town,
Singapore, São Paulo, Delhi, Mexico City

Cambridge University Press
The Edinburgh Building, Cambridge CB2 8RU, UK

www.cambridge.org
Information on this title: www.cambridge.org/9780521184991

First published 2012

Printed in the United Kingdom at the University Press, Cambridge

A catalogue record for this publication is available from the British Library

Library of Congress Cataloging-in-Publication data

Green, Anthony, 1966–
    Language functions revisited : theoretical and empirical bases for language
construct definition across the ability range / Anthony Green ; with contributions
from John L M Trim and Roger Hawkey.
      p. cm -- (English profile series; 2)
    Includes bibliographical references and index.
1. Language and languages—Ability testing. 2. Language acquisition. I. Trim,
J. L. M. (John Leslie Melville) II. Hawkey, Roger. III. Title. IV. Series.

    P53.4.G74 2011
    420.1'9--dc22

ISBN 978-0-521-18499-1

Contents

Acknowledgements	viii
List of abbreviations	x
Series Editors' note	xii
Preface	**xxi**
John L M Trim	
Some earlier developments in the description of levels of language	
proficiency	xxi
Scales and levels in modern languages	xxi
The Council of Europe modern languages projects	xxiii
The European Unit/Credit Scheme for Modern Languages	xxv
The Threshold Level	xxvii
Beyond the Threshold: an emerging system of levels	xxix
The Common European Framework of Reference for Languages	
(CEFR)	xxxiv
Introduction	1
Section 1: Theoretical Bases	
Chapter 1	
The theoretical foundations for functions in the Council of Europe	
modern languages projects and the Common European Framework	
of Reference for Languages	7
What are language functions in the CEFR?	7
A brief history of functions	11
Linguistic theory and the Council of Europe agenda	17
Communicative competence in applied linguistics and language	
education	19
Importance for functions	19
Functional progression between levels: what does the Council of	
Europe have to say?	29
Functional progression between levels: what do functionalist	
approaches to second language acquisition and interlanguage	
pragmatics have to say?	34
Conclusions	37

Chapter 2
Can Do statements as instructional objectives 39
Behavioural objectives 41
The proficiency movement 43
Use of behavioural objectives and proficiency scale descriptors
    in the CEFR 46
CEFR scale categories 50
Alternative approaches 61
Tension between purposes 69
Conclusions 70

Section 2: Empirical Bases

Chapter 3
Pedagogical perspectives on progression in functional abilities 75
Gathering higher level descriptions 77
Functional progression in language learning materials 78
    Methodology 78
    Locating materials 79
The relationship between the surveyed material and the CEFR 81
    The process of classification 82
    Illustrative case studies of the treatment of functions and Can
        Do statements in the materials database 86
    Relationship to the CEFR 86
    Treatment of functions/activities 87
    Analyses 89
Activities in Can Do statements 103
    Function words in the Can Do statements 108
Conclusions 112

Chapter 4
Progression in learner input 115
What makes an English text difficult for L2 readers? 116
The input texts 119
    The analysis tools 123
Analyses 124
Text characteristics 124
    Lexical and syntactic resources 124
Discourse characteristics 132
Nature of information 134
Content knowledge 135
Conclusions 142

Section 3: Connections in the English Profile

Chapter 5
Proposing a Can Do model for the English Profile   147

Chapter 6
Navigating the English Profile   159
Conclusions: functional progression   171

References and further reading   174

Appendices
Appendix A: C1 level Can Do specifications for Profile Deutsch   187
Appendix B: Functional progression in the T-series   203
Appendix C: Draft illustrative generative Can Do statements for the
              C levels   227

Author index   245
Subject index   248
Speech acts and functions index   253
Text type index   254
Levels index   255
Product index   256

Acknowledgements

I would like to thank the following: the series editors, Nick Saville and Mike Milanovic for initiating this strand of work and for commissioning the volume, and also for their insights, encouragement and support; Roger Hawkey, Annette Capel, Angeliki Salamoura and Luna Filipović for their invaluable feedback on the original manuscript; John Savage for his meticulous attention to detail; my colleagues at the Centre for Research in English Language Learning and Assessment, University of Bedfordshire – Cyril Weir, Stephen Bax, Liz Hamp-Lyons, Vladimir Žegarac and Fumiyo Nakatsuhara – for their suggestions; my family – my wife, Sachiyo and children, Richard, Maria and Alexander – for their forbearance and all of the many colleagues at Cambridge University Press, University of Cambridge ESOL Examinations, the Cambridge University Research Centre for English and Applied Linguistics and other partners and participants in English Profile around the world, far too numerous to list here, who have given me ideas and asked helpful questions. I would especially like to thank John Trim, both for contributing the preface to this volume and for his always perceptive guidance on the work of the English Profile.

I should like to dedicate this book to my mother, Sheila.

Abbreviations

ACTFL	American Council on the Teaching of Foreign Languages
AILA	Association Internationale de Linguistique Appliquée (International Association of Applied Linguistics)
ALTE	The Association of Language Testers in Europe
ASLPR	The Australian Second Language Proficiency Ratings Scale
ASTP	Army Specialised Language Programme (US)
AWEMAP	A Worldwide ELT EFL ESL EAL LEP ESOL Assessment Scales and Test Mapping Project
BBC	British Broadcasting Corporation
BEC	Business English Certificates (Cambridge ESOL)
BICS	Basic interpersonal communication skills
BNC	British National Corpus
CA	Conversation analysis
CAE	Certificate in Advanced English (Cambridge ESOL) (CAE now known as Cambridge English: Advanced)
CALP	Cognitive academic language proficiency
CCSARP	Cross-Cultural Speech Act Realization Project
CEFR	The Common European Framework of Reference for Languages
CERCLES	Confédération Européenne des Centres de Langues de l'Enseignement Supérieur (European Confederation of Language Centres in Higher Education)
CIEP	Centre international d'études pédagogiques (international pedagogical research centre)
CILT	The (UK) National Centre for Languages
CLB	The Canadian Language Benchmarks
CLC	The Cambridge Learner Corpus
CP	Cooperative principle
CPE	Certificate of Proficiency in English (Cambridge ESOL) (CPE now known as Cambridge English: Proficiency)
CSWE	Certificates in Spoken and Written English
DCT	Discourse completion task
EALTA	European Association for Language Testing and Assessment
ECML	European Centre for Modern Languages
ELC	European Language Council
ELP	European Language Portfolio

ELT	English Language Teaching
EP	English Profile
ESL	English as a Second Language
ESU	English Speaking Union
ETS	Educational Testing Service (US)
EU	European Union
FCE	First Certificate in English (Cambridge ESOL)
	(FCE now known as Cambridge English: First)
FINGS	Finland, Ireland, Norway, Greece and Sweden (a group of ALTE member organisations contributing to the development of 'Breakthrough' specifications for the relevant languages)
FSI	Foreign Service Institute
GEPT	General English Proficiency Test (LTTC Taiwan)
GESE	Graded Examinations in Spoken English (Trinity College, London)
GOML	Graded Objectives in Modern Languages
HKCEE	Hong Kong Certificate of Education Examination
IBT	Internet based test
ICFE	International Certificate in Financial English (Cambridge ESOL)
IELTS	International English Language Testing System (British Council, IELTS Australia, Cambridge ESOL)
ILEC	International Legal English Certificate (Cambridge ESOL)
ILR	Interagency Language Roundtable (US)
KET	Key English Test (Cambridge ESOL) (KET now known as Cambridge English: Key for schools)
KPG	Kratiko Pistopiitiko Glossomathias (The State Certificate of Language Proficiency, Greece)
LTTC	The Language Training and Testing Centre (Taiwan)
MEXT	(Japanese) Ministry of Education, Culture, Sports, Science and Technology
NATO	North Atlantic Treaty Organization
PET	Preliminary English Test (Cambridge ESOL) (PET now known as Cambridge English: Preliminary for schools)
PNG	Papua New Guinea
RLD	Reference Level Description
SLA	Second language acquisition
STANAG	Standardization Agreement (NATO)
T-series	The series of specifications developed by Jan van Ek and John Trim for the Council of Europe comprising Breakthrough, Waystage, Threshold and Vantage.

Series Editors' note

Like the first volume in the English Profile Studies series (Hawkins and Filipović 2012), this companion volume sets out to define 'criterial features', that is the specific properties of learner language that characterise L2 English at each of the CEFR levels. Together these two volumes summarise the outcomes of the first phase of the English Profile (EP) Programme which is an interdisciplinary project to develop Reference Level Descriptions (RLDs) for English to accompany the CEFR. See www.englishprofile.org. Both volumes seek to contextualise the EP research within the development of the CEFR itself as an evolving framework of reference dating back to the 1960s. A summary of the EP Programme and its objectives is set out below.

As the title suggests, Green's volume re-examines the use of language functions in defining language constructs across the ability range and in setting learning objectives which are sensitive to the proficiency level of learners. The book is in three main sections: Theoretical Bases; Empirical Bases; and Connections in the English Profile. He also provides readers with a comprehensive bibliography and suggested further reading, together with three helpful appendices illustrating Can Do statements which are discussed in the text.

In Section One he provides an accessible account of the *functional-notional approach* which now underpins the CEFR and which led to the use of Can Do statements within its Global Scale and bank of Illustrative Scales.

In keeping with the empirical stance taken within the EP Programme generally, in Section Two Green describes the empirical basis of his work. He includes here an account of the data collection and consultation which has informed his research, especially the data collected in the form of language learning materials aligned to the CEFR which are in use around the world. Through the EP Network (see below), the research team also consulted widely on the development of the new Can Dos for the C levels which are reported in this volume (Chapters 5 and 6).

In Section Three, Green suggests practical ways in which the existing Can Do statements in the CEFR can be expanded and refined with specific reference to English. His aim is to achieve better coverage across the top half of the framework (levels B2 to C2) with reference to contexts of use which are particularly relevant to learners of English.

In contrast to the first volume in the series which focuses on writing (*output*), this strand of the EP programme is primarily concerned with the *input* to the learners: in other words, the functions at each level of the CEFR that provide the learning objectives as part of a communicative syllabus, and the reading texts which are judged to be suitable for different levels and which are presented to the learners for pedagogic purposes. Green covers this topic in Chapter 4 in which he discusses progression in learner input and poses the question '*what makes English text difficult for L2 learners?*'. In answering this question, he discusses how software tools (such as Coh-metrix, Wordsmith Tools and RANGE) can be used to analyse and select texts which are suitable for specific levels and he illustrates his discussion with concrete examples. In keeping with the intention of the volume as a whole, his aim is to provide readers with practical suggestions and guidance which can usefully inform their own practice.

The revised English Profile Can Do statements which Green proposes in Section 3 are informed by a range of sources including: the CEFR illustrative scales themselves, international textbooks, examination handbooks, curriculum and syllabus documents sourced by EP partner organisations (e.g. the British Council, English UK), *the bank of descriptors for self-assessment in European Language Portfolios* (Lenz and Schneider 2004), online publications such as test specifications, proficiency scales, etc., and other materials from educational contexts (not publicly available).

As well as providing an account of the research undertaken within the EP programme, this volume makes a significant contribution by taking an historical perspective, clarifying the origins of the functional-notional approach and its impact on the CEFR. Green himself provides a detailed review of the relevant literature covering the concept of language functions and the use of Can Do statements for setting instructional objectives. In addition, the Preface to the volume provides a unique point of view from John Trim, coordinator of the authoring team which produced the CEFR and Director of the Council of Europe's Modern Languages Project from 1971 to 1996. Together with David Wilkins, he was responsible for initiating the project which led to the publication of the *Threshold level* in 1975.

Trim provides a comprehensive, eyewitness account of the history of the Modern Language projects and outlines the thinking which ultimately led to the publication of the CEFR 2001. He characterises the English Profile programme as the latest phase in a process of evolution and development which began many years earlier. By the 1970s it had become apparent that a *situational approach* which had caught on in some quarters in the 1960s could not provide a sound basis for developing language syllabi (see Wilkins 1976). The Council of Europe team felt that the way forward was to identify a *common core* of language relevant to all learners across many contexts or situations; this led to the Threshold concept and the 'action oriented' approach later found in the CEFR. The aim was to specify the functions that the target group of learners needed to accomplish through language based on analyses of their most relevant communicative needs. It had also become clear by the mid-1970s that it was not possible to divide up language learning into discrete modules, as in the proposed Unit-Credit system, and that the *notional-functional* syllabus associated with the work of Wilkins seemed to have greater potential.

Wilkins (1976:1) recommended that the meanings that learners might want to express should be organising principle, with grammatical structures as the exponents for realising those meanings. In his view, the *notions* (i.e. semantico-grammatical categories) and *functions* provided a rationale for selecting 'the language to which the learner will be exposed and which we will expect him to acquire'. As Green points out, the approach was clearly influenced by Hymes (1972) and a conceptualization of *communicative competence* which comprises both a 'linguistic' and a 'sociolinguistic' element. The sociolinguistic dimension includes the dynamic interaction that occurs between the context and the discourse produced. The interaction between context and the cognitive processes of the learner underpins a *socio-cognitive approach* to learning, teaching and assessment on which the CEFR itself is based, and which has been important in developing the EP programme of research.

In Green's volume this line of thinking is developed in Section 3 in which he proposes a new, *generative*, Can Do model. He highlights five elements which can be linked to specific contexts and which can lead to a more detailed and technical definition of the CEFR levels for English. These can be helpful in encouraging practitioners to develop and validate Can Do statements to fit more appropriately with their own context and purposes, while at the same time, finding a way to relate them coherently to the common framework. The component elements proposed by Green for additional Can Do statements include the following:

- The **social act** (function) or related **sequence of acts** (activity) that the learner might be expected to accomplish by means of the language.
- The **themes, topics and settings** in relation to which the learner might be expected to perform. In the CEFR, applicable themes are grouped under the four domains: educational, public, professional and personal.
- The nature of **the text** that the learner might be required **to process** as a basis for his or her own contribution or to demonstrate his or her comprehension.
- The nature of **the text** that the learner might be expected **to produce** or participate in producing to demonstrate (a specified degree of) understanding or to accomplish a task.

- The **qualities** that the learner would be expected to demonstrate in carrying out language activities (e.g. grouped under the CEFR headings of Linguistic, Pragmatic, Sociolinguistic and Strategic competences).
- Physical or social **conditions and constraints** under which the learner would be expected to perform.

A useful inventory of these refined and contextualised functions *for the C levels* is given in the Appendix C of the volume (i.e. by mode – spoken or written – and whether appropriate for interaction, production or reception).

In parallel, research is underway within the EP programme to specify language functions at the *lower levels (A1 and A2,)* and additional descriptors are being developed to specify functional objectives for younger learners of English who are studying the language as part of their school curriculum. It is hoped that this work will be reported in future EP publications.

Readers are also referred to the other appendices for useful taxonomies of Can Do statements. Appendix A provides an English translation by John Trim of the German Can Do specifications for C1 and C2 from *Profile Deutsch* (an RLD project for German); and Appendix B summaries the functional progression in the original T-series for English (A1 to B2+) – now freely available from the English Profile website.

The CEFR and the EP Programme

When the CEFR emerged in the 1990s, it was envisaged first and foremost as a planning tool which could provide a 'common language' for describing objectives, methods and assessment in language teaching, as put into practice in diverse contexts for many different languages. It was to facilitate the development of syllabuses, examinations, textbooks and teacher training programmes, and in particular, to stimulate reflection and discussion. As the CEFR authors themselves emphasise in their 'notes for the user': 'We have NOT set out to tell practitioners what to do or how to do it. We are raising questions not answering them. It is not the function of the CEFR to lay down the objectives that users should pursue or the methods they should employ.' (Council of Europe, 2001: xi)

The reference levels and original illustrative descriptors were intended to be used for the social organisation of learning and teaching within educational systems. These levels and descriptors were to provide a communication tool to assist practitioners in practical ways, having been selected and synthesised from existing scales which had been developed and operationalised in many diverse contexts. The Framework itself therefore built on the earlier specifications of level, such as Threshold, and language assessment systems in use in the 1980s and early 1990s (c.f. the work of ALTE members reported in Appendix D of the CEFR, 2001).

However, although the CEFR is an intuitively helpful descriptive scheme, in many cases the existing scales and related descriptors have **not** proved to be operationally adequate in their current form. So, while the CEFR can act as a focal point for reference purposes, it remains open to further development. In other words, the CEFR is 'not the finished article' but needs to be adapted or developed further for specific contexts (see Milanovic, 2009). John Trim succinctly points this out in the Preface:

> Overall, the apparatus of level description in the CEFR is rich and well differentiated for different purposes and users. Even so, experience over the past decade has shown that for high stakes purposes, particularly the valid and reliable calibration of qualifications and the tests and examinations leading to their award, the CEFR cannot be used as a 'stand alone' document. Indeed, it is probably impossible for any such document to be so used.

Importantly the CEFR is neutral with respect to the language being learned. This means that the users have to decide what actually gets taught or assessed in terms of the linguistic features of a specific language at each of the common reference levels.

It is partly for this reason that the Council of Europe has encouraged the development of Reference Level Descriptions (RLDs) for specific languages. RLDs seek to provide language-specific guidance for users of the Framework; the aim is to 'transpose' the Framework descriptors that characterise the competences of users/learners at a given level into the linguistic material which is specific to a given language (i.e. grammar, lexical items etc.) and considered necessary for the implementation of those competences. In providing a description of the language across all six levels, the grammatical and lexical progression which is central to the learning of that language can be addressed more precisely within the Framework concept. This is the aim of the EP Programme for English which was established by a core group of partner organisations in 2005 to address these issues. In particular it set out to make the CEFR more specifically explicit with regards to English language learning, teaching and assessment. Coordination of the programme is based at the University of Cambridge and involves interdisciplinary collaboration between several different departments. The core group was extended to create an English Profile Network from 2007 onwards.

The aims of the English Profile Programme can be summarised as follows:

- To set up and manage a collaborative programme of interdisciplinary research to produce *reference level descriptions (RLDs) for English* linked to the general principles and approaches of CEFR

- To provide a core set of reference tools for practitioners working in the field of English language education.

Several features of the English Profile distinguish it from other similar projects; these include:

- an empirical approach developed within a framework of interdisciplinary collaboration
- an agenda rooted in data-driven research
- a particular focus on the accessibility of outcomes and feedback to user groups using up-to-date technology.

Given the interdisciplinary nature of the research to be undertaken, the research teams are engaged in parallel and simultaneous investigations on a set of related research questions, observing them from different angles. The first two volumes in the English Profile Studies series bring together findings from two areas of investigation – grammar and functions.

The English Profile seeks to specify the 'salient characteristics', referred to as *criterial* features, which help to distinguish each proficiency level, from A1 to C2, of learner English. Criterial features are linguistic properties that are distinctive and characteristic of each of the levels but are not meant to capture all language features that a learner uses at a certain level. Criterial features describe changes from one level to the next and are important for both practitioners and theoreticians to know about. This approach is dealt with comprehensively in Volume one of the series, Hawkins and Filipović (2012), and a number of other accompanying publications (Hawkins and Buttery 2009, 2010; Salamoura and Saville 2009, 2010).

The *English Vocabulary Profile* (previously known and referred to in this Volume as the *English Profile Wordlists* (EPW)) is another outcome which complements the work on grammar and functions. It describes the vocabulary which learners of English are likely to know or might need to learn in developing their proficiency with reference to the CEFR. It is available as an interactive web resource, providing a huge searchable database of detailed information on the words and phrases that are appropriate for learners at each level.

The empirical approach taken within the EP for all three strands has made use of learner data, especially samples of writing and speech produced by learners at different levels of proficiency. The analysis of these data has produced informative results about the language of learners which contribute to an understanding of how the grammar and lexis of English is learned by different groups of learners. In addition to a focus on traditional grammatical and lexical features, psycholinguistic factors have also been taken into account, including the effects of language transfer (i.e. the impact of different first languages and learning contexts). This is adding to our understanding of how learners acquire English as some of the results would not be predicted from language acquisition theories or anticipated by researchers using intuition alone.

The Cambridge Learner Corpus (CLC) has been at the centre of this work to-date. This is a large learner corpus of written scripts from the Cambridge exams currently containing around 43 million words. It also has some important features which are not found in other L2 learner corpora:

- it is larger than most learner corpora (and continues to grow by around 3 million words a year)
- the scripts have been systematically categorised by their CEFR level according to reliable information captured during the examination process
- a large amount of information is stored about the learners, including their L1
- parts of the corpus have been coded for errors
- the corpus has been tagged and parsed using computer programmes developed by computational linguists at the University of Cambridge Computer Laboratory (Hawkins and Buttery 2009, 2010, Briscoe, Carroll and Watson 2006).

The information about the learners allows researchers to compare different L1 learners with respect to the English that they produce; 91 first languages are represented, over 20 of which with samples large enough for quantitative analyses to be carried out. The error coding and the parsing means that sophisticated kinds of grammatical analysis are possible, in addition to lexical analysis that can be carried out with concordance software.

A spoken learner corpus, although smaller than the written one, has provided data for EP researchers in addressing the spoken dimension of learner proficiency across the levels, (see for example McCarthy, 2010 on spoken fluency in L2). Work is now underway to construct much larger corpora of spoken data which will inform future iterations of EP research, including work on the phonological dimension.

The English Vocabulary Profile (noted above) has been substantially, but not exclusively, corpus-informed. Researchers at CUP have used the *Cambridge International Corpus*, (1.2 billion-words of written and spoken English) and the CLC in combination with other source material, including classroom-based sources, wordlists from leading course books and readers, and the content of vocabulary skills books. The Vocabulary Lists for Cambridge ESOL's Key English Test (KET – A2) and Preliminary English Test (PET – B1) examinations were also used; these have been in use since 1994 and have been regularly updated to reflect language change and patterns of use. Finally, although published thirty years ago, the *Cambridge English*

Lexicon by Roland Hindmarsh (1980) also proved informative and useful for cross-referencing as it too was organised by level.

In summary, the English Profile has begun an empirically-based approach to specifying more precisely how the CEFR can be operationalised for English. We hope that this in turn will lead to better and more comprehensive illustrative descriptors that will enable the CEFR to be well understood and appropriately used wherever English is being taught or assessed around the world.

This volume, together with the others in this series, will contribute to the growing toolkit of resources that the EP is now providing.

Nick Saville and Michael Milanovic
Cambridge
March 2011

References

Briscoe, E, Carroll, J and Watson, R (2006) *The second release of the RASP system*, paper presented at COLING/ACL 2006 Interactive Presentation Sessions, Sydney, July 2006.

Council of Europe (2001) *Common European Framework of Reference for Languages: Learning, Teaching, Assessment*, Cambridge: Cambridge University Press.

Hawkins, J A and Buttery, P (2009) Using learner language from corpora to profile levels of proficiency: Insights from the English Profile Programme, in Taylor, L and Weir, C J (Eds), *Language Testing Matters: Investigating the Wider Social and Educational Impact of Assessment*, Cambridge: Cambridge University Press, 158–175.

Hawkins, J A and Buttery, P (2010) Criterial features in learner corpora: Theory and illustrations, *English Profile Journal* 1.

Hawkins, J A and Filipović, L (2012) *Criterial Features in L2 English: Specifying the Reference Levels of the Common European Framework*, English Profile volume 1, Cambridge: UCLES/Cambridge University Press.

Hindmarsh, R (1980) *Cambridge English Lexicon*, Cambridge: Cambridge University Press.

Hymes, D (1972) On communicative competence, in Pride, J and Holmes, J (Eds) *Sociolinguistics*, Harmondsworth: Penguin.

Lenz, P and Schneider, G (2004a) *A Bank of Descriptors for Self-assessment in European Language Portfolios*, Strasbourg: Council of Europe.

McCarthy, M J (2010) Rethinking spoken fluency, *Estudios de lingüística inglesa aplicada (Universidad de Sevilla)* 9, 11–29.

Milanovic, M (2009) Cambridge ESOL and the CEFR, *Research Notes* 37, 2–5.

Salamoura, A and Saville, N (2009) Criterial features across the CEFR levels: Evidence from the English Profile Programme, *Research Notes* 37, 34–40, available online at: http://www.cambridgeesol.org/rs_notes/rs_nts37.pdf

Salamoura, A, and Saville, N (2010) Exemplifying the CEFR: Criterial features of written learner English from the English Profile Programme, in Bartning, I, Maisa, M and Vedder, I, *Communicative proficiency and linguistic development:*

Intersections between SLA and language testing research, Eurosla Monographs Series (1), 101–132.

van Ek, J A (1975) *The Threshold Level in a European Unit/Credit System for Modern Language Learning By Adults*, Strasbourg: Council of Europe.

Wilkins, D (1976) *Notional Syllabuses*, Oxford: Oxford University Press.

Preface

John L M Trim, March 2010

Some earlier developments in the description of levels of language proficiency

In this introductory chapter, John Trim draws on his personal involvement throughout the period as Director of Modern Languages Projects of the Council of Europe from 1971–97, as a co-author (with Daniel Coste, Brian North and Joseph Sheils) of the Common European Framework of Reference and as co-author (with Jan van Ek) of the Threshold series. He traces the work of the Council of Europe in Modern Languages over the past four decades and the developments that culminated in the publication of the Common European Framework of Reference for Languages (CEFR) in 2001. He shows how the ethos of the Council of Europe has informed its contribution to language education and the emphasis placed on plurilingual and pluricultural competences.

The responsiveness of the Council of Europe to the needs of users is apparent throughout. The needs of users shaped the system of levels that emerged with the expansion of the Threshold series and the development of the CEFR. Continuing in the same vein, the work of the English Profile should be understood as a response to the need for greater clarity and detail in level specification that has arisen as users engage with the CEFR itself.

Scales and levels in modern languages

Interest in the scaling of second language proficiency is a recent phenomenon. Indeed, the recognition of proficiency in the use of a modern foreign language as an educational goal in itself is of no great antiquity. Apart from a longer tradition in Europe of tutoring in French as a higher social accomplishment, the teaching of modern languages in schools and universities was long in the shadow of the classical languages. Modern languages were taught with the same values, aims and methods as Latin or classical Greek. In England, the state had no role in curricular planning. Teaching was examination-led, public examinations being in the hands of boards set up by universities to certify a sound general education by the completion of lower secondary education, acting also as a filter for more specialised courses in upper secondary education leading to university entrance. Emphasis was laid on formal mastery of the written language, free from grammatical error and demonstrating a broad vocabulary gained largely through the study of literary texts. Examinations consisted of two-way translation and essay-writing; concern with spoken language, examined through oral interview and dictation, was marginal. Syllabuses were opaque. Teachers were expected to gather what was required by studying past papers, while the examiners relied on cumulative experience.

While systems of this kind lasted, the question of levels of proficiency scarcely arose. The New English Dictionary, cited by Spolsky (1999), gives the first use of 'standard' as an educational concept in 1876 to refer to the following: 'In British elementary schools: each of the recognised degrees of proficiency, as tested by examination, by which children are classified. The sixth is the highest children are ordinarily expected to gain, the seventh being intended for those who will become teachers'. As foreign languages had no place in elementary education in this now long-superseded system, it is impossible to say on what basis standards would have been defined. More recently, school certification in modern languages, in line with that of other curricular subjects, was based on age-related examinations, held at the end of successive stages of the educational process, which screened the whole population. Given that the basis of assessment was essentially error-counting and that standards were norm-referenced, the grades awarded could not be interpreted as representing successive levels or stages in the process of developing language proficiency. In any case, that process was seen in purely grammatical and lexical terms, building up command of the formal structure of the language system step by step with little or no concern for overall communicative ability along the way. Thus, when in the mid-1980s the National Foundation for Educational Research was commissioned to investigate what children in British schools were able to do in a foreign language after two years of study, the teacher representatives on the Steering Committee for German insisted that no questions be asked about the past, since by the end of the second year the past tense had not yet been reached and it would be unfair to test what had not been taught. Modern foreign language teaching in schools was so insulated from contact with the reality of language use that no genuine challenge to communicate arose. What point would there be in articulating progression in language learning except in terms of the vocabulary and the grammatical categories and structures to be introduced, drilled and tested in a logical order by given points in the children's progression through their schooling? That ordering was left to the authors and publishers of standard textbooks, which teachers relied upon to provide the backbone structure of their teaching.

It is not surprising that the early development of language proficiency scaling took place late and outside the mainstream school sector. The first essay found by Spolsky (1999) was the *Language Ability Scale* published by Columbia University in 1938, which scaled abilities from the simple to the complex in the seven areas of the curriculum: silent reading, aural comprehension, civilization, speaking, grammar, translation and free composition (Sammartino 1938). The communication requirements of the military in the Second World War introduced a note of urgency and realism into the setting of learning objectives. Perspectives and courses were short-term. It seemed obvious to identify contact situations and the communicative abilities needed to deal with them. These could be scaled and personnel selected by ability to perform the tasks required, from the simple to the complex, according to their level of knowledge, skill and experience. Where special training was necessary, it must be as brief and as concentrated as possible, setting clear objectives and using methods in line with them. Spolsky cites Kaulfers (1944) as having proposed a more elaborate performance scale for aural comprehension for the (US) Army Specialised Language Programme (ASTP), containing such items as 'can understand the ordinary questions and answers relating to the routine transactions involved in independent study abroad'. This example, cited by Spolsky, shows already a number of features of subsequent scales: a brief, seemingly simple common-sense Can-Do formulation, relying on the reader's interpretation of words like 'ordinary' and 'routine'. Though Kaulfer's scheme was never implemented (ASTP being suspended in 1944), its approach was taken up in the influential 1957 Foreign Service Institute (FSI) scale, covering speaking, reading and writing at six levels. Over a period of years, this scale came to be adopted and adapted by other official bodies as a selection tool and became widely known in international applied linguistic and EFL circles.

The Council of Europe modern languages projects

The Council of Europe was founded in 1949 as an intergovernmental organisation, intended to strengthen the still fragile European pluralist parliamentary democracies in the aftermath of the collapse of the wartime alliance, the Communist take-over in Eastern Europe and the onset of the Cold War. At the centre of its concerns were the defence of human rights and the promotion of voluntary and equal co-operation among its member states, particularly in tackling social and cultural issues. In the language field, its activity started with the adoption of the Convention on Cultural Cooperation in 1954, under which member governments undertook to promote the study of their own language and culture in other member states and to facilitate similar action by other member states on their own soil. The first initiative on languages was taken by the French Government, which was impressed by the work of the USA's Center for Applied Linguistics and proposed the setting up of a European equivalent. When this project failed to command sufficient support, a 10-year Major Project was conducted in 1963–73, covering all educational sectors. In the first years, the main thrust was at school level, strongly promoting audio-visual methodology and in higher education, encouraging the development of Applied Linguistics.

It was in this context that I first became involved as Honorary Organiser of the Second International Congress of Applied Linguistics, held in Cambridge in 1969 under the auspices of the International Association of Applied Linguistics (AILA), set up on the initiative of the Council of Europe (Trim 2000). The Council's Committee for Out-of-school Education and Cultural Development was the last to become involved in the Major Project and did so from a different perspective. Its main concern was with the organisation of adult education, long the 'Cinderella' of educational provision. Whereas school curricula can be planned on a long-term basis, assuming that the child will continue to study full-time for the duration of a course spread over several years, the conditions of adult life make continuous long-term study impractical for all but a small number of strongly committed students. For most, the changing demands of vocational and family commitments make long-term advance planning hazardous. It is more appropriate to organise adult learning on the basis of short-term courses, to be followed as circumstances allow. There is, of course, the danger that such a pattern of learning will be superficial and fragmentary, but such dilettantism can be avoided if more substantial fields of study can be modularised. The attainment of particular modules can then be accredited to the student, and accumulated to attest an increasingly wide-ranging competence in the field concerned.

The Committee was interested in experimental work along these lines carried out in the University of Nancy and in 1971 an Intergovernmental Symposium was organised to consider its possible application in the modern languages field. The Symposium was held at the invitation of the Swiss Federal Government and hosted by the Eurocentres organisation at Rüschlikon. A 'situational approach' to the construction of modules was presented. As UK delegates, David Wilkins and I met to discuss the proposal in advance. We felt the approach to be attractive, but flawed. A 'situation' was represented by a contextualised dialogue, but we felt that a dialogue could only represent a unique event. A 'situation' was rather an abstract concept underlying a class of events. We should be looking for the component features of situations and for the patterns of communicative interaction that brought them together. These features might be found in the concepts, or notions, to be expressed (whether specific to the particular situation or more general, embodied in grammatical categories and very high frequency lexis) and the functional roles of component sentences in the communication process. I presented a short paper with a preliminary classification of language functions, published as an appendix to the Symposium report (Committee for Out-of-school Education and Cultural Development 1971).

The European Unit/Credit Scheme for Modern Languages

Following the Symposium, the Division of Out-of-school Education and Cultural Development set up a working party to investigate the feasibility of a European Unit/Credit Scheme for Modern Languages in Adult Education and invited me to take on the Chairmanship. My previous involvement in adult education was partly as an examiner for the Examinations in English as a Foreign Language of the University of Cambridge Local Examinations Syndicate (UCLES, now Cambridge Assessment) and particularly as author and methodological adviser for the broadcast language teaching programmes of the BBC in German, Italian and French. I had also served on the National Council for Educational Technology and been much influenced by the approach of its Director, Tony Becher. He held that the proper contribution of the Council to educational advance should lie less in the development of audio-visual aids than in the introduction of the concept of systems development from industrial organisation into educational thinking and practice.

Throughout my 25 years of working in the successive modern languages projects of the Council of Europe I attempted to promote, develop and refine this approach. Administrative planning, materials development and provision, teacher training, teaching, learning and assessment should be seen as interrelated aspects of one overall system. To ensure its coherence and efficiency, the many often independent agents and decision-takers involved should engage in direct interpersonal communication with each other, so as to become increasingly aware of their own distinctive role in the learning process in relation to that of others, coming to share common aims and to pursue clearly stated common objectives. The clear definition and common acceptance of learning objectives was seen as the central element in the system. Objectives should be based on: i) a careful assessment of the communicative needs and motivations of the learners concerned, ii) an appreciation of their relevant characteristics as learners (age, educational level, prior knowledge, etc.), iii) estimation of the human and material resources and of the time available, iv) an appraisal of the effects of the social context of learning. Once worthwhile, appropriate and feasible objectives have been agreed, suitable teaching materials and methods can be selected leading to their attainment and its assessment, attestation and certification.

In the Working Party, our first consideration was given to agreeing the fundamental principles and long-term aims of the project. In doing so, we had to bear in mind its context in the overarching aims of the Council of Europe: the defence and strengthening of human rights and pluralist democracy, improved mutual understanding and acceptance, maintenance of linguistic and cultural diversity, and voluntary co-operation among the peoples across a plurilingual and pluricultural continent. We saw our work as a contribution to the furthering of these aims. Accordingly, we did not set out to promote language learning simply as an end in itself, though some of the most gifted learners might see it that way. From our perspective, language learning was a necessary means for direct interpersonal face-to-face communication among people at all levels of society across the boundaries that had in the past separated them, producing prejudice, stereotyping and mutual hostility leading to the horrors of the two World Wars and now dividing East from West in a small but fragmented continent.

As we started work, the relaxation of restrictions on travel in our area and the dramatic improvement and cheapening of the means of communication of all kinds were opening horizons to all classes of the population. As our work progressed, socio-economic and political developments were making educational and vocational mobility a reality for more and more people. We believed that the strength of democracy lay with the independence of thought and action, combined with a strong sense of socially responsible citizenship, of all the people. We therefore sought to encourage language learning of a kind which would enable ordinary people to travel independently in a foreign language environment, not only transacting the business of everyday survival, but also making human contact with ordinary people they met, exchanging information and opinions, expressing and reacting to emotions and wherever possible developing good working relations. In this way, mutual understanding would be built on a solid basis in experience. We also sought to develop self-awareness and self-confidence in learners by making them more conscious of objectives and methods of learning, better able to exercise informed choice and to steer their own learning.

It will be seen that this approach did not attach great importance to defining a fixed set of levels through which all learners should pass. In principle, each learning situation should be analysed in its own terms, objectives set and pursued, the outcome assessed and the results fed back into the system, which should be as transparent as possible. We were, in fact, rather sceptical with regard to the concept of 'level'. The word seems to imply an even development of knowledge and skills, which not only is in conflict with the gearing of objectives to the distinctive needs of the individual learner, but is also incompatible with psycholinguistic reality. Using heuristic and recognition skills, any learner can understand much more than he or she can produce, especially if we compare reading, with access to reference materials under no time pressure, with holding a conversation in real time. There is also a tendency for the definition of low levels to become catalogues of incompetence and for high levels to be statements of an ideal proficiency unattainable under normal conditions by any but a tiny élite.

Of the scaled objectives available in 1971, most combined a sequencing of grammatical categories and structures, necessarily language-specific and unsuitable for a pan-European scheme, with vocabulary lists compiled on a lexicostatistical basis. This basis seemed to us suspect on a number of grounds. For one, with the corpora then available, statistical stability was reached only with a small number of words with grammatical functions. Otherwise, frequency varied widely with the nature of the texts on which the corpus was based. Another objection was the inverse relation between predictability and information value. Retaining only the high frequency words in a sentence, one may be left with: 'there's a big . . . .up there on that . . . .', which is much less informative than '. . . .eagle . . . . cliff-top.' Again, the polysemy of high frequency words, attested by the space given to them in major dictionaries, means that a word (e.g. 'like') cannot be taken as learned when first introduced in a course in one particular context. If different word uses are carefully distinguished, as is now being done in the English Profile vocabulary programme (see Capel 2010), their position in a frequency ranking may be greatly changed.

Level descriptions on a functional or Can Do basis also appeared to present some difficulties. If kept brief and 'user-friendly', easily understandable at first reading, they may be incomplete, leaving some criteria unstated, varying in this respect from one level to another, and tend to rely on qualitative adverbials such as 'simple', 'everyday', 'routine', 'predictable' etc., which remain undefined and capable of widely different interpretation. If, on the other hand, an attempt is made to make them fully explicit, they risk becoming unwieldy and rigidly prescriptive, leaving little or no room for flexibility, and may still be equivocal at some point. There was also the problem of how many levels should be differentiated. Practice varied from Cambridge's two to Trinity College's twelve. There seemed to be no logical basis for the segmentation of a continuous process. For these reasons we did not propose to base the unit/credit scheme on a closed system of defined levels.

The Threshold Level

We did, however, think that it might be possible to identify one natural break, which might be characterised as a 'level'. In the early learning of a second language, learners have only a severely limited, fragmented knowledge and ability to use the language, largely limited to the particular structures and vocabulary to which they have been exposed. It might be that at some point in the process these bits and pieces cohere into an overall communicative competence, with which the learner can cope, albeit in a very simple fashion, with the general demands of daily life. We termed this point, at which a communicative threshold seemed to be crossed, the 'Threshold Level'. We felt it to be of particular importance for our aim of making large numbers of European citizens able to travel as independent agents in a foreign environment.

In drafting the Threshold Level specification we drew upon a number of sources. We had before us the preliminary studies carried out by Richterich,

Wilkins, van Ek and myself (Trim Richterich, van Ek & Wilkins 1980), with a possible integrative framework developed by Klaus Bung (Bung 1973), who held the only research post to be funded in the project by the Council of Europe. Under the influence of J R Firth, I had for many years devoted the opening lecture of my university course in linguistics to an overview of the role of language in all aspects of human life and the relation of form to function. We were aware of Del Hymes' (1972) work on communicative competence and Austin's (1962) *How To Do Things With Words*. Anthony Peck brought the *Sprechintentionen* from the Nuffield Foundation's *Vorwärts!* project and Svanta Hjelmström the functional descriptors from the Linköping multimedia distance course *In the Air*. We made good use of a small book by H E Palmer and F G Blandford (1924) *Everyday Sentences in Spoken English,* which was organised on a functional basis and had been used for many years in UCL summer courses for teaching English intonation. In a 3-day workshop we drew up long unordered lists of categories for the various components of Bung's model, which were distributed by the Council of Europe to participants in the Rüschlikon Symposium and were warmly received by them, particularly by the German, Austrian and Swiss *Volkshochschulen*. Jan van Ek was then granted study leave by the Netherlands Government to rework and reorganise this raw material into shape as a coherent whole. The resultant work: *The Threshold Level in a European unit/credit system for Modern language learning by adults* was then published by the Council of Europe in 1975.

The descriptive model as elaborated by van Ek and further discussed in Chapter 1 has the following components:

1. The **situations** in which the language will be used.
2. The **topics** that will be dealt with.
3. The **language activities** in which the learner will engage.
4. The **language functions** the learner will fulfil.
5. The **behavioural specification** of what the learner will be able to do with respect to each topic.
6. The **general notions** the learner will be able to handle.
7. The **specific topic-related notions the learner** will be able to handle.
8. The **language forms** the learner will be able to use.
9. The **degree of skill** with which the learner will be able to perform.

This model and the way of thinking about the specification of language learning which it embodied rapidly became well-known, making *The Threshold Level* perhaps the most influential work of its time. It was taken up with particular enthusiasm by the EFL community, affecting all its agencies: syllabus guidelines, textbook writing and publication, teacher training, language testing, examination and qualification. The components which were most widely assimilated into standard practice were the language functions and specific notions, so that the approach became known as 'notional-functional'. The clarity of their structure, comprehensiveness and concrete practicality made them immediately useful in providing a backbone structure for textbooks and tests and spoke directly to felt user needs. The general notional component, which was more abstract and very largely expounded by grammatical classes and categories, received much less attention, leaving the false impression that the approach neglected the learning of grammar all told.

Beyond the Threshold: an emerging system of levels

The success of *The Threshold Level* made it the centre of attention and the starting point for further development for the next 15 years. It immediately caught the eye of the committee dealing with school education, which commissioned van Ek to compile *The Threshold Level for Modern Language Learning in Schools,* published by Longman in 1976. The main thrust of the successive Council of Europe projects in the language field in the eighties and nineties was to generalise the use of the model and the communicative approach to language learning, teaching and assessment across Europe. During this time 72 international workshops for teacher trainers were held in more than 20 countries and versions of the Threshold Level were produced for some 25 European languages. The first was for French: the other official language of the Council. Our French colleagues at Centre de recherche et d'étude pour la diffusion du français (CREDIF) were happy to move on from *Le Français Fondamental*, with its concentration on grammar and lexis, but feared that the concreteness and ubiquity of *The Threshold Level* would cause it to be established as *the* universal objective for early language learning, rather than as the exemplification of a model, addressed to one defined audience, which its author intended. This would prejudice the flexible application of the principles of learner-centred, needs-based provision central to the Working Party's ideology. They were therefore not content to limit themselves to an exact reproduction of van Ek's specification, but went on to attempt a much fuller account of the resources of the French language at a modest level, obliging users to make a selection according to their appreciation of the learning/teaching situation for a particular group of learners (Coste, Courtillon, Ferenczi, Martins-Batter & Pape 1976).

Despite the richness of *Un Niveau-seuil* (note the use of the indefinite article *un,* disclaiming unique status) and the valuable innovations it contained, it did not make the same impact, perhaps because of the greatly increased demands on the knowledge and skills of the users. Most teams developing Threshold Level descriptions for other languages followed the van Ek model, though they were encouraged to make such changes as they felt appropriate and innovations were welcomed. One innovation, which quickly became accepted into the normal pattern, was introduced by the German team in *Kontakte*, which attempted to draw upon both the van Ek and the CREDIF models. This was the functional category: 'organisation of discourse and communication repair' (Baldegger, Müller & Schneider. 1980).

The Threshold Level was produced as a concrete exemplification of an objective for a defined class of learner, based on an appreciation of their communicative needs. In spite of its title, it was not conceived as one of a set number of levels spanning the full range from absolute beginner to the highest level attainable by viable numbers of learners in adult education. The scheme presented in 1977 concentrated rather on the principles and procedures for the production of creditable modules, though some approach to a possible future system of defined levels was offered, exemplified by a scale of social communication skills I drew up and a more complete set by David Wilkins, which appeared as an appendix to the report.

The Threshold Level model did in fact develop into a more comprehensive series of specifications at successive levels, but it did so piecemeal, in response to user demand, not as a scheme designed as a whole. The first extension came about in connection with the Anglo-German broadcast-led multimedia course *Follow Me!*, which proposed to take the Threshold Level as its objective. Experience in the Viennese *Volkshochschulen* had shown that it could not be reached by the majority of adult education students in one year. A reduced objective was needed. J van Ek, L G Alexander and A Fitzpatrick therefore produced a cut-down version of the Threshold Level: *Waystage,* not then termed a level, since Threshold was believed to be the minimum able to constitute an across-the-board level of proficiency. In fact, one consequence of the Threshold Level being produced as a pioneering exemplification of an innovative model and not as part of a defined series of levels was a temptation to include more than the bare minimum. The authors of *Waystage* found that almost all the notional-functional coverage could be maintained and reduction achieved by eliminating redundancy in exponence.

In the 1980s, demand grew from major adult education institutions for a 'third level' for students wishing to progress beyond the basic competence in the language of everyday transactions and social interaction. This demand, resisted for some years, required a re-examination of the concept of 'level' and of the nature and scope of communicative objectives. What impelled students to continue with one language beyond Threshold, rather than to add a similar competence in another language? That would be more in line with the Council's promotion of European plurilingualism!

The answer might in some cases be in order to gain more advanced professional or vocational qualifications, but more generally in adult education we felt that it would probably be to overcome a sense of severe limitation, of being obliged to say what one could say rather than what one wanted to say, the sense of being unable to express oneself as a complete human being. This meant that at a higher level progress would be increasingly qualitative rather than quantitative, not merely adding to the range of functions (which at Threshold was in any case reasonably comprehensive, if at a simple and straightforward level) and an ever larger number of specific concrete notions, but also enriching the concept of communicative competence to take account of broader human, social and cultural factors. A series of studies was undertaken and published (Trim, Holec, Coste & Porcher 1984), on the basis of which van Ek produced a major study in two volumes: ('Scope' and 'Levels') on the definition of language learning objectives (van Ek 1985–86).

The way was now clear for a number of further developments. First, the existing *Threshold Level* and *Waystage* descriptions were revised and extended, so that 'those components of communicative ability which particularly allow it to be related to a wider educational context are identified and explicitly incorporated into the objective' (van Ek & Trim 1998b:6). The descriptions now included the following additional components:

- discourse strategies
- a socio cultural component
- compensation strategies
- a 'learning to learn' component
- a systematic grammatical summary
- selected intonation patterns.

This move from a highly specific pragmatic objective designed to meet the practical transactional and personal needs of a defined constituency to a more general educational objective was taken further in the definition of a higher level objective, though without losing sight of everyday purposes and interpersonal communication. This work was undertaken by Van Ek and Trim (2001) and given the title *Vantage,* signifying a somewhat higher viewpoint conferring an advantage to the learner. *Vantage* Level went beyond *Threshold* Level particularly in the following respects:

- the refinement of functional and general notional categories and exponents, notably in the expression of emotions and the conduct of discussion
- a considerable enlargement of concrete vocabulary in thematic areas relevant to the learner's developing needs and interests, making use of reference sources of all kinds
- recognition and limited control of important register varieties, formal and colloquial

- ability to understand and produce longer and more complex utterances, at both sentence and discourse levels
- increased range and control of goal-directed conversation strategies, allowing learners to converse in a more flexible and natural way.
- greater sociocultural and sociolinguistic competence, enabling the learner to respond more flexibly to the situations of use and the interpersonal as well as the social role relations appropriate to the situation
- improved reading skills applied to a wider range of texts, with increased reading speed and ability to select and understand more demanding texts and to differentiate their mode of reading, employing different reading strategies (scanning for key words, reading for gist, exact attention to detail) according to purpose
- higher level of skill in the processes of the reception and production of spoken language, with greater fluency and accuracy in speaking and, as a listener, better ability to cope with noise, distortion and interference as well as a greater variety of dialectal and idiolectal varieties.

'In all', the authors could now claim, '*Waystage, Threshold* and *Vantage* now offer to all practitioners a description of the language needed to assure a learner's ability to deal effectively with the challenges presented by everyday life, presented at three levels rising from a minimal equipment to deal with the highest priority needs, through the minimum needed to deal with the full range of requirements for a visitor or temporary resident, to an enriched equipment adequate to deal effectively with the complexities of daily living' (van Ek & Trim 2001:6). It should be noted that although the system was presented at three levels, it had not come about as an attempt to set up an overall system of clearly defined levels, but in response to successive user demands. The fact that the same descriptive model was used throughout, employing largely the same superordinate functional and notional categories, further weakened the distinctiveness of levels of proficiency. This has attracted criticism from those concerned with the clear differentiation of levels as a basis for the award of distinct qualifications, but it was in line with the general orientation of the Council of Europe's approach to adult education, since it made it easier for users to select from different level descriptions to establish profiled objectives in accordance with the needs and prior experience of particular learner groups.

This principle has also been followed in the more recent definition of a *Breakthrough Level,* setting possible objectives for the very first stage of language learning. By reducing exponents to the very bare minimum and making one exponent (e.g. 'sorry') serve as wide a range of functions as possible, it proved possible to maintain the same notional-functional categories to a far greater extent than expected. Taken together with paralinguistic resources, the general competences and previous experience of language structure and use, which mature adults can be expected to bring from their knowledge, understanding and experience of life and language, the 'maximal use of minimal resources can give learners a much more extensive communicative competence than is generally thought' (Trim 2009: 56). This fact is of importance in early language teaching to: a) those, such as work immigrants and refugees, who, from the start, have to face the full range of needs in everyday life, and b) those who are unable or unwilling to devote more than a brief period of learning in order to add some competence in a new language to their plurilingual repertoire. This latter function was applicable to the 'FINGS' group (Finnish, Irish, Norwegian, Greek, Swedish) in the Association of Language Testers in Europe (ALTE), which first set out to develop a 'Breakthrough' Level, but scarcely to English, where *Breakthrough* will be seen by most learners as the first step in a longer progress towards proficiency. That is certainly the perspective of very young learners, who lack the experience of life and language to make the optimal use of the limited language they are taught. This diversity of learner characteristics, needs and motivations makes the formulation of a Breakthrough Level a particularly complex undertaking.

Until this point, testing and assessment had not been central to the Council of Europe's approach, particularly in adult education. Following the initial publication of the *Threshold Level* in 1975, meetings of experts were held to consider 'how the attainment of operational objectives could be effectively monitored, in order also to provide learners, teachers and course organisers with continuous feedback on the effectiveness of the learning process' (Oscarsson 1980:vii). A study was commissioned from F E Chaplen of UCLES and a specimen Threshold Level test was produced and carefully validated by P Groot and A Harrison, but never published. Greater attention was paid to self-assessment. 'Especially in the Scandinavian context, the use of testing and evaluation as a way of enabling learners to structure their progress was of considerable importance, even more than general proficiency testing' (Oscarsson 1980:ix). In his study, Oscarsson (1980) gave examples of self-assessment forms using descriptors of a Can Do character, some on a 5-point, others on a 6 or 10-point scale, but these were not followed up. However, in the later years of the last century, the rapid expansion of educational, vocational and professional mobility gave much increased urgency to the portability of language qualifications. Young people across Europe were seeking employment abroad or applying to study at universities in other countries, but in many cases employers or university authorities were unable to form a proper estimate of the level of proficiency attested by the qualifications they had gained in their country of origin. In 1991, the Swiss federal government, facing a similar problem internally (Switzerland has no federal Ministry of Education and educational qualifications are awarded at

Cantonal level), hosted an Intergovernmental Symposium at Rüschlikon on *Transparency and coherence in language learning in Europe: objectives, assessment and certification* (see North 1992). The Symposium concluded that:

1. A further intensification of language learning and teaching in member countries is necessary in the interests of greater mobility, more effective international communication combined with respect for identity and cultural diversity, better access to information, more intensive personal interaction, improved working relations and a deeper mutual understanding.

2. To achieve these aims language learning is necessarily a life-long task to be promoted and facilitated throughout educational systems, from pre-school through to adult education.

3. It is desirable to develop a Common European Framework of reference for language learning at all levels, in order to:
   - promote and facilitate co-operation among educational institutions in different countries
   - provide a sound basis for the mutual recognition of language qualifications
   - assist learners, teachers, course designers, examining bodies and educational administrators to situate and co-ordinate their efforts.

The Common European Framework of Reference for Languages (CEFR)

Following the Rüschlikon Symposium, the Council of Europe agreed to develop a common European framework for languages, covering learning, teaching and assessment and set up a working party, with a small authoring group consisting of Daniel Coste (University of the Sorbonne, France), Brian North (Eurocentres, Switzerland) and John Trim (Centre for Information on Language Teaching and Research (CILT, now The National Centre for Languages, UK)). In the course of the 1990s the Framework went through successive drafts, was sent out to more than 1,000 experts for comment and suggestions for amendment and improvement and finally published, simultaneously in French and English (Council of Europe 2001), in the European Year of Languages, 2001.

The CEFR has three main aspects. One is an attempt to characterise comprehensively, transparently and coherently the act of language communication in terms of what competent language users do and the competences (knowledge and skills) that enable them to act. This 'action-oriented approach' is summarised as follows (Council of Europe 2001:2.1)

Language use, embracing language learning, comprises the actions performed by persons who as individuals and as social agents develop a range of **competences**, both **general** and in particular **communicative language competences**. They draw on the competences at their disposal in various **contexts** under various **conditions** and under various **constraints** to engage in **language activities** involving **language processes** to produce and/or receive **texts** in relation to **themes** in specific **domains**, activating those **strategies** which seem most appropriate for carrying out the **tasks** to be accomplished. The monitoring of these actions by the participants leads to the reinforcement or modification of their competences.

The key words in bold typeface represent the categories presented and exemplified in the language taxonomy, which takes up Chapters 4 and 5 of the CEFR and are glossed as follows:

Competences are the sum of knowledge, skills and characteristics, which allow a person to perform actions.

General competences are those not specific to language, but which are called upon for actions of all kinds, including language activities.

Communicative language competences are those which empower a person to act using specifically linguistic means.

Context refers to the constellation of events and situational factors (physical and others), both internal and external to a person, in which acts of communication are embedded.

Language activities involve the exercise of one's communicative language competence in a specific domain in processing (receptively and/or productively) one or more texts in order to carry out a task.

Language processes refer to the chain of events, neurological and physiological, involved in the production and reception of speech and writing.

Text is any sequence or discourse (spoken and/or written) related to a specific domain and which in the course of carrying out a task becomes the occasion of a language activity, whether as a support or as a goal, as product or process.

Domain refers to the broad sectors of social life in which social agents operate. A higher order categorisation has been adopted here limiting these to major categories relevant to language learning/teaching and use: the educational, occupational, public and personal domains.

A *strategy* is any organised, purposeful and regulated line of action chosen by an individual to carry out a task which he or she sets for himself or herself or with which he or she is confronted.

A *task* is defined as any purposeful action considered by an individual as necessary in order to achieve a given result in the context of a problem to be solved, an obligation to fulfil or an objective to be achieved. This definition would cover a wide range of actions such as moving a wardrobe, writing a book, obtaining certain conditions in the negotiation of a contract, playing a game of cards, ordering a meal in a restaurant, translating a foreign language text or preparing a class newspaper through group work.

The second aspect of the CEFR is the survey of methods of learning, teaching and assessment presented in Chapters 6, 7, 8 and 9. In addition to discussion of the curricular issues raised, these chapters aim to present users with an open, non-dogmatic account of the various options open to them, to encourage reflection on their own current practice, to consider alternatives and communicate to others their opinions and their reasons for holding them.

However, the aspect of the CEFR that has been most influential has undoubtedly been the scheme presented in Chapter 3 for establishing common reference levels for specifying language proficiency. The addition of a 'vertical dimension' to the Framework beside the 'horizontal' taxonomy of language use and competences is said to be that it 'enables learning space to be mapped or profiled, even if simply, and this is useful for a number of reasons:

- The development of definitions of learner proficiency related to categories used in the Framework may assist in making more concrete what it may be appropriate to expect at different levels of achievement in terms of those categories. This in turn may aid the development of transparent and realistic statements of overall learning objectives.
- Learning which takes place over a period of time needs to be organised into units which take account of progression and can provide continuity. Syllabuses and materials need to be situated in relation to one another. A Framework of levels may help in this process.
- Learning efforts in relation to those objectives and those units need also to be situated on this vertical dimension of progress – i.e. assessed in relation to gains in proficiency. The provision of proficiency statements may help in this process.
- Such assessment should take account of incidental learning, of out of school experience, of the kind of lateral enrichment outlined above. The provision of a set of proficiency statements going beyond the scope of a particular syllabus may be helpful in this respect.
- The provision of a common set of proficiency statements will facilitate comparisons of objectives, levels, materials, tests and achievement in different systems and situations.

- A Framework including both horizontal and vertical dimensions facilitates the definition of partial objectives and the recognition of uneven profiles, partial competencies.
- A Framework of levels and categories facilitating profiling of objectives for particular purposes may aid inspectors. Such a Framework may help to assess whether learners are working at an appropriate level in different areas. It may inform decisions on whether performance in those areas represents a standard appropriate to the stage of learning, immediate future goals and wider longer-term goals of effective language proficiency and personal development.
- Finally, in their learning career students of the language will pass through a number of educational sectors and institutions offering language services, and the provision of a common set of levels may facilitate collaboration between those sectors. With increased personal mobility, it is more and more common for learners to switch between educational systems at the end of or even in the middle of their period in a particular educational sector, making the provision of a common scale on which to describe their achievement an issue of ever wider concern'.

This powerful justification of the articulation of the continuous process of language learning into a sequence of defined levels leaves open, of course, the number of levels to be recognised. There appear to be no natural breaks. Whilst it was at first thought that the *Threshold Level* identified such a break (as the name implies), the subsequent development of *Vantage*, *Waystage* and *Breakthrough* greatly weakened that claim. Ultimately, the decision is dependent on the exigencies of the social organisation of learning, not in the nature of language itself.

The CEFR segments progress in language learning into three bands: A (*Basic User*), B (*Independent User*) and C (*Proficient User*). Each band is subdivided into upper and lower levels, producing a basic 6-level scheme. Each level is characterised by descriptors, which have been selected and synthesised from an overall bank of descriptors taken from 30 scales drawn up by various institutions for various purposes, mostly between 1980 and 1993. The selection was made in a project of the Swiss National Science Research Council by a process described in the CEFR Appendix B and in greater detail in Chapter 3 and in North and Schneider (1998). The aim, as set out in CEFR Appendix A, was to produce descriptors which were **positive** (describing competence, not incompetence), **definite** (avoiding vagueness and the mere use of undefined adverbials of quality, e.g. a few/some/many/more/most), **clear** (jargon-free and written in simple syntax with an explicit logical structure), **brief** (up to about 25 words and capturing the essential rather than trying to be exhaustive) and **independent** (rather than having meaning only in relation to other

Proficient User	**C2**	Can understand with ease virtually everything heard or read. Can summarize information from different spoken and written sources, reconstructing arguments and accounts in a coherent presentation. Can express him/herself spontaneously, very fluently and precisely, differentiating finer shades of meaning even in more complex situations.
	C1	Can understand a wide range of demanding, longertexts, and recognise implicit meaning. Can express him/herself fluently and spontaneously without much obvious searching for expressions. Can use language flexibly and effectively for social, academic and professional purposes. Can produce clear, well-structured, detailed text on complex subjects, showing controlled use of organisational patterns, connectors and cohesive devices.
Independent User	**B2**	Can understand the main ideas of complex text on both concrete and abstract topics, including technical discussions in his/her field of specialisation. Can interact with a degree of fluency and spontaneity that makes regular interaction with native speakers quite possible without strain for either party. Can produce clear, detailed text on a wide range of subjects and explain a viewpoint on a topical issue giving the advantages and disadvantages of various options.
	B1	Can understand the main points of clear standard input on familiar matters regularly encountered in work, school, leisure, etc. Can deal with most situations likely to arise whilst travelling in an area where the language is spoken. Can produce simple connected text on topics which are familiar or of personal interest. Can describe experiences and events, dreams, hopes & ambitions and briefly give reasons and explanations for opinions and plans.
Basic User	**A2**	Can understand sentences and frequently used expressions related to areas of most immediate relevance (e.g. very basic personal and family information, shopping, local geography, employment). Can communicate in simple and routine tasks requiring a simple and direct exchange of information on familiar and routine matters. Can describe in simple terms aspects of his/her background, immediate environment and matters in areas of immediate need.
	A1	Can understand and use familiar everyday expressions and very basic phrases aimed at the satisfaction of needs of a concrete type. Can introduce him/herself and others and can ask and answer questions about personal details such as where he/she lives, people he/she knows and things he/she has. Can interact in a simple way provided the other person talks slowly and clearly and is prepared to help.

descriptors in the scale). In its simplest form, the resulting scaling is presented in CEFR Table 1 (Council of Europe 2001:24):

In this table, each level is defined by a number of descriptors. Each descriptor is introduced by 'can', and all would seem to satisfy the above criteria of *positiveness, clarity, brevity* and *independence*. That of *definiteness* is more problematic, e.g. the distinction between 'familiar everyday expressions' (A1) and 'frequently used expressions related to areas of immediate relevance' (A2). The distinction clearly depends on the interpretation of *familiar, everyday, frequently* and *immediate*, which are undefined. The examples given are strongly indicative, but not definitive, even as further developed with 'strong' interlevels (Council of Europe 2001:3.5). The scale will certainly perform a useful function in giving learners, teachers, employers, parents etc. a reasonably clear and user-friendly picture of what to expect from a learner at one of the six levels of proficiency, but it may not satisfy a further criterion not so far stated: **operational adequacy**, in those cases where decisions have to be made which have important consequences, e.g. in the calibration of educational and vocational qualifications to assure their portability. It was, after all, this prospect that has led governments and educational institutions, not only in Europe but across the world, to welcome the CEFR as a universal point of reference.

A simple scale of this kind, however carefully formulated, cannot bear this weight. The CEFR therefore expands and supplements this scale by a number of others. Table 2 separates the basic language-using activities: listening. reading, spoken interaction, spoken production and writing, presenting them in a form suitable for learner self-assessment. Table 3 separates the qualitative aspects of (spoken) language use: range, accuracy, fluency, interaction and coherence. Backing these 'global' scales are others, for a variety of reasons not always complete, dealing with the particular activities and competences set out in Chapters 4 and 5. Concreteness is also supported by the association of Levels A2, B1 and B2 with the detailed specification of successive objectives in *Waystage, Threshold* and *Vantage*, though it has to be remembered that that series was developed quite separately from the CEFR levels by very different procedures, so that exact equivalence is not guaranteed.

The English Profile is a means of further exploring or giving form to these levels. In the case of *Vantage,* particularly, the intention was to carry learners who had reached Threshold Level with the same needs and perspectives 'a stage further'. In terms of the 6-level system of the CEFR, given that Threshold is equated with Level B1, 'a stage further' would seem to correspond to B2. This would be close to the authors' intentions. However, since no higher objectives were developed above Vantage in the T-series, its upper limit is not defined and some criteria statements, especially with regard to discourse structure and sociocultural competence might perhaps be considered to be appropriately situated at B2+ or C1 level. The issue is further addressed in this volume. The English Profile is a means of further exploring or giving form to these levels.

Since the CEFR is intended to be used in connection with any language, it is necessarily non-language-specific. This means that when dealing with the formal aspects of language, it cannot go beyond identifying the grammatical and lexical categories that may figure in the analysis and description of languages and perhaps the broadest principles of progression (e.g. from simple to more complex). It cannot lay down an order of progression, which may vary, not only from one language to another, but also, with respect to each target language, the learner's mother tongue. For instance, word order in subordinate clauses in German presents English learners with greater problems than

Dutch learners, which may affect the stage in learning at which complex sentences may replace sequences of simple sentences. Similarly, English phrasal verbs may present fewer problems to speakers of German than to speakers of Romance languages. As a result, the CEFR may appear to be underspecified in respect of grammar and lexicon.

No-one would deny that, for any particular language, grammatical and lexical progression is of central importance and is not merely a secondary consequence of notional-functional progression. However, the two are intimately related, so that excusive attention on the one may seriously distort the other, as in the case above of refusing to speak of the past until the past tense was introduced after more than two years of study. The necessary reconciliation has to be made and the optimal progression has to be established separately for each target language (L2) in turn and in principle for each source language (L1). Accordingly, a number of language-specific projects have been, or are being, undertaken. The first of these was *Profile Deutsch*. The authors of *Kontaktschwelle,* drawing upon both *Threshold Level* and *Un Niveau-seuil,* had produced a considerably enriched version of the Threshold Level for German. In terms of the CEFR, the material presented spanned the range A1 to B2. A trinational team, from Germany, Austria and Switzerland, was commissioned to reorder the material, separating out what was appropriate to each of these levels, supplementing where necessary to cover significant differences of usage in the three countries. The team then went on to add a specification for Levels C1 and C2, not in the original material and not fully specified in the CEFR. It was decided that learners reaching the C levels were so diverse and specialised that it was inappropriate – and perhaps impossible – to specify the additional grammar and lexicon required at these levels. Instead, they elaborated and exemplified a rich apparatus of Can Do descriptors, for the activities and competences presented in the CEFR, both global and detailed. An English translation of the specification for C1 is appended (that for C2 being very similar), since the formulations may be found helpful for those developing similar specifications for other languages. An important innovation was the provision of a computer disk containing the material, with a software program which would enable a user to make a selection across levels according to learner needs and motivations, so that what was on offer was the basis for an indefinite number of profiled objectives. Hence the title of the work: *Profile Deutsch* ('Profiles for German').

Overall, the apparatus of level description in the CEFR is rich and well differentiated for different purposes and users. Even so, experience over the past decade has shown that for high-stakes purposes, particularly the valid and reliable calibration of qualifications and the tests and examinations leading to their award, the CEFR cannot be used as a 'standalone' document. Indeed, it is probably impossible for any such document to be so used. What it can do is to stand as a central point of reference, itself always open to amendment and further development, in an interactive international system of co-operating institutions, linked by sound, genuine working relations and sharing common values and aims, whose cumulative experience and expertise produces a solid structure of knowledge, understanding and practice shared by all. It is entirely in the spirit of the Council of Europe if this structure is built, not by central directive but by free voluntary cooperation. To encourage such co-operation, the Committee of Ministers, the highest organ of the Council, issued a Recommendation to member governments, recommending them to ensure that all tests and examinations leading to officially recognised qualifications under their jurisdiction are linked to the CEFR and asking them to encourage and support teacher trainers, course developers and language testers in linking their work to the CEFR. Much progress has already been made, notably in the production of a manual, with supporting materials, for relating examinations to the CEFR (Council of Europe 2009). All the developments described here form the background to the major project for the description of English: *English Profile*, of which the work reported in this volume is part.

Introduction

The stated aim of the English Profile Programme (EPP) is 'to investigate what learner English is really like at each level of the influential Common European Framework of Reference (CEFR)' (Cambridge Assessment 2007) in order to provide reference level descriptions (RLD) (Council of Europe 2005) that will elaborate and exemplify the CEFR levels for the English language (see Saville & Hawkey 2010).

The English Profile starts from the stance that the CEFR provides a well-grounded, pedagogically motivated view of the development of communicative language abilities, representing 'the culmination of 30 years of experience. . . in developing and implementing curricula, syllabuses and teaching materials at different "levels" of foreign language development' (Hulstijn et al. 2010, p.13) and backed by 'much consultation on several draft versions (1996, 1998), which were widely circulated before the final text was ready' (Saville & Hawkey 2010). Now available in 37 different language versions, it is clear that the CEFR has had a substantial impact on language teaching and assessment around the world and is a widely valued resource.

This volume does not, however, claim to provide the full picture of 'what learner English is really like', of how English language learners develop their communicative competence, or even how this might be reflected in the language functions that they produce. Rather, the work reported here represents initial steps along one of many strands in a much wider and more open-ended research process. Arriving at such a picture will require a great deal more activity in the functional, grammatical and lexical areas where work is already well underway. It also requires the opening out of the research programme into such vast areas of inquiry as spoken production, interaction and reception and sociolinguistic, pragmatic and strategic competences: areas where English Profile work is only just beginning.

As the subtitle of this volume suggests, the work reported here involves both theoretical and empirical perspectives on how and how well learners identified as being at the different levels of the CEFR are able to use English. This work is most specifically concerned with exploring the highest levels in the scheme, the C (*Proficient User*) levels (C1: *Effective Operational Proficiency* and C2: *Mastery*) in terms of communicative functions (Wilkins 1972a), language functions (van Ek 1975), or simply *functions* (all three terms are used interchangeably in the CEFR).

Like the first volume in this series, Hawkins and Filipović (2012), this volume represents a quest for what they have termed 'criterial features': specific properties of learner language that appear to particularly characterise L2 proficiency at each level of the CEFR. Taking a complementary perspective to that of Hawkins and Filipović, who are concerned in the first instance with grammatical properties, and Capel (2010) who is concerned with vocabulary, this volume begins by investigating this criteriality from the point of view of language functions. Hawkins and Filipović are concerned in the first instance with learner production and look for evidence to the Cambridge Learner Corpus (CLC), a growing corpus of roughly 40 million words made up of Cambridge ESOL examination scripts and so including written English produced by learners from around the world. In this volume, we are more concerned with the input to the learner: the functions that are taught and the texts that are presented to learners judged to be at different levels of the CEFR. In this, the CLC cannot help. The primary data source here will be English language learning materials.

The concern with a functional (rather than a grammatical or lexical) progression across the ability range is particularly apposite because, in the 'action oriented approach' of the CEFR, the primary concern is not with what learners know about a language, or even about what aspects of the language they are able to use, but rather with how they use the language: what they *can do* with it in social contexts – and this is what functions are intended to capture. As John Trim, the director of the Council of Europe's modern languages projects from 1971 to 1997 (see Preface, above), expresses it in the foreword to the *Threshold* specification (Trim in van Ek 1975:1), 'the grammar and the lexicon is not an end in itself, it is simply a tool for the performance of the communicative functions, which are what really matter'. Our focus here is on what the proficient English language users at a C1 or C2 level are usually able to do that learners at lower levels of the framework are typically unable or less able to do with the linguistic resources available to them.

This English Profile contribution begins by investigating the C levels because no comprehensive CEFR language proficiency level specifications for the two advanced levels C1 and C2 have yet been published for English. The CEFR directs readers to *Threshold 1990* (van Ek & Trim 1998b) and the other volumes of the so-called T-series – *Breakthrough* (Trim 2009), *Waystage* (van Ek and Trim 1998a), *Vantage* (van Ek & Trim 2001) – but none of these separately addresses the C levels (although as Trim reminds us in the Preface to this volume, *Vantage* does cover language use beyond *Threshold* – i.e. at B2 and above). The C levels are also the least clearly specified in the CEFR: a number of the illustrative scales for C1 and C2 state, '*as B2*' or '*no descriptor available*' and we are told that relatively few C2 level descriptors from existing schemes were available to the developers (The CEFR: Council of Europe

2001:221). Methods developed for this investigation may subsequently be used in revisiting the descriptions for the A and B levels.

In carrying out this investigation, we are faced initially with issues of definition: a) what are communicative language functions? and b) what, in functional terms, is meant by the C levels in particular and by functional distinctions between levels more generally?

Section 1 (Chapters 1 and 2) looks for answers to these questions from the CEFR and other related Council of Europe documents and through the wider theoretical literature in Applied Linguistics and allied fields. In Chapter 1, the focus is on the theoretical sources for functions and their role in Council of Europe modern languages projects while Chapter 2 investigates the role of functions and related 'Can Do statements' in the CEFR: the starting point and informing framework for the English Profile.

Section 2 (Chapters 3 and 4) is concerned more with practice than with theory and explores ways in which functional levels have been operationalised in English language education around the world. Two research projects, currently in progress, are described. The first looks for common themes in Can Do statements used to set objectives in English language learning and assessment. Building on this first study, which identifies the importance of *texts* to level definitions, the second study considers how the CEFR levels are reflected in the reading comprehension texts presented in English language materials.

On the basis of the review in Section 1 and the empirical research in Section 2, Section 3 (Chapters 5 and 6) proposes a set of illustrative Can Do statements to supplement the CEFR and looks forward to the future development of the English Profile as a resource for teachers, syllabus designers and assessors. Chapter 5 describes the elements of the proposed Can Do statements and explains how these relate to the CEFR model of communicative competence. Chapter 6 shows how the elements of English Profile research can be brought together to form a coherent resource for educators to draw on and to which they may contribute.

Section 1
Theoretical Bases

1 The theoretical foundations for functions in the Council of Europe modern languages projects and the Common European Framework of Reference for languages

What are language functions in the CEFR?

In building detailed reference level descriptions based on the Common European Framework of Reference (CEFR) (Council of Europe 2001), 'it is important' as Hulstijn, Alderson & Schoonen (2010) suggest, 'to emphasise that the 2001 version of the CEFR itself did not suddenly appear out of nothing' (p.12). The CEFR not only reflects the 30 year history of the Council of Europe projects, to which Hulstijn et al allude, but also the longer traditions of linguistic analysis and language pedagogy that are concerned with language as a means of social interaction. This chapter traces some of the precedents for functions in these traditions and considers the part they came to play in the CEFR model of communicative competence.

Influenced by speech act theory and by the emergence of sociolinguistics as well as by wider socio-economic issues (Milanovic & Weir, forthcoming), the adoption of communicative language functions by the Council of Europe led the English language teaching profession in the social turn that it experienced during the 1970s and 1980s: a process that is still underway in many parts of the world. In this shift of emphasis, English language teaching moved from a structural to a communicative paradigm as educators became increasingly concerned with the ways in which language may be used meaningfully in social contexts. The growth in interest in the use of language for communication led to new insights, which in turn fed back into the Council of Europe projects (see Trim, in Preface).

The starting point for the system of levels that led to the CEFR was the concept of a stage in the language learning process at which knowledge of the language begins to 'cohere into an overall communicative competence, with which the learner can cope, albeit in a very simple fashion, with the general demands of daily life' (Trim above, p. xix). This was conceived as a *threshold* or critical point in the language learning process associated with a radical change in the ability to use a language. It was considered to be the lowest level at which it would be meaningful to speak of a general level of language proficiency and so would provide a logical objective for basic language learning programmes. The specification of this as a learning objective in the form of the *Threshold Level* (1975) also marked the crossing of a first threshold in the development of what would eventually become the CEFR.

The institutional context is important. The Council of Europe has been involved in the promotion of the teaching and learning of foreign languages throughout its history. Linguistic diversity is seen to be a defining and enriching feature of the European identity and language learning as essential to mutual understanding, to participation in a fully European culture and to continuing economic and social progress. The Council of Europe has committed itself to the democratisation of education: languages being regarded as a resource that should be accessible to all rather than to a social or professional élite.

Approaches to education at the Council of Europe provided the impetus for the modern languages projects. During the 1960s, recognising the need for greater flexibility in education in the face of rapid technological and societal change, the Council of Europe supported the concept of 'permanent education' (Schwartz 1969), subsequently recast as 'lifelong learning'. Traditional school-based education was regarded as 'an institution that tried to prepare the generation of tomorrow by instilling in their minds the culture of the past' (Council of Europe 1973:4). Such an institution, with its orientation towards developing 'know-how' rather than the required 'know how to become' (p.7), could not equip learners to cope with the rapidly changing world beyond the classroom and the 'growing gap between the sum of knowledge available and the sum of knowledge taught' (p.2). Europeans would need a form of education that would give them access to the new technologies and new areas of knowledge as they emerged. Schwartz (1969, 1974) proposed that in a suitably flexible approach to education, subjects (whether traditionally academic or vocational) would not be taught or assessed as monolithic wholes, but broken down into modules, which could be accessed as (or if) they became relevant to the needs of the learner. Teachers would play a more facilitative part as learners took greater responsibility for their own learning choices. Learner-centredness and learner autonomy were at the heart of developments from the beginning, together with a strong supporting role for educational technology and new media.

A Symposium was convened in 1971 at Rüschlikon in Switzerland on the theme of *Languages in Adult Education* to discuss a modular 'unit/credit' approach to language learning. It was quickly recognised that it would not be possible to divide up language learning into a set of discrete modules that could be dealt with in any arrangement, and a working party was established to explore alternatives (see Trim, above).

As Trim makes clear in the Preface to this volume, the *situational approach* then in vogue was discussed as a possible vehicle. The approach was pioneered by A S Hornby (1954–56;1959), following in the footsteps of other global best-selling authors of the 1930s to 1950s, such as Laurence Faucett, Michael West and Charles Eckersley. Faucett's *Oxford English Course* (1933), West's *Learn to Speak by Speaking* (1933) materials and Eckersley's four-volume *Essential English for Foreign Students* (1955) followed similar patterns. The starting point for each teaching unit would be a situation considered to be relevant and of interest to foreign learners. These were presented in the form of texts or dialogues covering paradigmatic grammar points, followed by practice exercises and tests. Typically, each book would be restricted to a certain number of new words, based on the ideas on vocabulary limitation of West (1953) and Faucett, Palmer, Thorndike & West (1936). The approach was exemplified in contemporary British ELT textbooks for adult learners such as *English in Situations* (O'Neill 1970), the *Kernel Lessons* series (O'Neill, Kingsbury, Yeadon & Scott 1971) and *New Concept English* (Alexander 1967).

Although the situational approach offered a contextualised alternative to the grammar-translation then dominant in schools across Europe, it seemed to the Council of Europe working group to be too limiting. There were too many uses of language which could not readily be captured through an analysis of situational scenarios so that the situational learner might be left 'unprepared for anything out of the ordinary' (Wilkins 1976:18). Furthermore, there seemed to be a *common core* of language that all learners would need and that would be of value across most contexts or situations that learners might encounter. Specifying the language associated with specific situations and organising the syllabus on this basis appeared unnecessarily restrictive.

Wilkins (1972a, 1976), the member of the Council of Europe working party tasked with outlining the common core linguistic and situational content of the system, suggested an alternative: turning the traditional structural syllabus on its head. Instead of taking grammatical structures as the basis for syllabus design, he recommended that the meanings that learners might want to express should be the point of entry, with grammatical structures relegated to the role of exponents: the linguistic tools for realising meanings.

Semantico-grammatical categories and *functions* would provide the common component. The semantico-grammatical categories are categories of meaning such as time, quantity and space that 'interact significantly' (Wilkins 1972a:3) with traditional grammatical and lexical categories and so can usually be more or less straightforwardly mapped onto them (e.g. temporal relations are expressed by tense, quantity is expressed by grammatical number). Functions are expressions of feeling and attitude that do not typically correspond to grammatical categories (there are no grammatical categories that straightforwardly convey, for example, apology or sympathy). Wilkins argued that these categories could provide a clear rationale, from the standpoint of learner requirements, for selecting 'the language to which the learner will be exposed and which we will expect him to acquire' (Wilkins:1). In the T-series, Wilkins' semantico-grammatical categories became *notions*. As Johnson (1982:38–39) among others has pointed out, the label 'notional syllabuses' used in the title of Wilkins' 1976 book is often misinterpreted. For Wilkins (1972a) both functions and semantico-grammatical categories are notional or semantic in the sense that they prioritise meaning in the same way as do 'notional' grammars. Wilkins (1976) in fact advocates that both semantico-grammatical categories and functions should be considered in syllabus design and the term notional-functional is more often used to characterise his overall approach (Richards and Rogers 2001; Brown 2007).

Notions may be general or specific. *General notions* are concepts that learners may need to refer to whatever the situation. These include *deixis, dimension, direction* and *duration*. In contrast, *specific notions* are related to topic and situation so that, in *Threshold*, the specific notional category of *occupation* (within the theme of *personal identification*) includes *baker, butcher* and *businessman*. *Functions* describe the social actions that people intend to accomplish through language and are expressed in *Threshold* in terms like '*expressing agreement with a statement*' or '*showing that one is following a person's discourse*'. In the English Profile, general notions are identified most readily in the work of Hawkins and Filipović (2012) on grammatical progression while specific notions have been subsumed within the broader remit on vocabulary (Capel 2010).

The notional-functional approach seemed particularly promising to educators in that it 'presented to many people for the first time the possibility of describing, at a new and higher level of generality, that which learners need to learn and hence which teachers need to teach' (Strevens 1980:116). Functions would seem to have had a greater impact on language pedagogy than their communicative team-mates' notions. This is perhaps because it was functions that were 'the most original part of the framework' (Wilkins 1976:23), notions being more difficult for users to distinguish from the traditional categories found in pedagogic grammars and word lists (Widdowson 1990:42): grammar explanations found in *Kernel Lessons Intermediate* (O'Neill et al 1971), for example, already had a distinctly notional flavour. Although the fashion for basing syllabuses on notional-functional principles has been largely superseded (by task- and content-based models), functions themselves have survived and continue to play an important role, taking their place alongside the more traditional grammatical and situational elements: 'woven indelibly into the fabric of language teaching' as Johnson (2006:417) expresses it.

A brief history of functions

The Council of Europe has, over the 40 years since the unit/credit scheme was first mooted, drawn on a wide range of ideas in developing the concept of language functions. In the following section I will briefly review some of the more prominent theories that have informed their thinking.

Origins for this conception of language function and its dependence on context as well as form have been traced in the 'social acts' of the Scottish Enlightenment philosopher Thomas Reid (1710–96), in the same term as used by the legal theorist Reinach (1913 cited in Mulligan 1987) as well as in the later work of Wittgenstein (1955) and Austin (1962). By the time of the first Rüschlikon Symposium in 1971, the idea that meaning and its relation to context should be a central concern was already well established in British linguistics, especially through the London School associated with J R Firth (see for example Firth 1957:93–118). This contrasted with the situation in the USA where the structuralist linguistics of Bloomfield and his followers (see Bloomfield 1933), which prioritised the study of language as a decontextualised system, was in the ascendancy. However, American sociolinguistics was an early influence through the work of Hymes in particular, with its insistence that 'communicative competence' includes being 'able to accomplish a repertoire of speech acts, to take part in speech events, and to evaluate their accomplishment by others' (Hymes 1972:277).

For Hymes (1974:52), speech acts are units within *speech events* (such as private conversations, lectures, formal introductions) analogous to nouns within sentences. A speech event is a bounded by a beginning and end and is governed by rules or norms. Just as one speech act may occur in different speech events (a joke in a conversation or in a lecture) so speech events may occur within different situations (a conversation might occur at a party or during a break in a tennis match). As we will see in Chapter 3, the need for units beyond the function would emerge as an important theme in the development of the Council of Europe projects and Hymes' *speech events,* picked up in later models of communicative competence such as Celce-Murcia, Dörnyei and Thurrell (1995), certainly resonate with the *language activities* of the CEFR.

Firth's thinking had been much influenced by Malinowski, a social anthropologist, whose ethnographic studies of the organisation of Polynesian societies led him to recognise the importance of 'context of situation' – the context in which an utterance is spoken – as well as the 'context of reference' – the topical content of a text – in explaining linguistic choices (e.g. Malinowski 1935). He was the first to use the term, 'phatic communion' (Malinowski 1922:315) to characterise conventional greetings, gossip and other exchanges that served the primary purpose of 'creating an atmosphere of sociability' between individuals rather than conveying information; an idea picked up in the *socialising* functions of the T-series. Firth analysed language in its relationships with contextual factors such as the 'non-verbal action of participants', the 'relevant objects' that surrounded the speakers and 'the effect of verbal action' (Robins 1968:28). By the 1930s, he was already identifying *functions of speech* (such as *address; greetings; farewells, adjustments of relations, creating solidarity*) in terms of their social value as 'acts' (Robins, *loc cit.*). Firth is acknowledged by Trim in the Preface to this volume as a particular influence on the CEFR.

For those working empirically from the analysis of observed language use in the tradition of Malinowski and Firth, classification of functions is made or refined according to the exigencies of the data. This is true whether the work is in the more distanced or etic orientation of discourse analysis (e.g. Sinclair & Coulthard 1975) or in the more embedded, emic orientation of conversation analysis, linked to Garfinkel's (1974) ethnomethodology, which interprets conversation from the point of view of the participants (e.g. Sacks, Schegloff & Jefferson 1974). In both approaches, functions are understood in relation to the specific speech event or text in which they play a part. For example, Pike (1967) – the originator of the emic/ etic dichotomy – used observations of social events to examine the conventions framing certain human communicative behaviours.

Others have eschewed performance data, relying on introspection in looking for more universally applicable functional categorisations. The philosopher Searle (1969, 1975, 1979), building on the earlier work of Austin, is identified with the development of speech act theory. In his *How to Do Things with Words*, Austin (1962) had introduced the distinction between three acts that we may perform whenever we say something:

- a locutionary act – producing a recognisable grammatical utterance. A speaker states '*It is cold in here*'.
- an illocutionary act – the performance of an act in saying something. Depending on the context and the manner of speech, the speaker may have said '*It is cold in here*' simply to inform the addressee, or as a way of requesting the addressee to close the window. The utterance carries an illocutionary force representing the speaker's intent. The Council of Europe functions mainly concern illocutionary acts.
- a perlocutionary act – the effect brought about on the feelings, thoughts or actions of either the speaker or the listener: the addressee closes the window as a result of what the speaker has said.

Searle (1979:22) argued that 'if we adopt the illocutionary point as the basic notion on which to classify uses of language, then there are a rather limited number of basic things we do with language'. He made a distinction between illocutionary *verbs* – the verbs that can be used to report speech acts (such as apologise, beg, complain, demand) – and illocutionary *acts*, which he considered to be much more limited in number. He built on Austin's (1962) classification (verdictives, expositives, exercitives, behabitives and commissives) in suggesting a taxonomy of speech acts based on 12 dimensions of variation, the three most important being the *illocutionary point* (the purpose of the act), the *direction of fit* between words and the world and differences in the psychological state expressed (the sincerity condition). Application of these conditions yields the five basic speech acts in Table 1.

Table 1 Searle's (1969) five speech acts

Speech acts	Illocutionary verbs	Illocutionary point	Direction of fit	Sincerity condition	Example utterance
Assertives	affirming boasting concluding	true/ false proposition	word to world: The speaker's words represent the world	belief	*Pragmatics is a division of linguistics. I won the race.*
Directives	asking begging commanding	make the addressee perform an action	world to word: The speaker elicits action to make the world match the words via the addressee	wants, wishes, desires	*Bring me a cup of coffee. May I leave?*
Commissives	arranging betting committing to	bind the speaker to doing something in the future	world to word: The speaker intends to adapt the world to fit the words	intention	*I'll drive. I bet it's going to rain.*
Expressives	apologizing berating congratulating	express how the speaker feels about the situation	N/A	various	*I'm sorry. Well done!*
Declarations	appointing awarding conceding	change the state of the world in an immediate way	Both word to world and world to word: The words come to match the world and the world matches the words as a result of the utterance. Depends on the nature of speaker and addressee roles.	N/A	*You're fired! (employer to employee) I hereby sentence you to five years in prison (judge to prisoner)*

Although Searle's system might appear attractive as a basis for classification, Sarangi and Coulthard (2000:xvii) suggest that, being based in introspection rather than observation 'the [speech act] approach has many drawbacks for those attempting to adapt it to investigate naturally-occurring data'. Of course it is naturally occurring language that learners have to handle and that is the chief concern of the CEFR. In relation to the debate between speech act theory and text or speech based systems of analysis, Flowerdew (1990) points to a 'basic theoretical problem of the conflict between an all-purpose system, which is likely to have defects in relation to specific situations in which it is applied and a system derived from one narrowly defined situation, which is liable to lack applicability to other, more general situations'. The wording of the Council of Europe functions is intended to be widely interpretable and so is based on the everyday expressions used by teachers – having something in common with the use of 'native terms' in the ethnography of speaking (Hymes 1974) – referring to acts that adult learners might need to accomplish in specific situations. The generalisability of the system comes from the familiarity of the common core of situations and functions that apply across a wide range of language use contexts; its specificity comes from local needs analysis and flexible local application and refinement of the scheme.

Developing an adequate *general* theory for the interpretation of utterances is challenging for linguistics, just as it is for language learners, precisely because there is often no clear relationship between the grammar of an utterance and the speech act that it realises. Jakobson (1960:354), reminding us of the key role played by phonology in realising functions (as later reflected in the 1990 revision of Threshold) refers to an exercise adapted from the famous director Stanislavski in which an actor is asked to generate 50 different meanings from one phrase merely by 'diversifying its expressive tint'. According to Jakobson, the intended implications of most of these variations were accurately recognised by listeners. But even if we include phonology, linguistic form is not sufficient to account for variation in the function of utterances: the situational context in which an utterance is made must also be considered.

Reflecting this lack of congruence between form and function, Searle (1969) makes a distinction between *direct* speech acts, in which the illocutionary force is reflected in the structure of the utterance (declarative-as-representative: *it's cold in here [as a straightforward observation]* or imperative-as-directive: *'close the door!'*), and *indirect* speech acts in which it is not (declarative-as-directive: *it's cold in here [meaning 'close the door!']*). If communication is to be successful, the addressee must distinguish between the primary illocutionary force of an utterance – which reflects the intended perlocution – from secondary illocutionary acts (which may be implied by the grammar: what van Ek (1986:33) refers to as the 'conventional meaning').

Searle envisages that the process by which the addressee understands that something other than the literal meaning is intended must involve a form of conversational implicature. Searle's own system of implicature is in part derived from Grice's (1975) well-known conversational principles such as the Cooperative Principle (CP) and its maxims of quantity ('give the right amount of information'), of quality ('try to make your contribution one that is true'), of relation ('be relevant') and of manner ('be perspicuous'). According to Searle, if communication is to be successful, the addressee must appeal to what they know of the conversational context for the utterance, drawing on background knowledge and the assumption that the speaker is being relevant and co-operative in the interaction.

Further developments of Grice's (1975) principles of relevance to speech act production, sequencing and comprehension are found in Sperber and Wilson's (1995) relevance theory, Brown and Levinson's (1987) conceptions of face and politeness strategies and Leech's (1980) politeness principle which encompasses communicative aspects such as tact, modesty and maximising agreement. All of these may affect the selection of forms in realising functions. The original Threshold (1975) specification paid little attention to implicature and the intensifying or modifying effects of linguistic choices, but, as we will see, this was taken up in later revisions.

Jakobson, already encountered above, is another influential figure in the functional description of language. Although working within the structuralist paradigm, unlike Bloomfield, Jakobson (1960) was concerned with the role of context in communication. His scheme, elaborating on Bühler (1990) and later adopted by Hymes (1964) conceives of six functions of language, all of which may be recognised in a text, but in different hierarchical configurations. Each function is closely associated with one of the constitutive factors of a speech event or text (Figure 1). In this conceptualisation,

Figure 1 Factors involved in verbal communication and their associated functions, adapted from Jakobson (1960:354, 357)

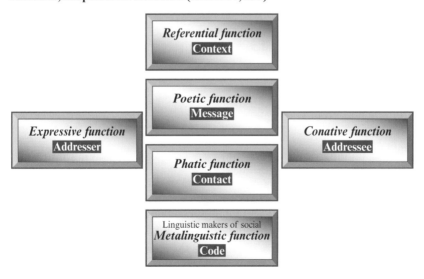

all verbal communication entails an addresser directing a message to an addressee. For communication to be successful, addresser (speaker/writer) and addressee (hearer/reader) must share an understanding of the context; a common code, or language; and a 'physical and psychological connection' (channel), 'enabling both of them to enter and stay in communication' (Jakobson 1960:353).

As set out in Figure 1, each function predominates in certain kinds of speech event or text. However, any text is likely to fulfil a number of functions. Advertisements, for example, may seek to attract our attention (phatic function), convey information about a product (referential function), make use of alliteration or other forms of word play (poetic function) and convey positive feelings about the product (emotive function), but their primary purpose is to persuade us to buy (conative function). News reports, on the other hand are primarily referential, but may also involve alliterative (poetic), attention-getting (phatic) headlines or openings. The possibility that an utterance may fulfil a number of functions is taken up by the T-series, but is not pursued. No guidance is given in *Threshold* on how or why learners might use multifunctional utterances.

Table 2 Jakobson's (1960) functions of language

Function	Purpose	Sentence/ text types	Examples
Expressive	expressing emotions, attitudes, opinions	interjections	*'Tut! Tut!'* *'Ouch!'*
Referential	informing describing	statements news reports	*'Pragmatics is a division of linguistics'*
Poetic	word play and rhyming	word play, alliteration, punning, rhyming poetry	*'I like Ike'* *'Many a mickle makes a muckle'*
Phatic	making and sustaining contact	greetings attention getting	*'Hello. How are you?'* *'Can you still hear me?'*
Metalinguistic	checking and repairing communication	language teaching and learning grammar books	*'I don't follow you – what do you mean?'* *'This animal is called a "gavagai"'*
Conative	persuading addressing	imperatives vocatives	*'Drink up!'* *'Hey, Joe!'*

Sometimes in his earlier work referred to as a neo-Firthian, Halliday (1970) also views language as a systematic resource for expressing meaning in context, but builds on Firth and Jakobson by considering the role of linguistic form in the exchange of meaning, concluding that 'both the general kinds of grammatical pattern that have evolved in language, and the specific manifestations of each kind, bear a natural relation to the meanings they have evolved to express' (1994:xviii). In understanding the choices available to the language user in a given context, it is necessary 'to look at both the system of language and its functions at the same time' (Halliday 1970:142).

In his unifying systemic-functional approach Halliday (1985) suggests three metafunctions that most language use will fulfil: the ideational, the interpersonal and the textual. The ideational function is concerned with ideas or concepts (the experiential function) and their interrelationships (the logical function). In realising the experiential function, the speaker is likely to refer, among other things, to participants (people, objects, abstract ideas – usually realised as nouns) and processes (actions, events and states – usually realised as verbs). Realising the logical function involves relations of co-ordination or subordination between parts of an utterance or text.

The interpersonal function embraces most illocutionary acts. It involves informational interaction (similar to Searle's assertive acts or Jakobson's referential function), social interaction (which parallels Jakobson's phatic function), instrumental interaction (directives and commissives/conative function) and expressive interaction (expressives/expressive function).

The textual function involves the organisation of information through, for example, placing phonological stress on a certain word to indicate the informational focus: compare 'Joe would like a cup of *coffee*' (i.e. Joe wants coffee rather than tea) with '*Joe* would like a cup of coffee' (i.e. Joe, not Mary wants the coffee) or using pronouns to avoid repetition of elements that have previously been mentioned: 'I saw Joe this morning. _He_ was drinking some coffee'.

Linguistic theory and the Council of Europe agenda

In the same year that his initial proposals for the unit/credit system appeared, Wilkins also published *Linguistics and Language Teaching*. In this book (Wilkins 1972b), he set out his belief that linguistic theory could help in building 'understanding of the nature of language and consequently of the nature of language learning' but that insights from theory might not offer 'specific points of information that can be built into language teaching' (Wilkins 1972b:217). Wilkins and his Council of Europe colleagues did not attempt to apply the ideas of Searle, Halliday or Hymes directly to language teaching, but drew on them eclectically to suit their purpose of building an approach to teaching and learning that would prioritise learner needs.

In this spirit, Wilkins does not adopt a Hallidayan systemic-functionalist analysis – 'Halliday's three-fold division of "functions" does not parallel the division into three types of meaning that is proposed' (Wilkins 1976:21) – but does borrow from his terminology. For Wilkins (1976, *loc cit.*), like Halliday, the *ideational* is semantic and encompasses 'events, processes, states and abstractions', embracing 'all the semantic information to be found in a grammar, a dictionary and a thesaurus' (Wilkins 1972a:3). However, Wilkins has a different purpose from Halliday. By adopting a notional approach to grammar (Lyons 1970) (with a debt to Jespersen, Zuidema and others, Trim 2007), he neatly absorbs and recasts the familiar traditional pedagogic grammatical syllabus while prioritising meaning over structure. Tense and case are not discarded from the functional-notional scheme, but become the means by which learners can convey 'universal, presumably innate' (p.9) notions of time and agency. This ideational type of meaning is expressed through the *general notions* in the T-series (Table 3).

Table 3   Categories of semantico-grammatical meaning in Wilkins (1972a) and general notions in Threshold 1990

Wilkins 1972a	Threshold 1990
1. Time: point of time; duration; time relations; frequency; sequence; age	1. Existential existence/non-existence; presence/absence; availability/ non-availability; occurrence/ non-occurrence
2. Quantity: grammatical number; numerals; quantifiers; operations	2. Spatial location relative position; distance; motion; direction; origin; arrangement; dimension
3. Space: dimensions; location; motion	3. Temporal points of time; divisions of time; indications of time; duration; earliness; etc. (27 categories)
4. Matter	4. Quantitative degree; quantity; number
5. Case: agentive; objective; dative; instrumental; locative; factitive; benefactive	5. Qualitative physical; evaluative
6. Deixis: person; time; place; anaphora	6. Mental reflection; expression
	7. Relational logical; possessive; contrastive; action/event; temporal; spatial
	8. Deixis definite; indefinite

A second type of meaning is *communicative* (Wilkins 1972a, 1976) and concerns the social meaning of the utterance in context – its illocutionary force – which is not readily traceable through (even a notional) grammar. The units of communicative meaning are, of course, the functions. The third type of meaning, modal, concerns the attitude of the speaker towards what he is saying (Wilkins 1976:22) and includes scales of certainty, intention and obligation. For Wilkins, modal meaning is intermediate between the ideational and the communicative types of meaning and in *Notional Syllabuses* (1976:66) becomes a separate category (modality – scale of certainty: *personalised, impersonalised*; scale of commitment – *intention, obligation*), but van Ek in *Threshold* (1975), and subsequently in the other T-series specifications, follows Wilkins (1972a) in treating modal meanings as functional (within the category of 'expressing and finding out attitudes').

Wilkins' conceptualisation of functions began to find its way into the models of communicative competence that, inspired particularly by the work of Hymes (1972) and of Savignon (1972) (who first applied the term 'communicative competence' to the teaching and learning languages), accompanied and informed the movement towards communicative language teaching and assessment during the 1970s and 1980s.

Communicative competence in applied linguistics and language education

Importance for functions

In his extension of the influential model first proposed by Canale and Swain (1980), Canale (1983) included four components of communicative competence. Functions were a focus for a *sociolinguistic competence* that concerned the ability to use language to fulfil communicative functions in social contexts. The other components of the model included grammatical competence (relating to underlying grammatical principles), discourse competence (concerned with the combination of utterances in forming a coherent text or interaction) and strategic competence (concerned with the strategies that learners might use to compensate for their shortcomings in other areas of competence and to maintain or repair communication – such as repetitions and reformulations).

Bachman (1990) and Bachman and Palmer (1996) considerably extended this model, emphasising the role of context and of the topic knowledge and personal characteristics of the learner in what they term *communicative language ability*. In the Bachman and Palmer model, language knowledge is divided into *organisational knowledge* (comprising grammatical and textual, or discourse knowledge) and *pragmatic knowledge*. Within *pragmatic knowledge*, contrary to Canale (1983), *functional knowledge* is distinguished from *sociolinguistic knowledge* (knowledge of dialects, registers, natural or idiomatic expressions, cultural references and figures of speech). Four functions are included: *ideational* (the way we convey meanings and experiences), *manipulative* (using language in an instrumental way to achieve ends), *heuristic* (using language to extend our knowledge of the world around us) and *imaginative* (using language to create imaginary worlds for aesthetic effect). Note that again, despite the Hallidayan terminology, these are all illocutionary (indeed in the earlier, 1990 version of the model, Bachman uses the term *illocutionary competence* to refer to them).

With the intention of more explicitly embedding lists of speech acts and functions (of the kind appearing in the Council of Europe outputs) in their pedagogically oriented model of oral communication, Celce-Murcia, Dörnyei and Thurrell (1995) develop Bachman and Palmer's (1996) conception of functional knowledge in their component of 'actional competence' (they also suggest a parallel 'rhetorical competence' for written language). This actional competence consists of 'competence in conveying and understanding communicative intent . . . based on the knowledge of an inventory of verbal schemata that carry illocutionary force (speech acts and speech events)' (p.17). In common with Bachman and Palmer (1996), they see functions as distinct from sociolinguistic competence and link them with pragmatic knowledge. They suggest that actional competence is made up of two major components: knowledge of *speech act sets* and knowledge of language functions (in seven categories: *interpersonal exchange, information, opinions, feelings, suasion, problems, future scenarios*). Speech act sets, a term derived from Cohen and Olshtain (1991), are identified with speech events (see above) and reflect the common patterns and sequences that are often associated with interrelated speech acts. The importance of such sequences was also being increasingly recognised in the Council of Europe projects (see below) and is reflected in the 'verbal exchange patterns' discussed in *Threshold 1990* (van Ek and Trim 1998b).

The CEFR model, based on van Ek (1986), makes a similar distinction to Canale and Swain's (1980) between *linguistic, sociolinguistic* and *pragmatic competences* as elements in the communicative language competence construct. Sociolinguistic or *sociocultural competences* (as they appear in the T-series) include such elements as markers for social relations, politeness conventions and register differences, while the pragmatic competences include both *functional competence* and *discourse competence* (Figure 2). Linguistic competences (*lexical, grammatical, semantic, phonological, orthographic and orthoepic* (to do with 'correct' pronunciation) are also specified. These are included 'to identify and classify the main components of linguistic

Figure 2 *Communicative competences* **in the Common European Framework of Reference (CEFR) (Council of Europe 2001:108–121)**

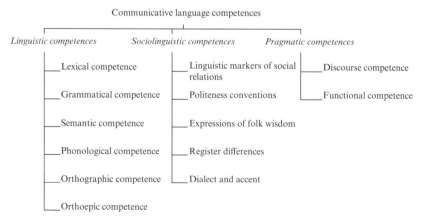

Communicative language competences

Linguistic competences   Sociolinguistic competences   Pragmatic competences

Lexical competence	Linguistic markers of social relations	Discourse competence
Grammatical competence	Politeness conventions	Functional competence
Semantic competence	Expressions of folk wisdom	
Phonological competence	Register differences	
Orthographic competence	Dialect and accent	
Orthoepic competence		

competence defined as knowledge of and ability to use the formal resources from which well-formed, meaningful messages may be assembled' (*ibid.* 109). As we are reminded all along the route towards insights into functional progression, language functions cannot be conceived without their structural exponents.

The Common European Framework of Reference (CEFR) includes a brief overview of functional competence (see below), but refers readers to the T-series for detailed listings relevant to each of the levels (p.30). All of the T-series volumes follow the same basic pattern of specifying learning objectives in terms of situations, activities, functions and notions. Van Ek sets out the basic approach in straightforward terms and is worth quoting at some length:

> In order to define the learning objective for a target-group we first have to specify the situations in which they will need the foreign language. Specifying a situation means stating the roles a language-user has to play, the settings in which he will have to play these roles, and the topics he will have to deal with . . .
>
> Once we have determined the situations in which the members of the target-group will want to use the foreign language we can try to specify just what they will have to be able to *do* in those situations . . .
>
> First we specify the language activities the learner will be likely to engage in . . . [such as] understanding the weather-forecast on the radio or . . . summarising orally in a foreign language a report written in one's native language . . . [then] we try to specify for what general purposes the learner will have to use the foreign language, what language functions he will have to fulfil. For instance, he may have to give information about facts, he may wish to express certainty or uncertainty, whether he considers something right or wrong, he may wish to express gratitude, he may wish to apologise.
>
> But the learner will have to do more than fulfil such general language functions. He will not only have to give information in the abstract, but he will want to give information about *something*, he will wish to express certainty or uncertainty with respect to *something*, he will want to apologise for *something*. In other words, he will need the ability to refer to things, to people, to events etc, and to talk about them. In order to do all this he will have to be able to handle a large number of *notions* in the foreign language. What notions he will need depends to a large extent on the topics he will deal with. If he is dealing with the topic "weather" he will have to handle notions such as *fair, sunshine, to rain* etc.
>
> When the specification of a language-learning objective has been completed up to this point we can determine what actual *language forms* (structures, words and phrases) the learner will have to be able to use in order to do all that has been specified. These forms are determined by considering each of the language-functions and notions separately and establishing how they are realised in a particular language – in other words by establishing their *exponents*.

The final component of a language-learning objective is a statement about the degree of skill with which a successful learner will be expected to be able to do all that has been specified, in other words how well he will have to be able to do it. It is very easy to do this in general terms, but very difficult, if not impossible to do it with anything approaching the degree of exactness we can achieve for the other components of the definition (Van Ek 1975:4–5).

In the current version of Threshold – *Threshold 1990* (van Ek and Trim 1998b) – the reader is presented with lists of functions selected to 'meet the most likely and urgent needs of the learners' and representing a surprisingly precise 'average learning load of two to three years for courses of average intensity, i.e. two to three hours per week, 35–40 weeks a year' (van Ek and Trim 1998b:27) or 'an average of 375 learning hours – including independent work' (p.8). Surprising in its precision not only because of the known variability in rates of language learning associated with factors such as individual aptitude and language distance, but also because we have been told that the increased flexibility of the revised objective 'makes an assessment of the learning load in terms of "an average number of learning hours" even more difficult' (p.8). The CEFR repeats the advice that, 'extreme caution should be exercised in using any scale of levels to calculate the 'mean seat time' necessary to meet particular objectives' (p.18). With the increasing diversity of language learning environments, this caution may have even greater justification today.

The categorisation of functions in Threshold adapts Wilkins (1976) (see Table 4). The functions are presented in the form of a branching system that makes increasingly fine distinctions (Figure 3) and provides illustrative exponents for each.

Table 4 Functional categories in Wilkins (1972a, 1976) and Threshold (1975)

Wilkins Modern Languages 1972a	*Wilkins Notional Syllabuses 1976*	*van Ek Threshold 1975*
1. Modality 2. Moral discipline and evaluation 3. Suasion 4. Argument 5. Rational inquiry and exposition 6. Personal emotions 7. Emotional relations 8. Interpersonal relations	1. Argument 2. Emotional relations 3. Judgement and evaluation 4. Personal emotions 5. Rational enquiry and exposition 6. Suasion	1. Imparting and seeking factual information 2. Expressing and finding out intellectual attitudes 3. Expressing and finding out emotional attitudes 4. Expressing and finding out moral attitudes 5. Getting things done (suasion) 6. Socialising

Figure 3 Sub-categories associated with the function of 'socialising' in Threshold 1990

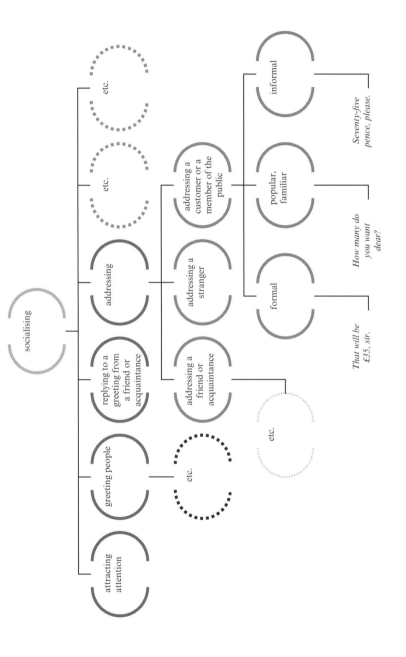

The listings are derived from speculative needs analyses based on the proposal by Richterich (1972), representing the language required for adult language learners to 'conduct the necessary business of everyday living when abroad with a reasonable degree of independence' (van Ek & Trim 1998b:1). Richterich (1983) collects 11 case studies 'in identifying language needs', all of them submitted to the Council of Europe Secretariat in 1980. If not fully empirical – in the sense that the analyses are not based directly on representative samples of learner language – the intention is nonetheless to capture the variation in uses of language that emerges from the investigation: 'the list represents a deliberate selection for T-level' rather than 'an exhaustive list' (van Ek 1975:19). At the same time, the specification is intended to be quite comprehensive in scope and, as we have seen, the functions are intended to generalise across situations.

It can be seen from Figure 3 that the branching arrived at is not simply a matter of drawing ever finer distinctions between illocutionary verbs (as between greeting and addressing), but also incorporates sociolinguistic constraints such as degrees of acquaintanceship, levels of formality and background knowledge. Taking account of interpersonal and contextual variables, in *Threshold 1990* there is a differentiation between greeting i) friends and acquaintances, ii) strangers and iii) members of the public (Figure 3) and a distinction (not shown in Figure 3) between responding to a greeting from a friend or acquaintance '*when in good health*', '*when in poor health*' or '*when recovering from an illness*'. We are also told that '*Good morning/afternoon/ evening*' is more formal than '*Hallo*' when greeting people.

Such differentiation may be a response to criticism of the original *Threshold* specification (1975) for its failure to take account of sociolinguistic issues (Flowerdew 1990). In his criticism, Flowerdew points to a lack of guidance on the effects of choosing '*I'd like*', '*I want*', or '*may I have*' in grading expressions of wants/desires. However, these continue to be listed as parallel choices in *Threshold 1990* (van Ek & Trim 1998b, Chapter 5) (see Appendix B).

Reflecting this and other feedback received, new insights gained in the intervening years as well as the possibilities suggested by the different approaches taken in specifications developed for other languages – especially *Un Niveau Seuil* (French) and *Kontaktschwelle* (German) – a number of changes were made to the *Threshold* specification between 1975 and 1990. Although it is, in the main, direct functions that are presented, in both the 1975 and 1990 versions a few conventional indirect functions – such as '*can I . . .*' for requests – are included in the listings (as in Table 5). It is stressed that the limited listing of indirect functions 'does not mean that the indirect fulfilment of language functions should be avoided in course materials designed for Threshold Level [as] an attempt to do so might lead to highly unnatural language use' (van Ek & Trim 1998b:28). In *Threshold 1990*, guidance

Table 5 Exponents of *expressing wants/desires* in Threshold 1990

2.23	expressing wants/desires

2.23.1 I'd like + NP
I'd like an ice cream

2.23.2 I'd like + to + VPinf
I'd 'like to .wash my hands.

2.23.3 I want + NP, please
I .want a cup of tea, .please.

2.23.4 I want + to + VPinf, please
I want to .go to the toilet, please.

2.23.5 (please) may I (+ VPinf)
Please may I .have a drink.

2.23.6 Can I have + NP (please)
Can I .have my bill, please?

on when and why indirect realisations of functions may sometimes be more appropriate is provided in a new chapter (van Ek and Trim 1998b, Chapter 11: Sociocultural competence).

Another of Flowerdew's (1990) objections is that *Threshold* (1975) does not refer to 'intermediate' categorisations of the kind made by Leech (1981). Leech observes that a tag question such as 'you will come, won't you?' is neither a clear-cut order, nor simply an invitation, but something in between the two. Again, such considerations are addressed in Chapter 11 of *Threshold 1990* (Sociocultural competence): in this case, in some detail (Table 6).

The T-series also acknowledges that utterances may be multi-functional ('one may seek factual information while at the same time expressing surprise', van Ek 1975:19), but as with indirectness, the issues that this raises are bypassed in the presentation of the lists of functions in Chapter 5 of *Threshold 1990* (van Ek & Trim 1998b) on grounds of convenience and practicality.

Roberts (1983) raises the issue of intonation. He objects that 'all students have to be helped to recognise that there is a connection between function and attitude on the one hand, and stress and intonation on the other', observing that available functional materials, including *Threshold* 1975, had failed to provide sufficient direction.

The 1990 version of Threshold does include guidance on intonation patterns. There are also changes in the arrangement of some of the functions, the collapsing of the three 'expressing and finding out' categories of functions in *Threshold* 1975 (Table 7, categories 2–4) to one in 1990 (category 2) and the addition of two new functional categories in the 1990 specification (categories 5 and 6 in Table 7). The scheme adopted for *Threshold 1990* (van Ek & Trim 1998b) is now used to cover all four levels in the T-series (see Appendix B).

Table 6 Offers, invitations and politeness conventions in *Threshold 1990* (van Ek and Trim 1998b), Chapter 11

Offers and invitations are very much subject to politeness conventions, but in a complex way, since they attempt to persuade the partner to act in a certain way, but in the interests of the partner rather than of the speaker. Invitations and offers may be strong or weak.

A 'strong' offer or invitation, making it easier for the partner to accept, may be conveyed:

* by using an imperative as though it were an order:
  e.g. Let me help you.
    Give me that case to carry.
    Come and spend the day in Oxford.
* by expressing obligation or necessity:
  e.g. You must let me carry that case.
* by demanding a promise:
  e.g. Promise you will come to dinner with us.
* by demanding confirmation of an imputed intention:
  e.g. You will be our guests| won't you?

Note the use of low falling intonations with strong offers and invitations.

A 'weak' offer or invitation makes it possible for the partner to decline:

* by using an interrogative question regarding the partner's intentions, desires, needs or ability.
  e.g. Are you coming to dinner?
    Would you like some help with that problem?
    Do you need any help?
    Can you come to dinner next Wednesday?

Especially weak are offers that:
a) require the partner to admit that he/she is unable to refuse:
  e.g. Can you manage?
    Are you stuck?
b) are negatively phrased:
  e.g. I don't suppose you could do with some help?
    You don't require assistance |do you?

Note the prevalence of rising intonation with weak offers. Strong offers can be accepted without demur, or confirmation can be invited:
e.g. Are you sure?
   Is that all right?

A weak offer or invitation is not usually accepted without demur. More commonly, a repeated offer is invited:
e.g. Won't that be too much trouble?
   Can you spare the time?
   It's very heavy| that case.

or a weak rejection is offered:
e.g. No, thank you|I don't want to ˇbother you.
   I'm sure you're much too busy.

This allows the partner to withdraw the offer or invitation:
e.g. Well| as a matter of fact| I am rather busy.
   Right then | So long as you can manage.

or to repeat it, usually in a stronger form:
e.g. No|really | I'd like to help.
   No| do come | We'd very much like you to come.

The declining of a strong invitation is usually accompanied by an apology, or a reason for declining an offer:
e.g. Well thank you| but I'm ^sorry| I'm afraid I have another engagement.
   No thank you|I don't smoke.
   Thanks| but it's easier by myself.

A suggestion for further contact, or even an invitation to visit, may be a polite or a well-intentioned way of ending a contact. Its formal acceptance need not entail a firm commitment on either side:
e.g. A: Do visit us next time you're in London.
   B: Thank you|I will.

Table 7 Functional components and chapter titles in *Threshold* 1975 specification compared with the 1990 edition

Functional categories		Chapter titles	
Threshold 1975	*Threshold 1990*	*Threshold 1975*	*Threshold 1990*
1. imparting and seeking factual information	1. imparting and seeking factual information	1. Objectives in a unit/credit scheme	1. The objective: levels of specificity
2. expressing and finding out intellectual attitudes	2. expressing and finding out attitudes	2. Language learning objectives	2. The objective: general characterisation
3. expressing and finding out emotional attitudes	3. getting things done (suasion)	3. Language learning objectives in a European unit/ credit system	3. The objective: extended characterisation
4. expressing and finding out moral attitudes	4. socialising	4. The threshold level	4. The objective: components of the specification
5. getting things done (suasion)	5. structuring discourse	5. Specification of situations	5. Language functions
6. socialising	6. communication repair	6. Language activities	6. General notions
		7. Language functions	7. Specific notions
		8. Topics: behavioural specifications	8. Verbal exchange patterns
		9. General notions	9. Dealing with texts: reading and listening
		10. Specific notions	10. Writing
		11. Language forms	11. Sociocultural competence
		12. Degree of skill	12. Compensation strategies
			13. Learning to learn
			14. Degree of skill

Another development from the 1975 specification in *Threshold 1990* (van Ek & Trim 1998b) is the greater acknowledgement of organisational influences on interaction and textual organisation such as juxtaposition (addressed in *Vantage*, Chapter 8), conversational gambits and routines (Keller 1981), schemata (Wunderlic, 1972), framing (Goffman 1974), scripts (Schank & Abelson 1977), genres (Swales 1990) and similar schema-based conceptions of the cultural knowledge and expectations that we bring to interaction. There is also recognition of the role of adjacency pairs and preference sequences (Sacks, Schegloff and Jefferson 1974; Schegloff 1992): 'function exponents are more likely to occur in sequences [which] exhibit certain regularities in the order of their elements. Thus, an apology will very often be followed by an explanation' (van Ek and Trim 1998b:82). As with issues of politeness and indirect functions, this is dealt with in the text (Chapter 8 in van Ek & Trim 1998b) rather than being integrated into the lists of functions (van Ek & Trim 1998b, Chapter 5).

Beyond offering a 'praxeogram' or 'general schema' for goods and services (reproduced in the CEFR on pp. 127–128) the newer specification does not attempt to offer comprehensive guidance on sequencing. This is on grounds that: 'to attempt to do so would be at once too restrictive and over elaborate' (van Ek & Trim 1998b:85).

Table 8 Functional categories in the T-series by level

Vantage	Threshold	Waystage	Breakthrough
1. Imparting and seeking information	1. Imparting and seeking factual information	1. Imparting and seeking factual information	1. The learner CAN impart and elicit factual information
2. Expressing and finding out attitudes	2. Expressing and finding out attitudes	2. Expressing and finding out attitudes	2. The learner CAN express and find out attitudes
3. Deciding and managing courses of action: suasion	3. Deciding on courses of action (suasion)	3. Getting things done (suasion)	3. The learner CAN get things done (suasion)
4. Socialising	4. Socialising	4. Socialising	4. The learner CAN socialise
5. Structuring discourse	5. Structuring discourse	5. Structuring discourse	5. The learner CAN structure discourse
6. Assuring and repairing communication	6. Communication repair	6. Communication repair	6. The learner CAN repair snags in communication

A distinction not found in the T-series is made in the CEFR between *macrofunction* and *microfunction*. This is not the same as the distinction more often made by applied linguists, as by Cook (1989), wherein macrofunctions stand in a superordinate relation to the microfunctions (the microfunction *request* is a category within the macrofunction of *directives*). In the CEFR, a microfunction is associated with an individual utterance or sentence (the kind of function that appears in the T-series listings). A macrofunction, on the other hand, is associated with the rhetorical purpose of an extended stretch of written text or spoken discourse and is identified in the CEFR with genre (p.93), parallel to speech events or speech act sets (see above). No comprehensive listing of macrofunctions is provided, but examples (p. 126) include *description, narration, commentary, exposition, exegesis, explanation, demonstration, instruction, argumentation* and *persuasion*.

We are told that, 'At higher levels of proficiency, the development of discourse competence . . . becomes of increasing importance'. There is therefore likely to be scope for specifying how macrofunctions and their associated 'text types' or 'genres' (Council of Europe 2001:123) relate to the CEFR levels, perhaps by identifying level-related differences in knowledge of 'conventions in the community concerning, e.g. how information is structured in realising the various macrofunctions (description, narrative, exposition, etc.)' (p.123).

Functional progression between levels: what does the Council of Europe have to say?

The CEFR offers guidance on what is *criterial* about each of the levels. The general characterisations (Council of Europe 2001:36) of the A and B levels describe progression in explicitly functional terms, but the C level includes very little that relates directly to functions. Level A2, for example seems to involve an increase in the range of interpersonal functions available to learners. Criterial (and clearly functional) abilities include to *greet people, ask how they are and react to news; handle very short social exchanges; ask and answer questions about what they do at work and in free time; make and respond to invitations; discuss what to do, where to go and make arrangements to meet; make and accept offers.* The illustrative scale for *sociolinguistic appropriateness* has A2 learners able to *perform and respond to basic language functions, such as information exchange and requests* and to *express opinions and attitudes in a simple way* (p.122), although there is no indication within the A2 specification of which functions are not 'basic'. Comparisons with B1 are, of course, possible ('a wide range of language functions'), but would breach the requirement for independence – descriptions should be self contained – and do not in any case make it clear how the user should determine whether a function is 'basic' or not.

At the B2 level learners are able to present and develop a coherent argument: *construct a chain of reasoned argument; develop an argument giving reasons in support of or against a particular point of view; explain a problem and make it clear that his/her counterpart in a negotiation must make a concession; speculate about causes, consequences, hypothetical situations; take an active part in informal discussion in familiar contexts, commenting, putting point of view clearly, evaluating alternative proposals and making and responding to hypotheses.* There is a growing role for textual functions supporting cohesion and conversation management – *plan what is to be said and the means to say it, considering the effect on the recipient/s* – and effective communication repair: *correct mistakes if they have led to misunderstandings; make a note of 'favourite mistakes' and consciously monitor speech for it/them; generally correct slips and errors if he/she becomes conscious of them* (Council of Europe 2001:35).

At C1 we are told that learners have a *fluent repertoire of discourse functions,* but the focus here is on the fluent and spontaneous nature of learner production, rather than on its range of functionality. The characterisation of the C2 learner concerns the 'precision, appropriateness and ease' with which learners manage the language. A C2 learner is said to be able to *convey shades of meaning precisely* and *has a good command of idiomatic expressions and colloquialisms with awareness of connotative level of meaning.* The higher level learner appears to have a developed pragmatic sensitivity to choices between functional exponents and to the role of *modification devices* (Council of Europe 2001:35).

Although functions are included in a number of the illustrative scales, they are (perhaps because of their recursivity) not scaled separately under the heading of '*Functional Competence*'. Instead, two generic qualitative factors are provided. Although these qualitative factors clearly do not relate exclusively to functions, they are said to 'determine the functional success of the learner/user' (Council of Europe 2001:128). They include:

a) *fluency, the ability to articulate, to keep going, and to cope when one lands in a dead end*

b) *propositional precision, the ability to formulate thoughts and propositions so as to make one's meaning clear.*

Included in the fluency scale are descriptions of hesitation and pausing behaviours; flow and tempo of delivery; degrees of ease/effort in production; naturalness and spontaneity; the degree of strain imposed on partners in interaction; the occurrence of false starts and reformulations (Table 9). The descriptors on the propositional precision scale relate to shades of meaning; modification and qualification; modality; degrees of informational detail or precision (Table 10).

Table 9 Spoken Fluency illustrative scale (Council of Europe 2001:129)

C2	*Can express him/herself at length with a natural, effortless, unhesitating flow. Pauses only to reflect on precisely the right words to express his/her thoughts or to find an appropriate example or explanation.*
C1	*Can express him/herself fluently and spontaneously, almost effortlessly. Only a conceptually difficult subject can hinder a natural, smooth flow of language. Can communicate spontaneously, often showing remarkable fluency and ease of expression in even longer complex stretches of speech.*
B2	*Can produce stretches of language with a fairly even tempo; although he/she can be hesitant as he/she searches for patterns and expressions, there are few noticeably long pauses. Can interact with a degree of fluency and spontaneity that makes regular interaction with native speakers quite possible without imposing strain on either party. Can express him/herself with relative ease. Despite some problems with formulation resulting in pauses and 'cul-de-sacs', he/she is able to keep going effectively without help.*
B1	*Can keep going comprehensibly, even though pausing for grammatical and lexical planning and repair is very evident, especially in longer stretches of free production. Can make him/herself understood in short contributions, even though pauses, false starts and reformulation are very evident.*
A2	*Can construct phrases on familiar topics with sufficient ease to handle short exchanges, despite very noticeable hesitation and false starts.*
A1	*Can manage very short, isolated, mainly pre-packaged utterances, with much pausing to search for expressions, to articulate less familiar words, and to repair communication.*

Table 10 Propositional Precision illustrative scale (Council of Europe 2001:129)

C2	*Can convey finer shades of meaning precisely by using, with reasonable accuracy, a wide range of qualifying devices (e.g. adverbs expressing degree, clauses expressing limitations). Can give emphasis, differentiate and eliminate ambiguity.*
C1	*Can qualify opinions and statements precisely in relation to degrees of, for example, certainty/ uncertainty, belief/doubt, likelihood, etc.*
B2	*Can pass on detailed information reliably. Can explain the main points in an idea or problem with reasonable precision.*
B1	*Can convey simple, straightforward information of immediate relevance, getting across which point he/she feels is most important. Can express the main point he/she wants to make comprehensibly.*
A2	*Can communicate what he/she wants to say in a simple and direct exchange of limited information on familiar and routine matters, but in other situations he/she generally has to compromise the message.*
A1	*No descriptor available*

These qualitative factors appear to reflect quite closely the criterial features of the C levels noted above from the general characterisations. At the C levels, the production of functions involves greater sensitivity to context (reflected in the use of modifying, qualifying and clarifying devices), greater spontaneity and less hesitancy than at the lower levels.

In terms of the topics and situations in which learners might be able to apply their functional competence, there is again relatively little to be said at the C levels (Council of Europe 2001:224). Appropriately enough, by the B1 *Threshold* Level, the learner is able to cope with *accumulated factual information on familiar matters* and *most topics pertinent to everyday life*. Beyond B1 there is only one mention of topic in the illustrative scales: the ability to provide a *clear detailed description of complex subjects*, which occurs at the C1 level on the illustrative scales for *sustained monologue* and *essays and reports*.

Turning from the CEFR to the T-series, there is no specification concerned exclusively with the C levels: the highest level *Vantage* specification (van Ek and Trim 2001) represents a level beyond *Threshold* (B1). In the CEFR *Vantage* is equated with B2 (p.23). However, according to Trim (see Preface), *Vantage* is not bounded in the same way as B2 and in some respects may go well beyond B2. The *Vantage* specification should therefore offer insights into the nature of language ability above the *Threshold* Level including C1 and C2, although it may have relatively little to say about what distinguishes B2 from the higher levels.

Wilkins (1976) illustrates the range of potential levels in communication around a particular notional-functional category, for example *definition,* where his examples include, '*Thyme is a kind of herb used in cooking*'and at a higher level of proficiency, '*A reversible reaction may be defined as a reaction which will proceed in either direction if conditions are arranged appropriately*'. The functional progression thus involves cumulative proficiency with the same function appearing at different levels, but expressed through different exponents.

As is clear from Appendix B, for the most part, the T-series adopts the same approach to progression. The same functions recur from *Breakthrough* (Trim 2009) up to *Vantage* (van Ek & Trim 2001) and progression is evident more through the increasing sophistication of the exponents than through the functions themselves. The intention from the earliest stage is to provide the broadest possible functionality from minimal resources.

In moving from *Threshold* to *Vantage*, there is a refinement of both functional and general notional categories, with more exponents provided for both. There is 'a more sensitive sub-categorisation of functions, particularly those in which a personal reaction, intellectual or emotional, is called for' (Van Ek & Trim 2001:22). This is perhaps most clearly marked in the functional categories of *expression of emotions* (expanded from 22 to 37 categories and sub-categories and from 102 to 194 exponents) and *suasion* (expanded from one category with seven exponents to eight sub-categories with 26 exponents) (Van Ek & Trim 2001:22). There is also a considerable expansion both in the 'common core' vocabulary and in more specialised vocabulary expressing specific notions in topic areas of interest to individual learners.

The *Vantage* learner has access both to more formal and to more colloquial language, and is starting to use variation more appropriately than those at lower levels. Learners gain an increased range and greater control of goal-directed conversation strategies together with a greater recognition and a limited control of important register varieties. This means that learners are 'more familiar with the conventions and able to act more flexibly with regard to formal and colloquial registers and the politeness conventions of a host community' (Van Ek & Trim 2001:18).

As in the movement from the B levels to the C levels in the CEFR, *Vantage* represents a qualitative development from *Threshold*: '*Vantage* as compared to *Threshold*, is marked by a relaxation of constraints, learners at *Vantage* level may be expected to communicate not only more effectively but also more efficiently and with greater ease in most of the communication situations in which they may find themselves' (Van Ek & Trim 2001:115).

Increasing proficiency gives the learner greater scope for creativity and for dealing with the unexpected: 'by *Vantage* level, greater control over greater linguistic resources enables the learner to rise above stereotypical schemata and to make more varied, flexible and effective use of principles of discourse structure and verbal exchange' (Van Ek & Trim 2001:23).

Table 11 Topics appearing in illustrative scales by CEFR level (Council of Europe 2001:224)

DESCRIBING & NARRATING

A1	A2	B1	B2	C1	C2
• where they live	• people, appearance • background, job • places & living conditions • objects, pets, possessions • events & activities • likes/dislikes • plans/arrangements • habits/routines • personal experience	• plot of book/film • experiences • reactions to both • dreams, hopes, ambitions • tell a story • basic details of unpredictable occurrences e.g. accident		• clear detailed description of complex subjects	

INFORMATION EXCHANGE

A1	A2	B1	B2	C1	C2
• themselves & others • home • time	• simple, routine, direct • limited, work & free time • simple directions & instructions • pastimes, habits, routines • past activities	• detailed directions • accumulated factual info on familiar matters within field			

RANGE SETTINGS

A1	A2	B1	B2	C1	C2
• basic common needs • simple/predictable survival • simple concrete needs: pers, details, daily routines, info requests	• routine everyday transactions • familiar situations & topics • everyday situations with predictable content	• most topics pertinent to everyday life: family hobbies interests, work travel, current events			

Functional progression between levels: what do functionalist approaches to second language acquisition and interlanguage pragmatics have to say?

Second Language Acquisition (SLA) research has not always proved to be readily applicable to language education and is more usually concerned with linguistic forms than with functions. However, it is important to consider what evidence exists for the acquisition of functional competence. Might there be observable acquisitional sequences of the kind found for the morpho-grammatical features explored in Hawkins and Filipović (2012, Chapter 4)? Do research findings support the Council of Europe specifications?

Although the earliest studies now date back over 30 years, research into developmental sequences in the acquisition of pragmatic abilities is still said to be in its infancy (Kasper & Schmidt 1996). A major project carried out in the 1980s, the Cross-Cultural Speech Act Realization Project (CCSARP) (*Applied Linguistics* 1983; Blum-Kulka, Kasper & House 1989), heralded an explosion of research into cross-cultural pragmatics, involving comparisons between native and non-native speaker realisations of various speech acts. However, (contrasting with a wealth of research on L1 child pragmatic development) this work has mainly been concerned with how L2 speakers comprehend or produce speech acts, rather than with the processes by which they learn to do so (see Bardovi-Harlig, Kasper & Schmidt 1996; Rose 2000; 2001). At the same time, the various functionalist approaches to SLA (Mitchell and Myles 2004) are more often concerned with what are termed notions in the CEFR scheme than with functions (see above). Attempts have been made, for example, to trace development in the linguistic expression of spatial and temporal relations or of modality, but functions or speech acts have attracted relatively little research.

Leech's (1983) distinction between *sociopragmatic* and *pragmalinguistic* knowledge is helpful in understanding the challenges that learners may face. Although most adults are aware of social conventions governing behaviour, these conventions may not transfer successfully across cultures (even when cultures share an L1). Sociopragmatic knowledge refers to this awareness of conventions governing behaviour – being aware for example, that in certain cultures rejecting an offer of food or drink may cause offence. Even if they have the linguistic resources to accept an offer, learners may fail to act appropriately because they are unfamiliar with the culturally conditioned expectations of their hosts. On the other hand, even when learners have sociopragmatic awareness, they may experience pragmalinguistic failure. They may lack the linguistic resources to support their illocutionary intent – not knowing appropriate phrases to indicate polite acceptance of the offer, or failing to recognise that an indirect offer is being made.

Kasper and Rose (2003) provide a useful overview of the relatively few developmental studies of interlanguage pragmatics, addressing both comprehension and production. These include studies that have concerned the speech acts (or functions) of apology (Blum-Kulka & Olshtain, 1986; Maeshiba, Yoshinaga, Kasper & Ross 1996; Rose 2000; Trosborg 1987), complaint (Trosborg 1995), invitation (Scarcella 1979), refusal (Houck & Gass 1996, Robinson 1992), request (Blum-Kulka & Olshtain 1986; Chiba 2002: Ellis 1992; Hassall 1997; Hill 1997; Rose 2000, Svanes 1992), response to compliments (Rose 2000), and suggestion and rejection (Bardovi-Harlig & Hartford 1993a).

These studies have generally shown the functions produced by learners becoming, with increasing language ability, more target-like: involving increasingly complex syntax and greater use of modification of the main speech act (the *head act*). Modification may be accomplished through internal modifiers including softeners such as hedges (*'kind of'*; *'I guess . . .'*) or downgraders (*'could you possibly . . .'*), intensifiers (*'I insist that you . . .'*) and external modifiers such as grounders (*'I don't have any money with me'*). Kasper and Rose (2003:307) suggest that, at least for requests, there is now sufficient evidence to suggest some developmental sequencing. Beginning learners tend to rely on pre-grammatical utterances, formulaic speech and direct rather than indirect requests. There is a gradual move toward conventional forms of indirectness, followed by the appearance of request modification as proficiency increases.

Developing the ability to control the form of speech act realisations in response to variation in the social context would seem to be particularly challenging. Kasper and Rose (2003) sum up the findings as follows: 'despite already possessing considerable universal pragmatic knowledge, adult L2 learners appear to require a great deal of time to develop the ability to appropriately map L2 forms to social categories. This appears to be especially true in foreign language contexts' (p.145). This is probably because the foreign language classroom provides fewer opportunities for developing sociopragmatic awareness than are available through immersion in a foreign culture.

Although much of the interlanguage pragmatics research involves L2/L1 speaker comparisons, Bardovi-Harlig and Hartford (2005) remind us that it should not be assumed that native speakers have a pragmatic mastery that non-natives lack or that observed differences between L1 and L2 speakers necessarily impact on the effectiveness of communication. Tarone (2005) suggests that an English for Specific Purposes (ESP) perspective might be a helpful one for conceiving pragmatic competence. ESP distinguishes between novices and experts according to their individual levels of awareness of the conventions associated with discourse genres rather than native speaker status. Hence 'a request may fail or succeed in a discourse community depending on whether its realization fits genre norms. All novices (native speaker or not) must master genre norms' (Tarone 2005:160).

Thomas (1983) makes the point that sociopragmatics are closely bound up with issues of personal and cultural identity and suggests that learners may not always need or wish to adopt the roles implied by the conventions of the target culture – in fact they may prefer to reject or subvert genre norms. The participants in the study by Siegal (1996), for example, although having both the sociopragmatic awareness of the conventions and the pragmalinguistic means to realise them, avoided adopting features of 'women's speech' in Japanese. The cultural basis of sociopragmatics makes such issues particularly sensitive for English language education, given the status of English as a global language and the questions that this raises about what might be suitable as a 'target culture'. In an interaction between, let's say, a Mexican, an Egyptian and an Indonesian at an international conference, which sociopragmatic conventions would the interaction be expected to follow?

The distinction made in the CEFR between *plurilingual* and *pluricultural* competences, makes operational definitions of pragmatic competence particularly difficult for those who, following the models of communicative language ability outlined above, may wish to isolate this aspect for testing. Hudson, Detmer and Brown (1995) suggest a range of indirect and direct techniques that may be used to test awareness of and production of speech acts for research purposes, but concede that their work is exploratory and, with a hint of understatement given the controversy that the topic has provoked (see for example Crystal 2003), that 'the role played by the "native speaker" as the standard against which performance is judged is far from resolved' (Hudson, Detmer and Brown 1995:66).

The evidence from tests of pragmatics on developing competence is mixed. Using discourse completion tasks (DCT – short written dialogues with a gap to be filled with an appropriate speech act) in both constructed (written) and selected response (multiple choice) formats together with self-assessment questionnaires, Liu (2006) found little (multiple choice) or no (written and self-assessed) significant relationships with TOEFL scores. On the other hand, Roever (2005), using similar multiple-choice and short-answer measures in a web-based test of pragmalinguistic knowledge of speech acts (requests, apologies and refusals), conversational implicature and interactional routines (associated with greetings, introductions, telephone interaction, meals etc.), found a positive relationship between language proficiency and knowledge of speech acts and implicature, but found that awareness of conversational routines was more closely associated with exposure to an English-speaking environment than with classroom-based learning. An unfortunate shortcoming of much of the interlanguage pragmatics research acknowledged by Hudson, Detmer and Brown and by Roever is that the most popular elicitation method, the DCT, may in fact be a poor predictor of performance in unscripted interaction (Bardovi-Harlig & Hartford 1993b, Golato 2003).

O'Sullivan, Weir and Saville (2003) investigate functions in language tests from a different perspective. Their study involves comparisons on the basis of a checklist of language functions, between the language that test tasks are designed to elicit and the language that is actually produced by test takers. The checklists proving to be operationally effective for the practical analysis of large quantities of oral test data, this approach may, as O'Sullivan et al suggest, allow for meaningful comparisons to be made between learners performing similar tasks at different CEFR levels. However, the checklists do not include issues such as turn length, awareness of routines and sociolinguistic variation that the interlanguage pragmatics research suggests may be criterial at the higher levels.

The suggestions in the T-series that speech acts can be realised through different exponents at different levels and that sociolinguistic variation is a high-level skill both receive some support from research into the use of functions by learners. However, the available evidence is perhaps too limited in scope (only a handful of speech acts have been studied) and methodology (unrepresentative, small scale case studies or unrealistic DCT) to provide many substantial insights into functional progression. There is scope for projects related to English Profile to make a substantial contribution in this area.

Conclusions

This chapter has reviewed functions and functional progression as conceived in the work of the Council of Europe. This has provided a general picture of the functional capabilities of the C level learner. Functional competence is seen to develop iteratively and to involve elements of both linguistic and cultural knowledge. At the C (*Proficient User*) levels, learners are likely to have both a repertoire of more formulaic functional exponents and the potential for more creative realisations. They will probably be confident in the use of implicature and familiar with a wide range of conventional indirect speech acts. They will be able to deal flexibly with a range of situations. They are likely to be able to make use of a range of internal and external modifiers to shape their own production to suit audience, purpose and context, with an awareness of the social implications of choices between exponents and modifiers.

Since the 1970s the work of the Council of Europe, mediated through language syllabuses, course materials and tests, has of course had a profound impact on language teaching and testing practice. However, the CEFR is neither the beginning nor the end of the story. The CEFR levels are intended to provide 'an adequate coverage of the learning space relevant to European language learners' (Council of Europe 2001:23) engaged in socially organised and publicly recognised learning. In other contexts and for other purposes, the description of different learning spaces with levels above or below those of the CEFR may be appropriate. Equally, it is acknowledged that the CEFR levels represent an attempt to capture a 'wide, though by no means universal, consensus on the number and nature of levels appropriate to the organisation of language learning' (Council of Europe 2001:22–23): a consensus that predates and continues to exist alongside the framework. A re-examination of this wide consensus as it relates to the English language (and so passes beyond the scope of the CEFR) is imperative for the English Profile. The continuing use of language functions and associated concepts in language classrooms and examination halls, filtered through the accumulated experience of teachers and testing professionals, should provide a rich vein of evidence on the nature of this consensus as it relates to functional progression and, as the focus of this book, to the C levels. The following chapter therefore pursues the question of functional progression in language learning materials: curricula, textbooks, examinations and associated materials.

2 Can Do statements as instructional objectives

Chapter 1 explored the heritage of language functions in Council of Europe modern languages projects and the T-series, which provide reference level descriptions and specific linguistic exponents for a set of language learning levels. We have already seen that the T-series represents a set of objectives for language learners founded on the concept of a 'common core' of situations for language use and of pertinent linguistic knowledge. The T-series objectives start from a classification of notions and language functions – useful categories for a reformed meaning-based pedagogy – presenting lexical and grammatical forms – the currency of the traditional syllabus – as their exponents. Progression is represented in the T-series through the expanding repertoire of exponents that the user can bring to bear on the situations they encounter as they pass from one objective to the next.

Trim notes in the Preface to this volume that at *Breakthrough* Level there are challenges in accommodating both those who, as migrants, may need to use their limited linguistic resources to meet immediate needs and those who are working towards higher level goals without any imminent requirement for communication. It is apparent that as learners move beyond the Threshold Level it becomes increasingly difficult to identify a 'common core' in the diversity that opens up. Those who become more proficient may simply wish to improve their ability to carry out the kinds of task envisaged at the *Threshold* Level, but with greater fluency or with a wider range of language: as Trim expresses it in the Preface, 'to overcome a sense of severe limitation, of being obliged to say what one could say rather than what one wanted to say': more a qualitative than a quantitative improvement. Others (and perhaps this is more often true of learning English than any other language) might study with a view to achieving quantitative changes, engaging in further language learning to carry out a wider range of tasks – especially tasks associated with 'more advanced professional or vocational qualifications', in order to access academic study, professional practice, commercial negotiation, international diplomacy and so forth.

Such uses of language carry learners in divergent directions: professional and academic specialities are partly constituted by distinct vocabularies, social roles and modes of expression. Most adult users of a language will need to find accommodation, travel, make purchases and socialise and can work towards a shared repertoire of words and expressions to do so. Relatively few will expect to write extended reports, give presentations or carry out sensitive negotiations: if they do, they will generally use a more specialised language for these purposes. Equally, those who become immersed in a specific speech community may adopt an identifiable variety of English: fluent, colloquial, but socially restricted. Higher level objectives are more diverse and more localised as a result: common interpretations harder to reach, comparisons of performance harder to make.

While the T-series is generally focused on qualitative development in relation to a defined range of functions, the panorama is necessarily rather broader for the CEFR. Firstly, in the CEFR prominence is given to the hierarchical system of levels and so to what distinguishes one level from another both quantitatively (in terms of the range of language activities that learners can undertake) and qualitatively (in terms of how well they can perform). For *Breakthrough* (Trim 2000), *Waystage* (van Ek & Trim 1998a), *Threshold* (van Ek and Trim 1998b) and *Vantage* (van Ek & Trim 2001), in contrast, the emphasis is on a comprehensive description of content at a single level for a defined group of learners. Secondly, the descriptions in the CEFR are not limited to English, but apply across languages and so linguistic exponents are not (and cannot be) included. Thirdly, where the T-series objectives are almost exclusively concerned with spoken interaction, the CEFR descriptions give more equal weight to receptive, productive and interactive uses of language. Fourthly, the CEFR scales are not organised around notions and functions, but around more broadly defined *competences, strategies* and *language activities*. As progression moves centre stage in the CEFR, so functions move away from the spotlight. It is, however, suggested that an analysis of the 'functions, notions, grammar and vocabulary necessary to perform the communicative tasks described on the scales could be part of the process of developing new sets of language specifications' (Council of Europe 2001:30) or reference level descriptions (RLD). In developing RLD for English Profile, it is important to investigate the CEFR scales themselves, how they represent progression and how they relate to functions (and, indeed, to the notions, grammar and vocabulary addressed in related English Profile projects).

It is important at the outset to remember, as Hulstijn et al (2010) remind us, that 'in a very important sense, the CEFR scales themselves are *not* new: they are based upon decades of experience in building, using and, presumably, refining scales in the light of experience' (p.14). The CEFR thus incorporated a pre-established consensus on levels of proficiency expressed through the scales that existed at the time. What most clearly sets the CEFR apart from its predecessors is the 'significant empirical research' (Hulstijn et al 2010:13) that went into the scale development.

The descriptors that make up the scales presented in the CEFR (and so help to distinguish one level from the next) take the form of positively worded Can Do statements. They are said to draw on three main sources; '(a) the theoretical work of the [CEFR] authoring group, (b) the analysis of existing scales of proficiency and (c) practical workshops with teachers' (Council of Europe 2001:30). We return to this process when we explore the foundations and development of the CEFR later in this chapter. First, as in Chapter 1, we explore precedents. The following section locates the sources for the Can Do descriptors and levels adopted in the CEFR in educational behavioural objectives and the proficiency movement. This is followed by an evaluation of the process by which the framework was developed.

Behavioural objectives

Wilkins (1976:13) makes the point that objectives of the kind espoused in the CEFR project are 'behavioural (though not behaviourist)' in the sense that they, in line with the 'action oriented approach', are based on 'the purposes for which people are learning language and the kinds of language performance that are necessary to meet those purposes'. The following paragraphs provide a very brief outline of the use of behavioural objectives in educational contexts and the implications of the approach for the CEFR and the English Profile.

The mastery learning movement (Block 1971; Bloom 1968) is based on Carroll's (1963) conception of *learning aptitude*. For Carroll there is variation between learners in the *rate* at which they might learn, but not in the eventual knowledge or ability that they might be able to attain. With its emphases on individuating learning – reducing variation in achievement by increasing variation in teaching (Bloom 1968) – and assessing progress formatively against clearly defined behavioural objectives, mastery learning appears, via the concept of permanent education (see Chapter 1), to have had a strong impact on a number of aspects of the development of the CEFR. This is evident from the attention given in the framework to the role of the learner and to achieving coherence between language learning contexts: socially organised learning within language programmes and individual learning pathways across programmes or outside formal education (Schärer and North 1992).

An important element in mastery learning is the use of *objectives* or intended outcomes which specify the observable behaviours that should result from successful learning, appealing to authentic, real-world applications (Block, 1971). Carroll (1971:31) argues that 'it is most essential . . . to be able to state as exactly as possible what the learning task is, particularly its objectives, in testable form. That is, a teacher must be able to determine when a student has mastered a task to a satisfactory degree'. Given such measurability, student progress may be tracked against objectives and feedback provided on task performance, with corrective instruction – employing alternative methods – provided to learners who do not achieve the intended objectives (Bloom 1968). Mastery learning ideas on the need for flexibility in teaching approaches are echoed by van Ek (1981). In setting out the need for objectives in the Council of Europe programme, he argues that these should be explicit, but flexible and allow 'maximum scope for differences between individual learners' (p.17).

In his classic text on the preparation of behavioural objectives, Mager (1991:21 – first published in 1962) suggests that three elements should be specified if an objective is to support mastery learning: performance, condition and criterion. The *performance* is a statement of what a learner should be able to do to demonstrate competence (the Can Do element), the *condition* states relevant constraints under which the learner will be expected to perform and the *criterion* sets out the level of performance that will represent success. An example given by Mager (1991:63) is 'Given a DC motor of ten horsepower or less that contains a single malfunction, and given a set of tools and references [the condition], be able to repair the motor [the performance]. The motor must be repaired within forty-five minutes and must operate to within 5 percent of factory specifications [the criterion]'. Similar requirements continue to inform the design of 'outcomes statements', 'competencies' and 'standards' in general education – see for example Spady's (1994) requirements for 'content', 'competence', and 'context'.

The need for clarity in defining conditions (context) and criteria (competence) as well as performance (content) was recognised by van Ek (1986), who writes:

> In dealing with levels it will be convenient . . . to distinguish between what learners can do and how well they can do it, and to describe what learners can do in terms of the tasks they can perform and the language content they have at their disposal in performing them. In our further discussion, then, we shall adopt the following scheme, which, in fact, underlies most current level descriptions:

What		How well
Task	Content	Quality

> Task, content, and quality – it should be recognised – are not discrete parameters. What a person can do implies an ability to handle language content as well as a particular manner of doing it (quality). Yet, it is convenient to distinguish the three aspects in level descriptions, tasks being particularly described with a focus on discourse competence and content in relation to linguistic and sociolinguistic competence. Quality is a feature of all the various aspects of communicative ability.

Hence for van Ek (1986, p.131) 'Level-descriptions are not complete without indications as to how well the learner is supposed to be able to perform the tasks specified in them'. Similarly, in the CEFR (p.180), it is said that:

> Experience has shown that the consistency with which teachers and learners can interpret descriptors is enhanced if the descriptors describe not only WHAT the learner can do, but also HOW WELL they do it.

The T-series is, in the main, concerned with 'what' rather than 'how well': the objectives they represent are 'a set of content specifications rather than performance criteria' (Schärer & North 1992:12). The T-series specifies the functions and notions that learners will need and the exponents that might be taught, but does not indicate how accurately or under what conditions learners should be expected to use the listed exponents. In this chapter, we will see that this 'what/how well' distinction is operationalised differently in the CEFR.

The proficiency movement

While mastery learning has its origins in educational psychology and general education, a second influential current sprang from a language learning context. The scales of language proficiency developed in collaboration by the American Council on the Teaching of Foreign Languages and the Educational Testing Service (ACTFL/ETS 1986), building on the work of the US Foreign Service Institute (FSI) (Herzog n.d.), gave rise to what has been termed the '*proficiency movement*' (Clark & Clifford 1988, Kramsch 1986).

Although originating in instruments designed for the judgement of performance on oral interview tests, over time the application of proficiency scales was broadened. They came to be used, in much the way that the CEFR is intended, to inform language programmes, textbooks, and assessments (Liskin-Gasparro 1984). The 10-point ACTFL scales, like other widely applied proficiency systems, came to represent a shared understanding of levels so that educators working in different sectors felt that they had a clear idea of what was meant by a *Novice High* or *Intermediate Mid* level regardless of context (Chalhoub-Deville 1997).

Schemes that derive, like the ACTFL Proficiency Guidelines, from the work of the US Foreign Service Institute present a vignette or profile of typical learner abilities that is said to characterise an overall level of proficiency, or a level of proficiency in one of the traditional language skills (reading, writing, listening, speaking). The *0+ (Memorized Proficiency)* level on the *Interagency Language Roundtable* (ILR) scale for Reading (Interagency Language Roundtable 1985), is defined thus:

> *Can recognize all the letters in the printed version of an alphabetic system and high-frequency elements of a syllabary or a character system. Able to read some or all of the following: numbers, isolated words and phrases, personal and place names, street signs, office and shop designations. The above often interpreted inaccurately. Unable to read connected prose.*

The holistic nature of these scales requires the rater to arrive at a global judgement of a learner's level of language ability on the basis of observed performance. In the ILR scheme, the learner must fulfil *all* of the stated criteria in order to be judged to be at the level, while in other schemes (such as the *Australian Second Language Proficiency Ratings* – ASLPR) the learner is placed at the level which appears to most closely fit their abilities, i.e. the performance need not satisfy all of the descriptors at the relevant level. The CEFR bank of scales is illustrative (rather than definitive) and open-ended: users may supplement it to meet their needs. This, of course, means that it can only be compatible with a best-fit approach to global levels. However, such flexibility also raises questions; questions that are as pertinent to the CEFR as to ASLPR. How close does the fit have to be in terms of quantity: i.e. how many descriptors should apply in order to justify reporting to a broad audience that a learner should be placed at one level rather than another? Are all weightings equal? Or are certain scales more central to the definition of a level than others?

In common with behavioural objectives, proficiency scales describe performance in concrete terms to inform judgements about success: both describe outcomes of learning (North 2004) and what a learner can 'actually do in the language' (Ingram 1996:2) beyond the classroom. However, in proficiency scales more attention is generally given to criterion – or in van Ek's (1986) terms, quality (how well) and performance – than to the operative conditions. This reflects the use of the scales in oral interview settings where it was assumed that comparability of conditions was assured (although this assumption would later be demonstrated to be mistaken – see, for example, Lazaraton 1991, van Lier 1989).

It is perhaps unsurprising that proficiency scales, in spite of the objections of many applied linguists (Kramsch 1986, Lantolf & Frawley 1985, Savignon 1985) have come to be used as language learning targets – to 'represent a graduated sequence of steps that can be used to structure a foreign language program' (Liskin-Gasparro 1984). However, within language programmes, teachers often employ relatively inconsequential 'intermediate objectives' (Trim 1981) to motivate learners and to acknowledge success on specific learning tasks; they may be less concerned with how performance on a task generalises to performance beyond the classroom. In contrast to teachers and learners, external audiences such as sponsors and employers are more interested in what are sometimes called 'terminal objectives' or summative representations of learner proficiency – the 'end-results of the learning process' (Trim 1981).

Initiatives such as the Graded Objectives in Modern Languages (GOML) movement in the UK (Page 1992) and the Dutch National Action Programme on Foreign Languages (van Els 1992) (both influential in the initial development of the CEFR) sought ways to integrate the capacity of proficiency scales to locate learners on a generally interpretable continuum (that would cover a full range of functional language ability and have meaning outside the class-room) with the capacity of learning objectives to recognise the learning gains made by learners across a relatively narrow range of the putative proficiency continuum at different stages within a language programme.

The CEFR is similarly said to be capable both of informing mastery deci-sions and of locating a performance on the global continuum of proficiency (Council of Europe 2001:184). It is claimed that 'there is no need for there to be a conflict between on the one hand a common framework desirable to organise education and facilitate such comparisons, and on the other hand the local strategies and decisions necessary to facilitate successful learning and set appropriate examinations in any given context' (Council of Europe 2001:3). In other words, the descriptors may be used both with a retrospec-tive view towards the content of a learning programme at a given level that learners have completed (achievement) and a prospective view towards the level(s) of tasks that learners will be able to carry out beyond the classroom (proficiency).

It is emphasised throughout the CEFR and its related publications that the framework is intended as a resource for consultation rather than a package for implementation. It is designed to be 'open and flexible, so that it can be applied, with such adaptations as prove necessary, to particular situations' (Council of Europe 2001:7). The CEFR, in other words, is concerned with the common core language ability familiar from the early days of the unit/credit scheme (see Chapter 1) covering uses of language that will be pertinent to all learners. While it sets out to achieve this through *context-free* descriptors – not tied to specific situations – these are also intended to be *context-relevant* – it should be possible to apply them (or rather to adapt them) to a wide range of situations for language use while maintaining the shared understanding of levels that supports mutual recognition. As noted above, the extremes of the scale pose distinct challenges to any shared understanding: the development of the C levels is acknowledged to have been particularly problematic. It is also recognised in the CEFR that the wording of descriptors might need to be refined in the light of experience: 'the wording of the descriptors will develop over time as the experience of member states and of institutions with related expertise is incorporated into the description' (pp. 24–25).

There is no requirement for psychometric equivalence between tests or other forms of assessment used to match learners to CEFR levels in different contexts: no expectation that assessments should all be designed to a table of specifications directly derived from the CEFR, that they should employ similar item types in similar proportions, that they should possess the equiva-lent score means, variance and reliability that such equivalence requires (see Feldt and Brennan 1989). Rather, shared standards are to be maintained through a form of social moderation (Mislevy 1992): coherent application of the framework is dependent on interaction and consensus building among users. If the users, working in different settings and with different languages, are unable to define the levels and achieve general agreement on their broad meaning, the framework loses its value as a basis for mutual recognition. As the following sections will make clear, the potential for conflict between comparability and flexibility in interpretations of the CEFR is sometimes at issue, especially at the higher levels of the scheme where the statements are more abstract and qualitative in nature and learners' objectives tend to be more specialised and diffuse.

Use of behavioural objectives and proficiency scale descriptors in the CEFR

In 1991, following the fall of the Berlin wall, a second Rüschlikon Symposium (North 1992) launched another major Council of Europe initiative, this time recommending the development of a common European framework of reference for languages. By now, both graded objectives and proficiency scales were well established in language education and were the subject of a number of presentations at the symposium (in North 1992 see, for example, Page on GOML, Carroll on the ESU framework and North on proficiency scales).

Seeking to learn from and build on this experience, North (1993, 1994, 1996, 2000; North and Schneider 1998) incorporated both proficiency scales and learning objectives into the CEFR scale development process. The *ACTFL Proficiency Guidelines* and related proficiency scales such as the *Australian Second Language Proficiency Ratings* (ASLPR, Ingram 1990), the *Foreign Service Institute Absolute Proficiency Ratings* (Wilds 1975) and the *Interagency Language Roundtable Language Skill Level Descriptions* (Interagency Language Roundtable 1985) were included, as were such objectives-based schemes as the *English National Curriculum: Modern Languages* (1991) and the *Eurocentres Scale of Language Proficiency* (1993). Borrowing from both behavioural objectives and proficiency scales in this way sits well with the aim of building shared understandings between learner and teacher assessment of ongoing learning and consolidated summative information derived from programme external tests that may be used for certification and accountability.

The illustrative scales in the CEFR are made up of individual descriptors stripped from the sources listed above, among others (30 schemes altogether), giving an initial pool of 1,679 descriptors in total (North 2000). The descriptors were screened for repetition and edited to produce, 'positively worded, "stand-alone" statements that could be independently calibrated' (North 2000:184). As we shall see later in this chapter, because the CEFR draws on both behavioural objectives and proficiency scales, it has attracted much of the criticism directed at both approaches as well as doubts concerning the extent to which it is possible to reconcile diverse purposes within a single scheme.

Editing and trialling were intended to produce descriptors that would be suitable both as learning objectives and for distinguishing levels (North 2000). Five requirements for adequate proficiency descriptors emerging from North's study are listed in Appendix A of the CEFR (Council of Europe 2001:205–207):

Positiveness:	worded *'in terms of what the learner can do rather than in terms of what they can't do'.*
Definiteness:	*'describ[ing] concrete tasks and/or concrete degrees of skill in performing tasks'.*
Clarity:	*'transparent, not jargon-ridden'.*
Brevity:	*'a descriptor which is longer than a two clause sentence cannot realistically be referred to during the assessment process'.*
Independence:	*'describ[ing] a behaviour about which one can say "Yes, this person can do this"'.*

Note the similarities between positiveness and independence and Mager's (1991) performance, and between clarity and definiteness and Mager's condition and criterion in formulating behavioural objectives.

The descriptor statements resulting from the selection and editing processes were given to foreign language teachers in Switzerland in a series of workshops (North 2000, Council of Europe 2001, Appendix B). Two techniques were used to ensure that the descriptors would be meaningful to teachers. In the first, following Pollitt and Murray (1996), teachers were asked to view video recordings of pairs of students, to judge which student in each pair was the better and to justify their choices. The resulting comments were reconciled with or incorporated into the descriptor pool. In the second technique, based on Smith and Kendall (1963), pairs of teachers sorted descriptors into piles representing potential descriptive categories, discarding descriptors they were unable to sort and identifying those that they found particularly useful.

Two further techniques were used to establish the relative difficulty of the descriptors. In the first, groups of teachers (Swiss teachers of English, French and German) used the descriptors to assess learners in their classes; in the second, teachers used selected descriptors to rate video recorded performances. These ratings were compared in order to calibrate the difficulty of each descriptor on a common scale using Rasch measurement (Wright and Stone 1979). It is claimed that the scaling of these descriptors based on the rating of performance samples using Rasch analysis creates an atheoretical, but empirically derived and operationally useful scale of language ability, dealing with the question of the criterion or 'how well' (North 2000).

We have seen that the six 'reference levels' arrived at for the CEFR are said to represent a 'wide but by no means universal consensus on the number and nature of levels appropriate to the organisation of language learning and the public recognition of achievement' (Council of Europe 2001:22). In the 'branching approach' suggested, a broader distinction can be made between three superordinate levels of learner (A: basic, B: independent and C: proficient) and finer distinctions can be made within the CEFR levels so that the relatively small gains in language proficiency made within language programmes (achievement) can be captured and reported. Within the scales presented in the CEFR, lines are sometimes drawn between descriptors representing the criterion level and those said to be 'significantly higher', although not sufficiently high to meet the demands of 'the following level' (Council of Europe 2001:36). This branching gives rise to levels such as B1.1 and B1.2 or B1 and B1+ and allows for further subdivisions so that 'a common set of levels . . . can be "cut" into practical local levels at different points by different users to suit local needs and yet still relate back to a common system' (Council of Europe 2001:32).

The lack of a theoretical motivation for these levels has been a cause for reproach. One criticism often made of the *ACTFL Proficiency Guidelines*, and especially of their use in setting learning targets, is that they were not based on research into the nature of second language acquisition (see for example Kramsch 1986, Lantolf & Frawley 1985, Savignon 1985,). This criticism has been repeated with respect to the CEFR by Bausch, Christ, Königs & Krumm (2002) and by Hulstijn (2007). Although, unlike the ACTFL Proficiency Guidelines, the CEFR *categories* are based on a componential model of communicative language ability (van Ek 1986), Hulstijn notes the continuing lack of 'empirical evidence that, in following the overall oral proficiency scale, all learners first attain the functional level of A1, then the level of A2, and so on, until they reach their individual plateau'. Conversely, of course, it could be argued in defence of the CEFR that counter-evidence suggesting that learners do not all proceed in this way is equally sparse (North 2007a).

In similar vein, Weir (2005a) and Alderson (2004, 2007), referring to the receptive skills, argue that the scales fail to take sufficient account of the cognitive and metacognitive processes engaged by learners as they perform tasks at each CEFR level. Relevant parameters are listed in the framework (Council of Europe 2001:90–93), but as Alderson (2004) observes, the CEFR provides only 'a taxonomy of behaviours rather than a theory of development in listening and reading activities'. In the scale for *Overall Reading Comprehension*, by way of illustration, the descriptor '*Can read straightforward factual texts on subjects related to his/her field and interest with a satisfactory level of comprehension*' not only fails to define what is intended by '*straightforward*' and what degree of comprehension is meant by '*satisfactory*', but provides no details on the operations required to arrive at this level of comprehension. It is unclear, for example, whether, following the options set out on page 68 of the English version of the framework, learners should be able to read such a text for gist, for specific information, for detailed understanding or for implications; or whether it is being suggested that differences in reading purpose might have no impact on the difficulty of the reading task.

Aside from any theoretical shortcomings, Hudson (2005) has questioned the claim of empirical calibration, observing that, 'whereas the descriptors were empirically scaled based on performance ratings, the particular descriptors were not subsequently cast as actual test prompts and then calibrated again to determine if they still scale hierarchically' (p.218). Changes of purpose have been seen to have an effect on the relative difficulty values – Alderson, Figueras, Kuijper, Nold, Takala and Tardieu (2004) found that some descriptors shifted in rank when used for self-assessment. North (2000) acknowledges the further objection that the scales are empirical only to the extent that they calibrate teacher perceptions: they are not empirically derived from L2 learner data (a criticism later voiced by Hulstijn 2007).

It should also be noted that the CEFR scales are not exclusively made up of descriptors that have been scaled by the method described. Some re-combine elements of calibrated descriptors, others derive directly from the qualitative workshops and a few, mostly at the highest (C2) level, were written to fill in gaps. Scales that did not result from the calibration process are identified in the text.

To be interpretable, objectives require indications of performance (task, which answers the question *what?*), of condition (content, *in what circumstances?*) and of criterion (quality, *how well?*). North (2004), drawing a parallel between the *what/how well* distinction in the CEFR and the notion of content standards and performance standards in standards-based education (Mislevy 1995), equates 'how well' with the hierarchy of levels in the CEFR and 'what' with the scale categories. In the CEFR, the *horizontal* and *vertical* axes in tables such as the *self-assessment grid* (pp. 26–27) operationalise this distinction (Richterich and Schneider 1992). In the development of the CEFR, descriptors were mapped onto the vertical axis according to their relative difficulty. However, descriptors were also arranged by workshop participants along the horizontal axis in ways that might be meaningful for specific audiences, reflecting the diversity of contexts for use or reflecting differences of focus in terms of spoken or written; receptive, productive or interactive language use. Learners placed at the same global level, but with different needs, may set themselves objectives based on – or be assessed against – descriptors drawn from quite separate CEFR scales.

We have seen how North (2000), in calibrating the descriptors, addresses this 'how well' criterion by appealing to pooled teacher judgement – in the same way that tests of writing and speaking skills rely on the pooled expert judgement of their examiners. In the following section, we turn our attention to how the CEFR deals with the question of 'what': the horizontal categorisation of scales.

CEFR scale categories

In brief, the CEFR offers a variety of scales to illustrate the levels, intended to demonstrate the flexibility of the system with respect to a) the approach to objectives that the user may wish to adopt and b) the range of language use situations to which the framework can be applied. This is important to the English Profile because it suggests the diversity of functional uses of language envisaged at each level.

The *Common Reference Levels* are introduced via three tables in Chapter 3 of the CEFR. A *global scale*, which provides holistic summaries of the levels, is intended to convey the levels to the 'non-specialist user' (Council of Europe 2001:24); a *self-assessment grid* with distinctions between subscales for *reading, listening, writing, spoken interaction* and *spoken production* is designed for learner self-assessment (Council of Europe 2001:26–27) and a table of *qualitative aspects of spoken language use* is intended for the assessment of spoken performance (Council of Europe 2001:28–29). The latter has subscales for *range, accuracy, fluency, interaction* and *coherence* – criteria similar to those used in oral interviews and other tests of spoken language. These modes of presentation are intended to demonstrate the selectivity of the scheme for communicating flexibly to different audiences at different levels of detail, bringing different aspects of the learner's competence into focus according to purpose.

In addition to the three scales presented in Chapter 3 of the CEFR, over 50 further scales are provided to illustrate the levels. These cover three kinds of objective: *language* (or *communicative*) *activities, strategies* and *competences*. The range of categories is said to allow for the construction of scales that reflect specific contexts for language use within the four specified domains: *personal, public, occupational* and *educational* (Council of Europe 2001:45).

One perspective on the 'what' of the CEFR is van Ek's (1986) model of communicative competence (see Chapter 1 above), which provides the basis for the *linguistic, sociolinguistic* and *pragmatic competence* scales (Table 12). As the scales are intended to be illustrative, not all of van Ek's (1987) categories have associated scales: for example, semantic and orthoepic do not figure among the linguistic competence scales, but could be developed where the need arises.

These scales of linguistic competence sit comfortably within the tradition of analytic rating scales being used increasingly in tests of general language proficiency during the 1990s and, as we have seen, are readily combined into

Table 12 Communicative language competence scales (Council of Europe 2001 Chapter 5)

Communicative language competences	Sub-classification	Illustrative scales
Linguistic competences		1. General linguistic range
	Lexical competence	2. Vocabulary range
		3. Vocabulary control
	Grammatical competence	4. Grammatical accuracy
	Phonological competence	5. Phonological control
	Orthographic competence	6. Orthographic control
Sociolinguistic competences		7. Sociolinguistic appropriateness
Pragmatic competences	Discourse competence	8. Flexibility to circumstances
		9. Turn taking*
		10. Thematic development
		11. Coherence and cohesion
	Functional competence	12. Spoken fluency
		13. Propositional precision

also presented under interaction strategies

rating scales of the kind presented in Chapter 3 of the CEFR: *Qualitative aspects of spoken language use* (Council of Europe 2001:28–29).

However, models of competence are not seen to be the only perspective of value in delineating levels. According to the CEFR, because activities are visible in ways that cognitive processes and competences are not, 'progress in language learning is most clearly evidenced in the learner's ability to engage in observable language activities and to operate communication strategies. They are therefore a convenient basis for the scaling of language ability' (p.57). Correspondingly in Chapter 4 of the CEFR, Can Do statements are arranged into sets of scales relating to *language activities* and *working with text* (33 scales) and *strategies* (seven scales). As with competences, although large numbers of language activities and strategies are listed, the lists are not intended to be exhaustive and not all listed categories have scales associated with them. Rather, the scales are intended to be illustrative of the range of applications open to the user, who is encouraged to adapt the scheme in line with local needs. The language activities and strategies for which illustrative scales are provided are set out in Table 13 below.

Language activities, as defined in the CEFR, are an innovation derived from Trim (1973). North (2007a) traces similar suggestions for a more useful and better theoretically grounded pedagogic alternative to the traditional 'four skills' of listening, reading, writing, speaking in the work of Breen and Candlin (1980) Brumfit (1984) and Swales (1990). Distinctions are made between language activity types on the basis of the neurological and physiological processes of reception or production that they involve (Council of

Table 13 Scaled language activities and strategies (Council of Europe 2001 Chapter 4)

Mode	Illustrative scales: strategies	Category of activity	Illustrative scales: language activities
Production	1. Planning 2. Compensating 3. Monitoring and repair	Spoken production	1. Overall spoken production 2. Sustained monologue: describing experience 3. Sustained monologue: putting a case (e.g. in debate) 4. Public announcements 5. Addressing audiences
		Written production	6. Overall written production 7. Creative writing 8. Reports and essays
Reception	4. Identifying cues and inferring	Listening	9. Overall listening comprehension 10. Understanding interaction between native speakers 11. Listening as a member of a live audience 12. Listening to announcements and instructions 13. Listening to audio media and recordings
		Audio/visual Reading	14. Watching TV and film 15. Overall reading comprehension 16. Reading correspondence 17. Reading for orientation 18. Reading for information and argument 19. Reading instructions
Interaction	5. Taking the floor 6. Co-operating 7. Asking for clarification	Spoken interaction	20. Overall spoken interaction 21. Understanding a native speaker interlocutor 22. Conversation 23. Informal discussion 24. Formal discussion and meetings 25. Goal-oriented co-operation 26. Transactions to obtain goods and services 27. Information exchange 28. Interviewing and being interviewed
		Written interaction	29. Overall written interaction 30. Correspondence 31. Notes, messages and forms
Text		Written response to a spoken input Written response to a written input	32. Note-taking (lectures, seminars, etc.) 33. Processing text

Europe 2001:10). Thus language activities may require reception, production, interaction or mediation using spoken or written language, or both. '*Unidirectional activities*' as they are termed in the CEFR *Guide for Users* (Trim 2002:22) include productive language activities such as '*oral presentations, written studies and reports*' (Council of Europe 2001:14), and receptive language activities such as '*silent reading and following the media*' as well as the more academic: '*understanding course content, consulting textbooks, works of reference and documents*' (loc. cit.). Language activities that involve the user both as a producer and as a receiver include interaction – *transactions, casual conversation, informal discussion, formal discussion, debate, interview, negotiation, co-planning and practical goal-oriented co-operation* – or mediation: activities in which the user serves as a channel of communication – *summarising, paraphrasing, interpreting, translating*.

Language activities entail the exercise of communicative competences 'in a specific domain in processing (receptively and/or productively) one or more texts in order to carry out a task' (p.10). For example, in purchasing chocolate (a task in the public domain), a language user might activate her knowledge of words and grammatical forms (linguistic competence) to carry out the transaction (language activity). This might involve, perhaps, greetings, requests and thanks; ordered according to a mental schema or praxeogram for purchasing chocolate (pragmatic competence) with a suitable level of formality (sociolinguistic competence). Some elements of the *task* will be non-linguistic – handing over the payment and accepting change might, for example, be accomplished without words – but the linguistic elements constitute the language activity and the text. We are told that many situations in which learners may find themselves 'involve a mixture of activity types' so, for example 'in a school language class . . . a learner may be required to listen to a teacher's exposition, to read a textbook, silently or aloud, to interact with fellow pupils in group or project work, to write exercises or an essay, and even to mediate, whether as an educational activity or in order to assist another pupil' (p.57).

Language activities are to be distinguished from *texts*, although there is a very close relationship 'between the categories proposed for the description of language activities and the texts resulting from those activities' (p.97). Often the same word is used both for the language activity and for the type of text that results from it: '"translation" may denote either the act of translating or the text produced. Similarly, "conversation", "debate" or "interview" may denote the communicative interaction of the participants, but equally the sequence of their exchanged utterances, which constitutes a text of a particular type belonging to a corresponding genre' (p.97). The relationship between functions and language activities, echoing Hymes' (1974) distinction between speech acts and speech events (see Chapter 1), thus appears to parallel that between words and sentences or between sentences and texts. Functions are realised by a single utterance or sentence, language activities are made up of one or more utterances in a coherent sequence. The language activity scales thus may be considered to subsume the language functions of the T-series.

In carrying out *tasks* (defined as 'any purposeful action considered by an individual as necessary in order to achieve a given result in the context of a problem to be solved, an obligation to fulfil or an objective to be achieved' Council of Europe 2001:10), particularly where difficulties are encountered or anticipated, language users may draw on *strategies*. These are 'organised, purposeful and regulated line[s] of action' that relate the learners' resources (their competences) to what they seek to do with them (the language activities they engage in) (p.27). The CEFR exemplifies the range of strategic choices that a learner may face when carrying out a task: 'a learner at school who has to translate a text from a foreign language (task) may look to see if a translation already exists, ask another learner to show what he or she has done, use a dictionary, try to work out some kind of meaning on the basis of the few words or structures he or she knows, think of a good excuse for not handing in this exercise, etc.' (p.14). Strategic competence thus mediates and manages the relation between linguistic competences and language activities.

Just as the competence scales parallel the scales used in tests of speaking or writing that, like the *IELTS band scales* or the Cambridge *Certificate in Advanced English* (CAE) (now known as *Cambridge English: Advanced*) scoring grids for Writing or Speaking, followed a communicative competence model (Bachman & Palmer 1996, Canale & Swain 1980, van Ek 1986), so the overall language activity scales in Chapter 4 (*Overall Spoken Interaction, Overall Reading Comprehension* etc.) bear a strong family resemblance to the skills-based proficiency scales, like the ASLPR and ACTFL, that fed into their development.

North (2007) suggests that the divisions between language activities involving production, reception, interaction or mediation on the one hand and between spoken or written language on the other are better theoretically motivated than the traditional 4-skills model. However, the more specific language activity and strategy scales represent a development that goes well beyond any of the precedents listed by North.

The classification of language activities at this micro level originates in the workshops that North conducted with teachers (see North 2000) at which teachers sorted the available descriptors into categories (Table 14) according to macro activity on one dimension and, for production and interaction, broadly functional categories of *transactional, creative/interpersonal* or *evaluative/problem solving* language use on the other (although these categories are not included in the CEFR). Descriptors that were judged to be substandard or that could not be categorised in this way were discarded. Perhaps because the micro language activity categories are simply inherited from ideas embedded in the various schemes used in the CEFR development, they seem to lack

Table 14 Categories for communicative activities: interaction and production, from North (2007:4)

	Interaction		Production	
	Spoken	**Written**	**Spoken**	**Written**
Transactional	Service encounters	Form-filling	Formal	Formal
	Information exchanges	Notes &	presentations	reports
	Interviews	messages		
	Telephone transactions	Formal letters		
Creative,	Conversation	Personal	Describing, narrating and	
Interpersonal		letters	interpreting experience	
Evaluative,	Discussion	–	Putting a case	
Problem-	Negotiating			
solving	Formal meetings			

coherence. The pedagogic value of differentiating between *Interviewing and Being Interviewed* and *Information Exchange*, for example, is not immediately apparent.

Some of these micro language activities do seem to reflect widely known genres with recognisable (and so potentially teachable) boundaries and norms of behaviour; others do not. *Interviewing and Being Interviewed* (p.82), for example, are events with which most language users have some familiarity. Interviews occur as occupational *Events* in CEFR Table 5, defining *External Contexts of Use* (Council of Europe 2001:48–49) and can also be understood as texts (see above). Of course this is a broad category embracing a good deal of variation. In addition to various types of occupational interview (e.g. job interviews, performance appraisals), one might encounter interviews in the personal (e.g. counselling interview; interview to join a social introductions agency), educational (e.g. interview for school/college; oral examination) or public domains (e.g. immigration interview; police interview). However, most interviews share a common purpose: the transfer of information about one of the participants – the interviewee – (often concerning their qualifications, experiences, attitudes or personal qualities) to the other – the interviewer. Questions of course play a defining role; interviews are asymmetrical and the interviewer has a privileged right to ask questions and direct the interaction (Schegloff 1992). There is typically an element of formality and social distance. Functional and discoursal elements in an interview are likely to include greetings, lead-ins, exchanges of information and topic-related phases marked by transitions and closings. In short, interviews may be a useful descriptive category for pedagogic purposes.

In contrast to *Interviewing and Being Interviewed* or *Transactions to Obtain Goods and Services*, categories such as *Goal Oriented Co-Operation*, *Understanding a Native Speaker* or *Information Exchange* do not seem to reflect recognisable genres of speech event: we do not usually speak of goal oriented co-operation as an event in the same way that we speak of being interviewed. The examples given of co-operation – 'repairing a car, discussing a document, organising an event' (p.79) do not really clarify matters. Organising an event or repairing a car would seem to be *tasks* that might be accomplished using a number of strategies, calling different language activities into play (in the latter case the task could be accomplished through reading a manual, following verbal instructions, discussing options with a friend, explaining a fault to a mechanic, negotiating a price for the repairs). While it seems closer to the other examples of language activities, it also seems incongruous that 'discussing a document' is not positioned with the scales for informal or formal discussion.

While it makes the task of tracing functional progression more challenging, it is perhaps inevitable that language activities will overlap with each other as the heuristic categories used to characterise discourse so often do, but comparisons between descriptors on different scales do not always support the claims made for coherence (Council of Europe 2001:223). Alderson is critical of inconsistencies in the wording, which may reflect the varied provenance of the descriptors (Alderson et al 2004, Alderson 2007). Alderson et al (2004) note that eight different verbs are used to indicate understanding at level B2 (*understand, scan, monitor, obtain, select, evaluate, locate, identify*), but that no gloss is provided to explain the implications, if any, of using these different words.

To exemplify the inconsistency in the scales, *Interviewing and Being Interviewed* and *Information Exchange*, both scales for *Spoken Interaction* and clearly closely related, have a number of discrepancies. At A1, the questions to be put to the learner in an interview are '*spoken very slowly and clearly in direct non-idiomatic speech about personal details*'. Questions for information exchange are '*addressed carefully and slowly to him/her*' (note, in relation to Alderson et al's 2004 criticism of inconsistency in wording, the use of *addressed to* for one descriptor, *spoken* for the other), and, in another descriptor, are '*about themselves and other people, where they live, people they know, things they have*'. The small differences in the descriptors raise questions about salience: is it important that information exchange questions are put to the learner '*slowly*', but interview questions '*very slowly*'? Does this reflect a difference in the calibration of descriptors within the spread of the A1 level, or does it reflect a difference between interview and information exchange uses of language? Why is no mention made of '*idiomatic*' speech in information exchange? Does this imply that idiomatic usage is criterial in interviews, but not in information exchange? Do the '*personal details*' mentioned at A1 for interviews embrace details about '*people they know*' mentioned for information exchange?

Similar questions arise for other scales. For example, the productive language activities of making *Public Announcements* and *Addressing Audiences* are also clearly closely related – it appears from the scales that the key feature differentiating announcements from addresses is that the latter are open to questioning. The absence of a descriptor at a given level is said to reflect the fact that 'some activities cannot be undertaken until a certain level of competence has been reached, whilst others may cease to be an objective at higher levels' (p.25). At the A1 and C2 levels for announcements, we are told that there is *'no descriptor available'*, but descriptors are given for addressing audiences at both levels. This would appear to suggest, against common sense, that while it is possible for a learner at the A1 level to *'read a very short, rehearsed statement'* to an audience, it is not possible for them to read a short, rehearsed public announcement.

Even within scales, there can be considerable variation among descriptors in the extent to which they specify language activities, texts, topics or performance quality. In the scale for *Overall Spoken Interaction* (p.74) the B1 descriptors read,

> *Can exploit a wide range of simple language to deal with most situations likely to arise whilst travelling. Can enter unprepared into conversation on topics that are familiar, of personal interest or pertinent to everyday life (e.g. family, hobbies, work, travel and current events)*

The first refers to a domain (travel) and situations within that domain (*'most situations likely to arise whilst travelling'*) that imply certain functions and language activities. There is some indication of the qualities of the learner's language (*'a wide range of simple language'*), but the only indication of a criterion is that the learners will *'deal with'* the situations. The second descriptor, in common with many of those offered for the lower levels, describes a language activity: *'conversation'* and operative conditions: the speaker is *'unprepared'* and the topics are *'familiar, of personal interest or pertinent to everyday life'*. In this case, no criteria are suggested for the quality of the learner's contribution.

The C1 descriptors from the same scale are,

> *Can express him/herself fluently and spontaneously, almost effortlessly. Has a good command of a broad lexical repertoire allowing gaps to be readily overcome with circumlocutions. There is little obvious searching for expressions or avoidance strategies; only a conceptually difficult subject can hinder a natural, smooth flow of language*

In contrast to the B1 descriptors, these are almost exclusively concerned with quality or 'how well' (*'fluently and spontaneously without much obvious searching for expressions'*). These descriptors provide no guidance on the language activities or tasks in which the learner might be expected to participate, beyond the indeterminate *'express him/herself'*. Other than the limitations imposed by the *'conceptually difficult subject'*, there is no indication of the conditions or situational constraints under which the speaker might be asked to interact, perhaps implying that most forms of constraint are no longer criterial at this level. Among the linguistic competences, these C1 descriptors recur in the *Spoken Fluency* (*Functional competence*) and *Vocabulary Range* (*Lexical competence*) categories (but not on any other language activity scale). The first B1 descriptor is (in part) reflected in *Flexibility* (*Discourse competence*) and in part in the language activity of *Transactions to Obtain Goods and Services*, the second does not occur on the competence scales, but occurs in the language activity of *Conversation*. While such inconsistencies may be confusing for the user and may simply reflect the illustrative purpose of the descriptors, or shortcomings in their design, it is possible that they reflect important differences between the levels; the implications are not pursued. It may be that with progress through the levels activities become less salient and features of linguistic competence such as fluency and vocabulary range become more salient.

Hulstijn (2007) pursues this issue of vertical and horizontal progression. Echoing another criticism of the ACTFL Proficiency Guidelines made by Bachman and Savignon (1986), with implications for the notion of 'best fit' discussed above, he suggests that the division into linguistic competence and language activities confounds issues of quantity – the number of 'domains, functions, notions, situations, locations, topics, and roles' (de Jong 2004) that a learner is able to cope with – and issues of quality – the extent to which communication is effective and efficient. He questions whether there is any reason to suppose that a learner placed at B2 because they perform a certain number of language activities would necessarily be placed at B2 in terms of the qualities described on the linguistic competence scales (p.666). Rather, he suggests, there may be learners who are limited in terms of quantity, but able to perform their limited range of roles with high linguistic quality, while others may be able to operate in a wide range of contexts, but with only limited linguistic resources.

There is clearly a relationship between the two – it would be difficult to conceive of how responding to a basic form could provide evidence of a C1 or C2 level of communicative language ability, or how a timed academic essay could provide evidence of an A1 or A2 level – but it is less clear that 'a description of an event, a recent trip – real or imagined' (Council of Europe 2001:62), a B1 level activity, might not elicit 'clear, smoothly flowing, and fully engrossing stories' (loc. cit.), qualities associated with C2. But does the ability to write an engrossing story also imply that a learner could compose 'complex reports, articles or essays which present a case, or give critical appreciation of proposals or literary works' (loc. cit.)?

In view of such complexities, North (2000) has suggested that, 'Nobody has the same level across the 54 scales. Everybody has a profile': that the scales apply to aspects of competence rather than to learners. In performance a learner may, for example, display certain competences at C1 level, others at B2. It is therefore important to understand which scales do apply to the sample performances or tasks and which do not. To what extent can a given level (rather than a profile) characterise a learner, a task or a performance?

It is not clear whether each level of the CEFR represents an overall objective that can be *achieved* – in the sense, for example, that the French *Commission des Titres d'Ingénieur*, recognises a pass on B2 level Cambridge ESOL exams or a score of 750 on the TOEIC test as proof that a learner has achieved the CEFR B2 level (*Cambridge First* Newsletter 24, 2007, https:// www.toeicadvantage.com.fr) – or whether the range of domains and themes is too broad to allow for such a one-dimensional interpretation of the level: different domains, different operationalisation of skills and different weightings of these might lead to quite different interpretations of B2.

The TOEIC test, which embraces levels A1 to C1, is said to measure 'English-language skills in real, everyday business situations' while Cambridge FCE (now known as *Cambridge English: First*) is a test of general English proficiency that focuses exclusively on the B2 level. Neither test was developed to represent all facets of B2 as specified in the CEFR, but each was conceived for a different purpose. In other words (and quite apart from the psychometric qualities of the two tests), a score of 750 on the TOEIC test may have quite different interpretations to a passing score on Cambridge FCE, although both have been interpreted (by different procedures and by different individuals) to be located within the scope of B2. Not only is there no guarantee of horizontal alignment between B2 tests, there may be vertical differences to be considered as well. The Council of Europe Manual for *Relating Language Examinations to the CEFR* (Council of Europe 2009:4) tells us that 'B2 represents a band of language proficiency that is quite wide; the "pass" cut-off level for the different examinations may be pitched at different points within that range, not all coinciding at exactly the same borderline between B1 and B2'. In other words different test providers could make defensible claims that their tests were at the B2 level, but 'B2' scores on the two tests might represent significantly different levels of proficiency. There is similarly potential for confusion between score interpretations where passing scores on an existing test that predates the CEFR and without any clear link to it, are reported in relation to CEFR levels and situations in which a new test is designed to assess performance in relation to the CEFR construct and levels. Both situations are envisaged in the Manual for *Relating Language Examinations to the CEFR*, but a 'B2 level qualification' could mean something quite different in both vertical and horizontal terms according to which situation applies.

The question of how useful and appropriate it may be to seek an overall judgement of a learner's competence is one that requires further investigation. As the tasks that learners are asked to perform are likely to have a substantial impact on the nature and quality of the language that they will be able to produce, further work is required to tease out the relationship between elements of linguistic quantity and quality. The complex relationship between the two may partly explain why the higher levels of the CEFR may be inappropriate or unattainable for certain groups of learners – especially young learners (Little 2007) as the language activities envisaged at these levels 'lie beyond the cognitive and experiential range of children and the great majority of adolescents' (p.651).

The CEFR includes criticism of scales reviewed during the development for the use of vague language and qualifiers to define level differences. North (1992:167) gives an example from the ESU Framework (Carroll & West 1989) of distinctions being made between levels in terms of 'simple' and 'moderate speech situations' and between 'adequate' and 'good competence'. In spite of the criticism, such problems are not consistently avoided in the illustrative descriptors of the CEFR. In the *Grammatical Accuracy* scale (Council of Europe 2001:114), a B2 learner '*Shows a relatively high degree of grammatical control*' while a B2+ learner has '*Good grammatical control*' and C1, '*Consistently maintains a high degree of grammatical accuracy*'. In attempting to apply these descriptions, the user may wonder, 'relative to what?' or 'how consistently?', but no guidance is offered in the CEFR document. These descriptors fall short on the CEFR criteria of *independence, clarity* and *definiteness* as they fail to specify observable behaviours that would demonstrate the learner's ability and may only be interpretable in relation to each other.

Weir (2005a) argues that because the framework fails to spell out the operative contextual parameters that might define the level of performance – Mager's (1991) 'condition' – the framework is insufficiently explicit to inform test or task specifications. It is suggested in the CEFR that 'very detailed concrete decisions on the content of texts, exercises, activities, tests, etc.' (Council of Europe 2001:44) will be required on the part of users, taking into account the impact on student/test taker performance of variables such as physical conditions (e.g. levels of ambient noise), social conditions (e.g. relative status of interlocutors) and time pressures (e.g. conversational interaction allows participants little time to prepare their utterances). To assist users, a list of external conditions is provided (Council of Europe 2001:46–49), but these conditions are not systematically incorporated into or explicitly related to the level definitions. As Weir (2005a) has pointed out, this must seriously undermine the interpretability of the levels as it is unclear which conditions should apply when we judge what learners 'can do'. In other words it is not possible on the basis of the definitions provided in the CEFR to measure a learner's level.

The lack of guidance on criteria and conditions in the CEFR leads directly to questions about comparability. In posing the question, 'how does one know for certain that a test of Greek calibrated at level B1 in Finland is equivalent to a test of Polish considered to be at level B1 in Portugal?' Bonnet (2007:670) points to two threats to comparability: local norms and interlinguistic variation. In the absence of elaboration, exemplification and, most crucially, moderation of standards, it is likely that users in one setting may interpret the illustrative descriptors differently to users in another. It is possible that different interpretations of levels might develop so that, to take an entirely fictional example, a learner judged to be B1 in English conversation in one school in Finland might be rated as C1 at another in Portugal.

Teasdale and Leung (2000) raise the more general question of 'whether assessments can at the same time, adequately serve formative/diagnostic purposes whilst adequately performing as valid (in the psychometric sense) measurement instruments within particular contexts' (p.167). Arkoudis and O'Loughlin (2004) and Burrows (1998) point to the variation that teachers can exhibit in their interpretation of frameworks and to the ways in which they may adapt these to local circumstances in divergent ways. Such customisation is welcomed in the CEFR in its role as a heuristic for the elaboration of language programmes, but is likely to work against the comparability of outcomes from programmes purportedly situated at the same level.

The risks associated with such inconsistency are well illustrated by Crossey's (2009) account of the NATO STANAG 6001 scheme intended to provide agreed international language standards for military personnel. According to Crossey, faith in the scheme was undermined when it became clear that learners certified as being at a given level in one context did not satisfy the criteria as interpreted in another. Equally (although beyond the scope of a reference level description for English), the effect of language differences on the calibration of Can Do statements is far from clear. It is important that RLDs incorporate a mechanism for ongoing interaction between users so that common understandings can be fostered and maintained.

Martyniuk and Noijons (2007) in their survey of the use of the CEFR across Europe found that users 'stress the need for general clarification (such as comments on theoretical concepts, examples and good illustrations, sets of tasks for use in specific contexts)'. Further development of the sample materials provided by the Council of Europe or of open-access collaborative schemes such as WebCEF (www.webcef.eu/) or CEFtrain (www.helsinki.fi/project/ceftrain) might help to ground the CEFR levels in a way that meets these needs. On the other hand, the more detail that is provided, the greater the risk that *illustrative* tasks become *required* tasks and this distinction must be made unequivocal.

Alternative approaches

In appendices to the CEFR document itself, further alternative approaches to ordering and interpreting the levels are presented. One, DIALANG (Council of Europe 2001, Appendix C), offers scales for use as self-assessment instruments in the initial screening of test takers in a self-access, web-based diagnostic testing system. On the basis of the self-assessment, test takers are directed to the DIALANG test version covering the most appropriate CEFR levels. The DIALANG scheme also provides descriptors to be used in advisory feedback to test takers as part of the reporting process. The latter present the levels in terms of the text and content types that learners might be able to handle at each level and operative constraints or conditions.

These DIALANG scales seem to offer a more coherent way of conveying progression to users than the CEFR scales and are further developed in the Manual for *Relating Language Examinations to the CEFR* (Council of Europe 2009, Table A2 p.124). In this table, the scale categories are level-related indicators of *setting* (topics and situations); *action* (operations such as understand, follow, identify etc.); *what is understood* (i.e. information and attitudes expressed in the texts); *source* (i.e. text type) and *restrictions* (i.e. conditions and limitations). In these categories we have more consistent presentation of performance and condition, although criteria remain largely unstated. Similarly, North (2007), arguing for the coherence of the CEFR, shows how 'setting' (contextual features), 'speech' (rate and articulation) and 'help' (repetition and pausing behaviours on the part of interlocutors) distinguish the CEFR illustrative descriptors at different levels.

The integration of the ALTE and CEFR scales (Council of Europe 2001 Appendix D), making use of Rasch analysis, provides a helpful methodological precedent for assimilating new descriptors into the existing CEFR levels and provides an operational definition of learner level on the basis of responses to Can Do items. The ALTE descriptors are not derived from the CEFR, but were developed independently and were later anchored to the CEFR through the use of common items on self-assessment questionnaires so that both sets of descriptors could be located on the same measurement scale. A learner is said to be at level B2 if their overall response pattern indicates an 80% chance of endorsing a statement at that level. This definition was found to be compatible with success on Cambridge ESOL tests at the targeted levels.

The Council of Europe Manual for *Relating Language Examinations to the CEFR* (Council of Europe 2009) suggests a different general approach that institutions might take to determining 'how well' criteria. Adhering to one of a number of well established procedures for standard setting (see Cizek and Bunch 2007) panels of experts should be convened to recommend the most appropriate score on a test to represent the borderline between relevant CEFR levels. Such panels should first become familiar with the CEFR levels, arriving at a consensus on their interpretation before following steps to judge how many points on a test might best represent the relevant CEFR level or levels. A problem with this approach, from the point of view of mutual compatibility, is that as the different panels work independently of each other, each may arrive at their own consensus interpretation of the levels and there is no central authority to which all may refer or appeal.

Table 15 Salient characteristics: Reception (Council of Europe 2009:124–125)

	Setting	Action	What is understood	Source	Restrictions
C1	• Abstract and complex topics encountered in social, academic and professional life, whether or not they relate to own field/speciality	• Follow, maybe with a little difficulty • Understand	• Finer points of detail • Implied as well as stated opinions • A wide range of idiomatic expressions and colloquialisms • Register shifts • Implied attitudes and relationships	• Films with a considerable degree of slang and idiomatic usage • Poor quality, audially distorted public announcements • Lengthy, complex texts of various kinds • Extended speech – lectures, discussions, debates – even when not clearly structured • Complex interactions between third parties in interaction and debate • A wide range of recorded and broadcast texts, including some non-standard • Any correspondence	May occasionally need to: • confirm details (with dictionary, from speaker) if outside field • re-read difficult sections
B2+	• A wide range of familiar and unfamiliar topics encountered in social, academic and professional life	• Follow, maybe with a little difficulty • Understand		• Animated conversation between native speakers • Spoken language, live broadcast • Specialised texts (highly specialised if within field)	• Standard, non-idiomatic • Adequate discourse structure • Low background noise • May occasionally need to confirm details (with dictionary, from speaker) • if outside field • if above conditions not met

Table 15 Continued

	Setting	Action	What is understood	Source	Restrictions
B2	• Reasonably familiar concrete and abstract topics related to field of interest/speciality	• Follow, maybe with a little difficulty • Scan quickly • Understand (with a large degree of independence)	• Much of what is said • Relevance • Whether closer study is worthwhile • Specific details • Main ideas • Essentials/essential meaning • Complex lines of argument • Speaker/writer mood, tone etc.	• Discussion around him/her by native speakers • Long and complex texts • News items, articles and reports • Extended speech: lectures, talks, presentations, reports, discussions • Propositionally and linguistically complex text • Technical discussions; lengthy; complex instructions; details on conditions or warnings • Most TV and current affairs programmes • TV documentaries, interviews, talk shows, highly specialised sources • Announcements and messages • Most radio documentaries, recorded audio materials • Correspondence • Argumentative text	• Standard • Clearly signposted/signalled with explicit markers • If native speakers talking together modify language • If can re-read difficult sections
B1+	• Common everyday or job-related topics • Topics in his/her field of (personal) interest	• Follow, though not necessarily in detail • Scan • Understand	• Line of argument in treatment of the issue • Desired information • Straightforward factual information content • General message	• Longer texts • Different texts, different parts of a text • Argumentative text • Lectures and talks within own field • Large part of many TV programmes: interviews, short lectures, news reports	• Standard – (Familiar accent) • Straightforward • Clearly signposted/signalled with explicit markers

Level	Topics	Understand	Points	Materials	Speech conditions
B1	• Familiar topics regularly encountered in a school, work or leisure context • Topics in his/her field of (personal) interest	• Follow, though not necessarily in detail • Understand with satisfactory comprehension	• Main conclusions • Specific details • Significant points • Main points • Relevant information	• Majority of recorded and broadcast audio material • Extended discussion around him/her • Many films in which visuals and action carry much of the story line • TV programmes: interviews, short lectures, news reports • Straightforward newspaper articles • Straightforward factual texts • Short narratives • Descriptions of events, feelings, wishes • Detailed directions • Short talks • Radio news bulletins and simpler recorded materials • Everyday written materials: letters, brochures, short official documents • Simple technical information e.g. operating instructions	• Clear • Standard • Straightforward • Relatively slow
A2+	• Familiar topics of a concrete type	• Identify • Understand enough to meet needs	• Main points	• TV news items reporting events, accidents etc. in which visuals support the commentary • Basic types of standard letters, faxes (enquiries, orders, confirmations) • Short texts with simpler, high frequency everyday and job-related language • Regulations, e.g. safety	• Clearly and slowly articulated • Expressed in simple language

Table 15 Continued

	Setting	Action	What is understood	Source	Restrictions
A2	• Predictable everyday matters • Areas of most immediate priority: basic personal, family, shopping, local area, employment	• Identify • Understand	• Specific, predictable information • Topic of discussion • Changes of topic • An idea of the content • Main point • Essential information	• Simpler everyday material: advertisements, menus, reference lists, timetables, brochures, letters • Discussion around him/her • Short newspaper articles describing events • Factual TV news items • Short simple texts containing the highest frequency vocabulary including a proportion of shared international vocabulary items • Simple directions relating to how to get from A to B • Simple clear messages, announcements, recorded passages • Simple instructions on equipment encountered in everyday life (e.g. telephone) • Short simple personal letters • Everyday signs and notices: directions, instructions, hazards	• Clearly and slowly articulated

A1	• The most common everyday situations	• Identify
		
		• Understand
			• Familiar words, phrases, names
			• An idea of the content
			• (*Main point*)
				• Simple notices
				• Simpler informational material
				
				• Very short simple texts with visual support, a single phrase at a time:
				  • messages on postcards
				  • directions
				  • descriptions
					• Very slow, carefully articulated, with long pauses to allow assimilation of meaning
					• Familiar names, words and basic phrases
					• A chance to re-read/get repetition

Beyond the projects that have been part of the wider Council of Europe initiative (such as the ALTE Can Do study or DIALANG), other frameworks have been developed for similar purposes and these may suggest directions for further development of value to the English Profile. The approach adopted in the CEFR is contrasted by McNamara and Roever (2006) with schemes such as the Australian Certificates in Spoken and Written English (CSWE) or the related Canadian Language Benchmarks (CLB 2000) which also attempt to operationalise communicative competence as a framework of levels, but start from a systemic-functionalist conception of genre.

These schemes provide a much fuller elaboration of descriptors than the CEFR and offer sample tasks to exemplify levels. Such elaboration is intended to help test developers, teachers responsible for assessment and learners themselves to arrive at comparable understandings of learner abilities. In the *Canadian Language Benchmarks 2000* document, for example, the following Can Do statement is given for the skill of reading at 'Benchmark 5: Initial intermediate proficiency':

Table 16 Reading Benchmark 5: Initial intermediate proficiency (Pawlikowska-Smith 2000:89)

What the person can do	Examples of tasks and texts	Performance indicators
I. Social interaction texts • Obtain factual details and inferred meanings in moderately complex notes, e-mail messages and letters containing general opinions and assessments of situations, response to a complaint and expressions of sympathy.	C. S. W Read authentic notes, e-mail messages and letters (personal and public) containing general opinions, assessments of current affairs, response to a complaint/conflict, or expression of sympathy. Identify correctly specific factual details/inferred meanings.	• Identifies specific factual details and inferred meanings in text. • Identifies purpose of text, context of the situation, reader-writer relationship. • Identifies mood/attitude of writer and register of the text.

Note that this (Table 16) includes criteria for success (how well/criterion) as well as task definition (what: task/performance) and exemplification. A list of conditions (what: content/condition) is also provided – for Reading Benchmark 5 these include the following:

- Text is two or three paragraphs long and related to personal experience or familiar context.
- Text is legible, easy to read; is in print or neat handwriting.
- Tasks are in a standard format: with items to circle, match, fill in a blank, complete a chart, answer questions, etc.
- Learner is adequately briefed for focused reading (has at least minimal knowledge to activate knowledge schemata for top-down processing).

- Instructions are clear and explicit, for everyday situations, used with some visual clues, presented step by step. Pictures occasionally accompany text.
- Text has clear organisation.
- Text is two or three paragraphs long, printed or electronic.
- Language is mostly concrete and literal, with some abstract words.
- Context and topic are often familiar and partly predictable for learner.
- Content is relevant and can be related to personal experience.
- Text types: newspaper articles, educational/content materials, stories, encyclopedia entries, short reports (Pawlikowska-Smith 2002:p.88)

In a companion volume (*CLB Sample Tasks*) examples of representative tasks are offered for each of the three CLB domains of 'community access', 'study/academic' and 'workplace'. The following reading tasks are suggested for the academic domain at Benchmark 5:

Study/Academic tasks:

- Read a brochure about a training programme.
- Follow instructions regarding school assignments.
- Follow simple-language, user-friendly computer screen commands.
- Number a set of pictures in an appropriate sequence based on the information in the text. Identify pictures that do not belong in a story sequence.
- Skim 10 texts for 30 seconds each. Fill out a sheet with information on what each article is about, its purpose, if it is interesting or useful for you to read or not.

Guidance is also given on the proportion of items based on such tasks that a learner would need to answer correctly in order to achieve the benchmark (Pawlikowska-Smith 2000:146): see Table 17.

The extent to which the CLB tasks might, in fact, yield comparable tasks and comparable results across teaching and learning contexts is, of course, open to question – how long after all are 'two to three paragraphs' and how might one be sure that a learner is 'adequately briefed'? There is insufficient information on required item types to ensure the comparability of tasks produced by different teachers based on these lists and so any assumption that 80% correct responses on one task would be even very roughly comparable to 80% on another seems overly optimistic. Nonetheless the amplification of the Can Do is far closer to the level of detail that Weir (2005a) has called for. Providing a similar level of detail for purposes of illustration might benefit the interpretability of RLD for English. At the same time it should be recognised that detail is not synonymous with precision. The concern of

Table 17 Performance monitoring, evaluation and the Benchmark achievement report in CLB 2000 (Pawlikowska-Smith 2000:146)

1	Fewer than 50% of the items	Performance not successful relative to task requirements; learner responds correctly to fewer than 50% of the items (comprehension questions)
2	Fewer than 70% of the items	Performance marginally successful relative to task requirements; learner responds correctly to fewer than 70% of the items (comprehension questions)
3	70–80% of the items	Performance successful relative to task requirements; learner responds correctly to 70–80% of the items (comprehension questions)
4	More than 80% of the items	Performance very successful relative to task requirements; learner responds correctly to more than 80% of the items (comprehension questions)

the English Profile must be with efficiency: identifying and isolating those differences that are criterial in distinguishing levels.

The CSWE scheme goes even further than the CLB in supporting comparability in teacher assessment, providing sample tasks whose difficulty levels have been calibrated (using the Rasch model) for teachers to draw on when they assess learners (Brindley 2001). Of course, such calibration may be more meaningful when a scheme is designed to work within an educational programme (the case for the CSWE) than when it is intended to apply across programmes (the case for the CLB, the CEFR and the proposed English Profile RLD).

Tension between purposes

In addition to the criticisms considered above, a number of further questions have been raised in relation to Can Do based scales and frameworks that will need to be considered in the development of the English Profile. Brindley (1998) lists challenges encountered in the development of outcomes-based assessment. Some of these are equally applicable to proficiency scales and include issues such as comparability and consistency of judgements outlined above. Additionally, there is a danger, also seen in the mastery learning experience of the 1960s and 1970s that objectives can come to dominate the classroom. In finding an appropriate level of specificity in setting objectives, steering a course between the *Scylla* of inexplicit generalisation and the *Charybdis* of atomisation has proved to be a persistent challenge for educators (Brindley 1998, Popham 1973, Spady 1994). Almost every learning activity could be specified and recorded in terms of an objective, but this is administratively overwhelming and it is far from clear how data might be aggregated so as to be of use to stakeholders outside the immediate learning context.

A further objection to outcomes based schemes is that they 'obscure, deform and trivialize education' (Egan 1983 quoted in Lantolf & Frawley 1985). Objectives are said to be bureaucratic and coercive, serving to circumscribe learner roles and pushing teachers to work towards predetermined ends (Auerbach 1987). McNamara & Roever (2006) are concerned that the CEFR is achieving such dominance that it imposes its interpretation of language learning on previously diverse teaching and testing programmes: 'testing organizations wishing to operate in Europe . . . have had to align their assessments with levels of the CEFR, despite radically different constructs, as a pure political necessity. Funding for reform of school language syllabi. . . is tied to conformity to the CEFR in more than one European country' (pp. 212–213). This interpretation would seem to misrepresent the extent to which the CEFR has required users to adjust their approach towards teaching or testing languages. Linking of international tests to the CEFR such as the American *TOEFL* test, the Taiwanese *General English Proficiency Tests* or the Japanese *Eiken* suite of tests of English, for example, has been accomplished without any reported alteration to the test specifications (Tannenbaum & Dunlea & Matsudaira 2009; Wu & Wu 2007; Wylie 2005).

Morrow (2004) stresses that the framework is explicitly not intended as 'a set of suggestions, recommendations or guidelines' to be followed or implemented, and cites the case studies that he introduces as evidence for the diversity of ways in which it may be engaged with and interpreted. Although critical of some of these uses, Fulcher & Davidson (2007) take a less pessimistic view than McNamara & Roever (2006), seeing the framework's role in raising awareness as a key strength. In line with the ethos of the CEFR, RLD for English should be presented as a resource for teachers, course developers and other educators and should be developed in consultation and collaboration with users.

Profile Deutsch (Glaboniat et al 2005), a set of RLD for German (see Appendix A), makes use of information technology to allow users to approach the material from the point of view of either grammar or functions. In the *Profile Deutsch* interface, clicking on a function brings up grammatical and lexical exponents, clicking on a grammatical item brings up a list of functions that the item could be used to realise. The English Profile RLD should make use of similar technologies to allow users to access content in directions that are of most relevance to their requirements (see Chapter 6 for suggestions on how this might be done).

Conclusions

Case studies in using the framework have consistently called for further elaboration and exemplification of the levels (Alderson 2002, Figueras & Noijons 2009, Martyniuk 2011, Martyniuk & Noijons 2007, Morrow 2004). This need has been addressed by the Council of Europe through the provision of materials exemplifying the framework levels and the Manual for *Relating Language Examinations to the CEFR* (Council of Europe 2009). However, these materials remain sparse relative to the number of scales. The English Profile, with its substantial and expanding database of learner language, has a vital role to play in more fully exemplifying the levels for English.

Alderson (2004:1), reporting on the experience of applying the CEFR scales to the DIALANG diagnostic assessment project, identifies a key challenge for users; 'it is not easy to determine what sort of written and spoken texts might be appropriate for each level, what topics might be more or less suitable at any given level, and what sort of operation – be that strategy, subskill or pragmatic inference – or sociolinguistic context might be applicable at which level'. In addition to supplying language-specific specifications of grammar and vocabulary, the integration of cognitive and contextual parameters into the CEFR levels should be a key contribution of the English Profile. Work contributing to the Council of Europe (2009) Manual for *Relating Examinations to the CEFR* such as the task content analysis checklists (Alderson, Figueras, Kuijper, Nold, Takala and Tardieu, Association of Language Testers in Europe 2005) has provided a framework for approaching such work. Shaw & Weir (2007) and Khalifa & Weir (2009) have taken up the challenge and have already established how contextual and cognitive parameters relate to the levels of Cambridge ESOL examinations. This work needs to be applied more broadly in the English Profile RLD to indicate how level differences are operationalised in a range of settings.

Martyniuk & Noijons (2007) concluded from their survey that there was 'a considerable and quite urgent need to develop user-friendly sets of materials for mediating the CEFR to the different stakeholder groups: policy makers, curriculum developers, textbook developers, publishers, teachers, testers, parents of learners, employers. There is also a strongly felt need for national and international cooperation in interpreting and using the CEFR' (p.8). The English Profile will clearly need to extend the elaboration and exemplification of level-specific features of learner language, but also to encourage opportunities for exchange between users so that the social moderation of standards can be maintained.

Reference level descriptions will need to address the links between teacher perceptions as operationalised in the scales and observable learner performance. To become more amenable to measurement, the descriptors will need to be related to contextual and cognitive parameters. Extended specification of functions, notions, grammar and vocabulary with exemplars of the kind envisaged in the draft guidelines and exemplified by *Threshold* will not be sufficient to achieve this. In addition, there may a requirement for:

- extensive elaboration and perhaps revision of the terms used in the CEFR illustrative descriptors
- indications of the relationship between learner language skills and contextual parameters
- indications of whether and how the skills engaged by reading and listening tasks relate to the CEFR levels
- illustrative calibrated tasks
- support and guidance for application of the English Profile to language programmes
- development of an international community of users with opportunities to share experiences and understanding of the CEFR levels.

Section 2
Empirical Bases

3 Pedagogical perspectives on progression in functional abilities

Previous chapters have traced the theoretical grounds for and practical implementation of language functions in the CEFR and the T-series. The reviews in Chapters 1 and 2 have pointed to the complexity and interrelatedness of notions, functions, activities and their grammatical and lexical exponents as well as to the importance of considering them together within the wider context of communicative competences as envisaged in the Council of Europe projects and the English Profile.

Chapter 1 introduced the established wisdom that effective educational objectives need to specify three key elements: performance, condition and criterion. We have seen that Can Do statements in the CEFR scales rarely include all three. Although it might be expected that the *Activities* and *Strategies* scales might be more concerned with performance and the competence scales with criteria, this is not, in fact, the case. Compare the following two descriptors, one taken from an *Activities* scale and the other from a *Competences* scale.

> Activities: Spoken Production: Sustained Monologue – *C2: Can give clear, smoothly flowing, elaborate, often memorable descriptions.*
> Competences: Pragmatic Competences: Flexibility – *B1: Can adapt his/ her expression to deal with less routine, even difficult situations.*

Both indicate a performance: *give descriptions/adapt expression to situation*. The *Activities* descriptor specifies criteria (descriptions must be clear, smoothly flowing, elaborate and often memorable) without indicating operative conditions (constraints, texts, domains, tasks). The *Competences* descriptor specifies conditions (less routine, even difficult situations) without indicating explicit criteria for judging the adequacy of the performance.

The *Elaborated Descriptive Scales* used in DIALANG (Table C3 in Appendix C of the CEFR) suggest one way of bringing together elements from different scales to provide a consolidated overview of each level. The approach directs attention to the different elements of the objectives in a way that the *Global Scale* (Council of Europe 2001 Table 1, p.24) does not. The

DIALANG elaborated scale for Writing, for example (Table 18), includes three elements: i) *What types of text I can write* (which chiefly concerns performance: e.g. 'Can write a variety of different texts'); ii) *What I can write* (mainly concerning indicators of quality – criteria – e.g. 'Layout, paragraphing and punctuation are consistent and helpful') and; iii) *Conditions and limitations* (chiefly concerned with restrictions on the quality of the performance, rather than with the conditions under which the performance occurs e.g. 'Expressing subtle nuances . . . can be difficult'). The categorisation may be questionable – 'Can express oneself with clarity and precision' represents a markedly different interpretation of 'types of text' from the 'letters, postcards, notes, messages, notes, forms' listed at B1 – but the use of a framework of this kind helps to bring together the different perspectives that together define the level.

Table 18 Elaborated descriptive scales used in the advisory feedback section of DIALANG: *Writing* (from CEFR:240)

Writing	B2	C1	C2
What types of text I can write	Can write a variety of different texts.	Can write a variety of different texts. Can express oneself with clarity and precision, using language flexibly and effectively.	Can write a variety of different texts. Can convey finer shades of meaning precisely. Can write persuasively.
What I can write	Can express news and views effectively, and relate to those of others. Can use a variety of linking words use of to mark clearly the relationships between ideas. Spelling and punctuation are reasonably accurate.	Can produce clear, smoothly flowing, well-structured writing, showing controlled organisational patterns, connectors and cohesive devices. Can qualify opinions and statements precisely in relation to degrees of, for example, certainty/ uncertainty, belief/ doubt, likelihood. Layout, paragraphing and punctuation are consistent and helpful. Spelling is accurate apart from occasional slips.	Can create coherent and cohesive text making full and appropriate use of a variety of organisational patterns and a wide range of cohesive devices. Writing is free of spelling errors.
Conditions and limitations	Expressing subtle nuances in taking a stance or in telling about feelings and experiences is usually difficult.	Expressing subtle nuances in taking a stance or in telling about feelings and experiences can be difficult.	No need to consult a dictionary, except for occasional specialist terms in an unfamiliar area.

A further difficulty in attempting to build up a picture of this nature from the CEFR is the lack of detail on the C levels. The C1 and C2 levels are under-described – among the 31 scales for language activities, 17 provide no descriptor for C2 and six have no descriptor for C1. 'Conditions and constraints' are listed in Chapter 4, but their relation to the levels is not explained and they rarely appear in the descriptors. The criteria provided at the C levels often appear subjective (the meaning of 'smoothly flowing' or 'often memorable' may be open to a wide range of interpretations), but they are not exemplified.

To address such gaps, it may be helpful additionally to explore other pedagogic sources. Where communicative needs are taken into consideration, current practice in English language education could provide a valuable additional source of evidence, providing further detail relating to performances, criteria and relevant conditions that might enhance our definition of the C levels. A useful place to begin in the investigation of higher level English language learning would therefore seem to be the materials currently in use around the world that are directed at higher level learners. In effect shadowing, updating and expanding on the approach adopted in compiling the original CEFR scales (see CEFR Appendix B). In this chapter we describe a survey of the functions and activities (avowedly) addressed in current language teaching and testing materials designed for this audience.

Gathering higher level descriptions

Lenz and Schneider (2004a) provide a *Bank of descriptors for self-assessment in European Language Portfolios* which brings together Can Do statements from the CEFR itself, from the DIALANG and ALTE frameworks (which appear as appendices in the CEFR), from a number of European Language Portfolio models, and from the Bergen Can Do project (Hasselgreen 2003). This bank offers a useful starting point, but unlike Lenz and Schneider (2004a), our objective in the English Profile is not to supplement the CEFR by providing an extensive and expanding bank of descriptors. Rather, the intention is to synthesise and distil from a broad range of material the criterial features that would seem to distinguish most effectively between the levels for English.

As in the CEFR itself, the starting points in this project are pedagogic and functional: the focus is on functions and activities. We set out to discover what C level learners, '*proficient users*', are more likely to accomplish with their communicative language abilities than learners at the B2 level of '*independent users*' or below. This complements the investigation into the observed grammatical and lexical features of learner language covered in detail in the English Profile contributions of Hawkins and Filipović (2012) and by Capel (2010). In other words, while this volume deals with functions, Hawkins and

Filipović and Capel are mainly concerned with the *notional* categories of the Council of Europe model: Hawkins and Filipović with *general* and Capel with *specific* notions.

For a number of reasons, the description of the C levels is likely to prove a more challenging task than the development of the 'common core' descriptions available for the lower (A and B) levels of the CEFR in the T-series. With the progression through the levels summarised on pp. 33–36 of the framework (Council of Europe 2001), it is clear that the scope for divergence increases as learners gain access to more specialist vocabulary and may become increasingly encultured into localised discourse communities (whether regional, social, professional or academic) with associated language varieties. It also seems clear from a comparison of the descriptors that simple yes/no distinctions concerning what learners can (or cannot) do become more difficult to sustain at the higher levels.

The CEFR (Council of Europe 2001:6) stresses that at all levels learners may have an uneven or weighted profile of abilities – that they may for example be best characterised as B1 in one activity or area of competence and A2 in another. Given the broader variation in use that the C levels encompass it perhaps makes less sense to speak of a learner as being *at* C1 or C2 than it does to speak of him or her as having a C1 or C2 level in using English as a medical practitioner or as an engineer or in informal exchanges with speakers of a standard North American variety of English (or in some other relatively defined and restricted domain). At the C levels, lists of common core words or expressions (of the kind found in the specifications for *Breakthrough* or *Threshold*) are unlikely to capture such diversity. A similar conclusion was reached by the team developing the *Profile Deutsch 2.0* Reference Level Description for German (Glaboniat, Müller, Rusch, Schmitz & Wertenschlag 2005) which does not offer vocabulary lists at the C levels (see Introduction and Appendix A).

Functional progression in language learning materials

Methodology

The survey reported in this chapter is intended as a first step in specifying ways in which learners of English at the C1 and C2 levels might be expected to be able to make use of the language. The ultimate aim within the English Profile is a fuller description of the distinctive, criterial features of communicative English language use at the higher levels than is currently available; one that employs the organising principles of the CEFR itself to bridge the divide between the framework and the multiple and varied practice(s) of specifically *English* language teaching, learning and assessment. For this reason, the key outcome of the survey will be new, more operationally adequate Can

Do descriptors for English Profile that can be integrated with and serve to supplement those already available through the CEFR.

Following the draft *Guide for the Production of RLD* (Council of Europe 2005:6) a methodology was sought for generating these Can Do descriptions that would synthesise 'established knowledge concerning spontaneous oral usages' and 'the intuitive and reflexive command of the language possessed by knowledgeable and highly competent informers' as expressed through materials designed for the purposes of pedagogy and assessment. Like the CEFR itself, the project which is the focus of this Chapter synthesises the experience of language educators to mark out the extent to which certain language functions in English might be associated with the C1 and C2 levels.

Taking a step back from the CEFR document itself, this chapter draws on the collective experience and expertise of educators, course designers, testers and policy makers operating in a wide range of contexts. The intention is to find and capture areas of consensus on features of language use that are held to be indicative of the highest levels of socially organised English language learning: the C levels. To explore the nature of this consensus, meta-documents such as test specifications, proficiency scales, syllabuses, and textbook outlines are surveyed together with their support material in all media. These include English language curricula in various countries to cover the range of settings in which English is taught around the world. The materials included in the survey are claimed by their producers – or, where guidance from these was lacking, judged by English Profile researchers – to address at least the B2 level of the CEFR or higher. Listings of the language functions or activities (or both) that the various systems set out to teach or test were extracted from these materials. Indications of performance conditions and criteria for judgement that would help to define a C level performance were of particular interest.

Locating materials

As in other strands of the English Profile, the process began with materials produced by English Profile partner organisations (Cambridge University Press, University of Cambridge ESOL Examinations, the British Council and English UK) as well as the existing CEFR and related portfolio contributions. From this base, the scope was expanded to include the work of other institutions operating in a range of settings.

In summary, our sources included lists of functions and Can Do statements extracted from:

- textbooks sourced through Cambridge University Press
- examination handbooks from University of Cambridge ESOL Examinations
- curriculum and syllabus documents sourced by English Profile

Programme partner organisations such as the British Council, English UK and others
- the *Bank of descriptors for self-assessment in European Language Portfolios* (Lenz & Schneider 2004a)
- other publications disseminated by educational institutions available for download on the internet such as test specifications and handbooks, proficiency scales and support materials for textbooks
- bestselling international textbooks and related support materials provided by the publishers and identified via sales figures provided by the Bournemouth English Book Centre (a specialist supplier of English Language Teaching materials)
- additional materials not available from public sources, sourced from educational contexts in which the project team members had previous experience.

As our concern is with English language learning, we set out in the first instance to gather materials that would be used for English language, learning and most of the schemes that we included are exclusively connected with English. However, material was not excluded if, like the *ACTFL* scales or the *Canadian Language Benchmarks*, it covered other languages in addition to English.

A database was developed that would allow us to organise, store, and retrieve lists of function words and Can Do statements taken from specifications for each of the schemes included in the study. Because the database is designed to record the occurrence of functions and activities across the schemes, it facilitates comparisons between these. This allows us, for example, to search for common features associated with C level materials across contexts and to identify how the C levels might differ from B2. Further comparisons are made between the Council of Europe categories (Wilkins 1976, as discussed in Chapter 1) that form the basis for our definition of communicative language functions and the functions and activities described for each of the schemes analysed.

Lenz and Schneider (2004b) make the point that descriptor statements may be developed for a range of purposes, not all of which will be compatible with the definition of a broadly applicable level. They give the example of self-assessment scales designed for children. These may 'use short, simplified descriptors that often lack modifiers which would indicate what restrictions apply (e.g. "if spoken slowly and clearly")' (p.5). In adult contexts, such statements 'might be misinterpreted and seem to describe much more demanding tasks (and higher competences)' than is, in fact, the case. Lenz and Schneider also found descriptors that did not 'stand alone', but occurred in clusters – e.g. 'Provided that people speak slowly and clearly and I am very familiar with the topic, a) I can understand words and phrases in a conversation, b) I can understand the important information in a short announcement or message, c) I can follow the main points of a short story'. Because the objective in this English Profile project was to synthesise rather than to pool descriptors, such statements were not excluded, but were viewed as potentially useful indicators of the range of activities, conditions and criteria that might help to define the levels more adequately for operational purposes.

A more serious challenge noted in the review in Chapter 1 and illustrated by the case studies below is that pedagogic materials often employ idiosyncratic descriptive categories. The use of terms such as *tasks, activities, notions, functions* and *topics* in the materials may not necessarily reflect the ways in which these are understood in the CEFR. In some cases a 'function' in a textbook outline might not correspond to the Council of Europe definition: in others 'functions' are referred to by a different term, or are incorporated into Can Do statements. Indeed, arriving at a shared understanding of terms has proved to be a recurrent and sometimes intricate issue for the English Profile partners.

As might be expected in materials of this nature, definitions of terms were not usually provided. It was therefore unclear how far the different schemes shared an understanding of terms and how far the differences between them could be attributed to differences of theoretical approach or of definition. The strategy was to include all lists of 'functions', even where these did not conform to the Council of Europe definition, together with listings of Can Do statements (whether these concerned activities, strategies, competences or some other categorisation) and any listings we found of closely related categories such as 'speech acts'. No attempt was made to translate each scheme into a unified terminology, but it was anticipated that the resulting synthesis would require standardisation, definition and exemplification.

The relationship between the surveyed material and the CEFR

Given that the intention is to develop Can Do descriptors targeted at the C levels, it is clearly important to establish, at least in broad terms, the nature of the relationship between the collected materials and the CEFR. As the intention was to sample widely from a broad range of settings, unlike Lenz and Schneider (2004a), this project was not restricted to descriptors derived from or designed to be compatible with the CEFR. To establish how each scheme might relate to the CEFR, a process of interpretation was needed.

Linking to a framework such as the CEFR is not a straightforward matter: procedures for linking existing examinations to the Framework are the subject of an extensive manual and reference supplement produced by the Council of Europe (2009). This manual states that a testable claim for a relationship between a given level of a programme or testing system and the Framework requires extensive empirical evidence including learner performance data. It will be clear that the procedures adopted here do not meet such exacting standards and the links drawn are tentative rather than definitive. At this preliminary stage, however, the focus is on the descriptions used rather than the performances they describe – in the terms used by the Manual it is at the level of *specification* rather than of *standardisation*. If some of the Can Do statements that emerge are not seen by educators to reflect the C levels, this will become clear in later phases of the development process when statements are calibrated in relation to the CEFR level definitions. In short, for the purpose of the survey, relatively approximate links to the CEFR are sufficient at this stage.

The process of classification

The intention was to synthesise from the broad range of descriptive material collected an indication of functions and activities that might (at least in the perspective of the publishers, test producers and course providers concerned) characterise the C levels and help to distinguish them from B2. Partly because of this purpose and partly because of the uncertainty surrounding the relationship between the materials collected and the CEFR levels, unless an explicit claim was made by the providers, no attempt was made to differentiate C1 from C2 when judging which CEFR level they most closely reflected. This differentiation will be made later when the statements come to be calibrated and integrated into the CEFR scheme. In addition to material that was judged to be at the C (C1 or C2) levels, B2 material was also included in the analyses as a basis for comparison.

As conceived in the CEFR, the C levels are most often associated with tertiary education and with cognitively demanding occupational uses of language. Although some secondary school materials were found that did, in the judgement of the researchers, seem to reflect the C levels; notably in L1 'inner circle' English material (Kachru 1990) but also from ESL or 'outer circle' settings (such as Hong Kong, Lebanon and Papua New Guinea). Trim (2005) has stated that in EFL ('expanding circle') settings in Europe, 'As a very rough guide, A1 (*Breakthrough*) is appropriate to progress in the first foreign language at the 10 or 11 year primary/secondary interface, A2 (*Waystage*) to around 14, B1 (*Threshold*) to 16+, the lower secondary goal, B2 (*Vantage*) to 18+, the completion of upper secondary education, and C1 and C2 to specialist university level' (p.4). This also ties in with the evidence from informants working in the secondary school sector in Europe and the foreign language materials we collected from France and Germany that B2 is widely seen as a suitable, if sometimes challenging attainment target for matriculation across much of the European continent (see also the Eurybase database of Eurydice reports on European school-level language teaching programmes at www. eurydice.org/portal/page/portal/Eurydice/DB_Eurybase_Home).

That B2 is regarded in many systems as a challenging target for secondary school attainment meant that tertiary and vocational institutions were more usually the source for C level materials – secondary school level material being collected more for purposes of comparison. However, universities we contacted were not generally able to provide us with syllabus outlines that incorporated functions or activities. We were more usually provided by our informants with lists of textbooks to be covered in a course, often including books that we had also collected through the textbook strand of this project.

Because these often represent entry requirements for language learners progressing to tertiary institutions, we also took the decision to include language or communication requirements for upper secondary study or for matriculation taken from settings where English is the first language. This included schemes directed at immigrant students within national education systems (e.g. the WIDA – *World-Class Instructional Design and Assessment* – standards) and those directed at L1 speakers of English (the 'A' – Advanced – Level syllabus for *English Language* in England and Wales, used for matriculation) (see below for details of these schemes).

Of the material collected and entered to the database, curriculum documents proved to be the greatest challenge to source. Of those that were found, some were only available in the language of the country concerned. Rather than attempt to translate these and risk introducing descriptions that were not intended in the originals, the decision was taken to restrict the survey in the first instance to documents that included statements in English.

To date the following 46 schemes have been entered into the database. Between them, these include some 2,474 functions, activities or Can Do statements (declared or judged to be) at B2 and 2,142 at the C levels. Further items will be incorporated as they become available:

European Language Portfolio (ELP) models/CEFR related
Association of Language Testers in Europe (ALTE) Can Do project (Council of Europe 2001 Appendix D)
European Association of Language Centres in Higher Education (CERCLES): 29.2002 *ELP for University Students*
European Centre for Modern Languages (ECML) Bergen Can do Project
European Language Council (ELC): 35.2002 *ELP Higher Education*
Ireland: 14.2001: *ELP for adult newcomers preparing for mainstream vocational training and employment* (Irish ELP)
Sweden: 19.2001 *ELP 16+* (Swedish ELP)
Switzerland: 1.2000 *ELP Version for Young People and Adults* (15+) (Swiss ELP)

Syllabus and curriculum documents
Bogazici University (Turkey) – English language syllabus (n.d.)
Curtin University of Technology (Australia) – UniEnglish English language Self Assessment
(Curtin University n.d. http://unienglish.curtin.edu.au)

International Education Agency of Papua New Guinea – English Language
Curriculum (http://www.iea.ac.pg)
Japan Ministry of Education, Technology, Science, Sports and Technology
(MEXT) – The Course of Study for Foreign Languages
(http://www.mext.go.jp/english/shotou)
Republic of Lebanon – English Language Curriculum
(Centre for Educational Research and Development, Ministry of Education, nd:
http://www.crdp.org/crdp)
Sabanci University (Turkey) – English Language Syllabus (n.d.)
Singapore Ministry of Education – English Language Secondary School Syllabus
(Curriculum Planning and Development Division, 2001)
United Kingdom Adult ESOL Core Curriculum
(UK Department for Education and Skills 2001)
Ukraine Kherson State University 4th year Syllabus (Institute of Philology,
2005)

Language tests
Cambridge ESOL Main Suite Examinations: Certificate of Proficiency in English
(CPE), Cambridge Certificate in Advanced English (CAE) and Cambridge
First Certificate in English (FCE)
Cambridge ESOL Business English Certificates (BEC)
(Cambridge ESOL Handbooks, 2007)
Cambridge International Legal English Certificate (ILEC)
(Handbook for teachers, 2007)
Cambridge International Certificate in Financial English (ICFE)
(Handbook for teachers, 2007)
City and Guilds (C&G) International English for Speakers of Other Languages
International (International ESOL)
(Qualification handbook Revised 2005)
DIALANG Assessment Framework (DAF)
(The Dialang Partnership, Final version, November 1999)
Eiken Can Do List – Society for Testing English Proficiency, Japan
(English Translation, 2008: www.eiken.or.jp)
Graded Examinations in Spoken English (GESE) – Trinity College
(2007–2010 Syllabus, Trinity College London, 2006)
The Greek State Examination System to Certify Foreign Language Proficiency
(KPG)
(Information Booklet, Dendrinos, 2007)
Hong Kong Examinations and Assessment Authority, Hong Kong Certificate of
Education Examination (HKCEE) Syllabus for English Language
(Curriculum Development Council, 2007-CE ENG LANG, 2007)
International English Language Testing System (IELTS) band descriptors for
Speaking and Writing (public version)
(www.ielts.org)
London Tests of English
(Handbook, Pearson Language Assessments, Revised Edition August 2007)
Test of English as a Foreign Language (TOEFL) iBT Language Competency
Descriptors (Educational Testing Service 2004: www.ets.org/Media/Tests/
TOEFL/pdf/EngLangCompDescriptors.pdf)
Test of English for International Communication (TOEIC) Can Do Levels Table
(Educational Testing Service, 2006)

The European Language Certificates (TELC) Certificate in English for Business
  Purposes: Learning Objectives and Test Format
(WBT Weiterbildungs-Testsysteme GmbH 2001)

Proficiency scales and frameworks
ACTFL Proficiency Guidelines
(The American Council on the Teaching of Foreign Languages, 1999)
Canadian Language Benchmarks 2000: English as a second language for adults
(Pawlikowska-Smith, Centre for Canadian Language Benchmarks, 2000)
Indiana's English Language Proficiency Standards
(Adopted by the Indiana State Board of Education, November 2003)
Interagency Language Roundtable Language Skill Level Descriptions (ILR)
(Interagency Language Roundtable, July 1985)
NATO Standardization Agreement (STANAG) 6001 Language Proficiency
  Levels
(Military Committee Joint Standardization Board, NSAl0524–6001 [Edition 2],
  June 2003)
World-Class Instructional Design and Assessment (WIDA) Consortium: English
  Language Proficiency Standards for English Language Learners (Grades 9–12)
(State of Wisconsin 2004)

Textbook series
English for Academic Study (Garnet)
    Campbell and Smith (2009) *Listening*
    McCormack and Slaght (2009) *Extended Writing and Research Skills*
    McCormack and Watkins (2009) *Speaking*
    Pallant (2009) *Writing*
    Slaght and Harben (2009) *Reading*
face2face (Cambridge University Press)
    Redston and Cunningham (2007) *Upper Intermediate*
    Cunningham and Bell (2009) *Advanced*
Inside Out (Macmillan)
    Kay and Jones (2009) *Upper Intermediate*
    Jones, Bastow and Hird (2001) *Advanced*
Natural English (Oxford University Press)
    Gairns and Redman (2003) Upper Intermediate
New Cutting Edge (Pearson Longman)
    Cunningham and Moor (2005) *Upper Intermediate*
    Cunningham and Moor (2003) *Advanced*
New English File (Oxford University Press)
    Oxenden and Lathan-Koenig (2008) *Upper Intermediate*
    Oxenden and Lathan-Koenig (2010) *Advanced*
New Headway (Oxford University Press)
    Soars and Soars (2005) Upper Intermediate
    Soars and Soars (2003) Advanced
Straightforward (Macmillan)
    Kerr and Jones (2007) *Upper Intermediate*
    Norris and Kerr (2007) *Advanced*
Total English (Pearson Longman)
    Acklam and Crace (2006) *Upper Intermediate*
    Wilson and Clare (2007) *Advanced*

Illustrative case studies of the treatment of functions and Can Do statements in the materials database

In this section three schemes that were collected for the database (a test, a national teaching syllabus and a proficiency framework) are used to illustrate how the materials were incorporated into a practical database tool that would facilitate a comparative analysis of the B2 and C levels. The extracts from the three documents provided here exemplify many of the challenges experienced in extracting language activities and functions and the implications for the survey of the differences in approach taken by diverse institutions producing documents with a range of purposes. We discuss the three schemes in terms of their relationship to the CEFR, their presentation of activities and functions and the implications of these for the design of the database: the London tests of English, the Japanese Ministry of Education Course of Study for Foreign Languages and the NATO Standardization Agreement (STANAG 6001) Language Proficiency Levels.

Relationship to the CEFR

The London Tests of English claim equivalence between the London *Level A1 Foundation* and CEFR A1 and between each London test level and CEFR level up to *Level 5 Proficient* and C2. The test handbook makes the claim that, 'The alignment of the London Tests of English to the CEFR has been established by mapping of the test specifications to the CEFR descriptors and is reinforced by regular training of test writers and markers. Work is in progress to further improve the robustness of the alignment on the basis of empirical data' (p.6).

The preamble to the document raises questions about the 'robustness of the alignment' as it states that, 'Level 5 is the minimum requirement for undergraduate courses at many UK universities and institutes of higher education'. However, the entry requirements of most UK universities of a band score of 6.0 or 6.5 on IELTS or an internet-based TOEFL score of 90 to 100 indicate, on the basis of equivalences suggested by Cambridge ESOL and ETS, that, depending on institution and subject, B2(+) or C1 are generally accepted for this purpose, although de Jong (2009), for example, has questioned whether the different test providers have interpreted the CEFR in the same way in making these claims. It is not clear, without further evidence, whether this implies that the London Level 5 is, in fact a B2+/C1 test, that Level 5 test takers applying to university are being asked to perform at a substantially higher level than their TOEFL/IELTS counterparts or whether the TOEFL and IELTS alignments are considered to be at fault. Rather than attempting, without any firm basis, to disentangle these questions, the suggested equivalences were taken at face value and Level 5 (or at least the description of it provided through these specifications) was accepted as representing C2.

No reference was found to any direct mapping of the Ministry of Education, Culture, Sport, Science and Technology (MEXT) syllabus to the CEFR, but judged on the basis of the content description provided, the syllabus included material ranging broadly from A1 to B2. The Grade 2 level and pre-Grade 2 *Eiken* tests are used in Japan to represent benchmarks for terminal attainment at high school. A linking exercise carried out by the Society for Testing English Proficiency (STEP) (the non-profit foundation which provides the *Eiken* tests) identified pre-Grade 2 with A2 and Grade 2 with B1 on the CEFR.

The Worldwide ELT EFL ESL EAL LEP ESOL Assessment Scaler and Tests Mapping Project (AWEMAP) global proficiency scale map locates STANAG level 3 at the C1 level, based on work by Clifford and Lowe of the NATO Bureau for International Language Coordination (cited online), although the Linguapeace Europe Language Portfolio places STANAG level 3 at the B2 level apparently on the basis of a mapping exercise undertaken by the University of Westminster (see Lonergan 2006) and the latter is the equivalence employed here. As with the other schemes included in the analysis and referred to in the literature review, convincing evidence of the relationship between the STANAG scales and the CEFR is not yet available. The equivalences used in the database must also therefore be regarded as contingent and are certainly open to refinement.

Treatment of functions/activities

The London Tests of English specifications do not include a section dedicated explicitly to functions. It is stated that at Level 5, candidates should be able to, 'understand stated and unstated functions', but further details of these functions are not provided for the user. The specifications do include Can Do statements that set out the 'performance required' at each of the five levels in the suite. Distinctions are made between the papers with separate lists given for the receptive activities addressed in the written Listening and Reading tests and for written production addressed in the Writing Test. These lists are headed, 'Specific Assessment Objectives for the Written Test' (for the Reading and Listening tests) and 'Communicative tasks' (for the Writing test).

Many of the statements in the lists do explicitly or implicitly incorporate functions or activities; both in productive use, e.g. 'respond to and express qualified opinions and arguments in a variety of ways' and through identification of activities in spoken or written input, e.g. 'recognise how the writer tries to influence other people through choice of language and content'; 'identify the purpose and register of the spoken discourse'. Other statements refer to characteristics of the language or texts involved; e.g. 'read lengthy, complex literary texts'. Note how such descriptions relate to e.g. Bachman and Palmer's (1996) pragmatic competence or the CEFR *macrofunctions*. Further lists cover 'Themes and Vocabulary' and 'Language

Content'. Themes and Vocabulary has a semantic focus of more relevance to specific notions than functions, while Language Content focuses on register, grammar, cohesion and range of vocabulary: aspects of linguistic, sociolinguistic and pragmatic competence in the CEFR scheme.

The schemes analysed varied in the extent to which they offered separate descriptions according to mode (production/interaction/reception/mediation) and channel (spoken/written). The London tests do make a distinction in their Can Do listing between the Reading and Listening papers, although the differences often involve minimal rewording. In this extract, the differences in the wording of the Reading and Listening descriptor are italicised, with the distinct wording for Listening in parentheses; 'recognise how the *writer tries* [*speakers try*] to influence other people through [*their*] choice of language and content'.

There are some statements that occur only for one paper: 'select, extract, synthesise and summarize the relevant information from the written discourse' appears for Reading, but not Listening while there is no parallel for Reading in the Listening statement, 'recognise the speakers' use of language and stylistic devices to convey ideas, feelings, attitudes and points of view'. A somewhat different approach is taken to the Oral test; the specification provides a brief list of Can Dos, but also refers the reader to the '*Communicative Tasks listed in syllabus for written test*', thus implying that the test taker will be expected to perform the same functions or activities in spoken interaction as in written production. At Level 3 (B2) for the Writing test these include, *inter alia*, such functions or activities as, 'introduce others; make comparisons; make and refuse formal and informal requests'.

The MEXT syllabus does suggest lists of functions for the different educational levels, but makes no distinctions by mode or channel. Unlike the London tests there are also some lists of language use situations (including phone calls, speeches, magazines, skits) and of specific grammar points (Subject+*seem* etc. +to-infinitive), but there are no lists of communicative activities, of notions or of lexical categories. Can Do statements are not provided.

Functions are listed under the category headings of, '*Smoothing human relationships*'; '*Transmitting feelings*'; '*Transmitting information*'; '*Transmitting ideas and intentions*' and '*Instigating action*'. Not all of the functions here appear in Wilkins (1976) or in *Vantage – celebrating* (listed under 'transmitting feelings') and *treating* (listed as an 'instigating action') in the MEXT syllabus, do not – but the MEXT lists appear very brief in comparison to the Council of Europe work and the extent to which they are intended to specify the functional aspect of the syllabus for each level is unclear. It is apparent that the lists are not intended to be exhaustive as each ends with 'etc.' but it is not apparent how much more this 'etc.' implies. The list for *Transmitting information*, for example, includes only 'explaining, reporting, describing, giving reasons, etc.' The lists of 'Examples of Functions of

Language' were included in the database as they are presented here; i.e. there was no attempt to address the shortfall implied by the 'etc.'.

The STANAG scales, like the London Tests, offer Can Do statements describing aspects of linguistic competence as well as activities and functions. These statements are provided separately for the 'four skills' of listening, speaking, reading and writing. For example, at Level 3 in Listening, the descriptor includes, 'Can readily understand language that includes such functions as hypothesising, supporting opinion, stating and defending policy, argumentation, objections, and various types of elaboration'. However, in common with the Can Do statements used in the London tests, not all of these statements include functions (e.g. 'Can follow accurately the essentials of conversations among educated native speakers').

As with the London tests, some statements are very similar across the skills – e.g. the following for Writing and Speaking (differences in the wording of the Speaking descriptors are italicised, with the Speaking wording in parentheses) 'Can *write about* [*discuss particular interests and*] special fields of competence with considerable ease'. Other descriptors are unique to skill – there is no clear parallel in Writing for the Speaking statement, 'Can reliably elicit information and informed opinion from native speakers'. The sets of level descriptors for all four language skills were included in our database.

Analyses

Large numbers of Can Do statements and functional descriptors were collected from a wide range of materials with the objective of synthesising a set of statements that would serve both to supplement the sparse C level descriptors available in the CEFR document and to more fully address the classic requirements for objectives: performance, condition and criterion.

The collected statements were analysed with two questions in mind. First, are there functions that only become available to learners at C level? Addressing this question involved tracing the occurrence of function words in the collected materials. If function words could be identified that were exclusively or predominantly used at the C levels, this might be a sign of *criterial* differences between the B and C levels. The second question concerned the extent to which the wording of statements at the B2 and C levels might indicate differences in how well learners are expected to carry out functions or activities and the conditions under which they might be expected to perform. To address this question a range of text analysis tools were used in the study to compare the statements, highlighting relevant conditions and criteria.

1. Are there functions that only become available to learners at C level?

The Threshold Level and the related publications at lower levels use the following broad categories of communicative function: *Imparting and Seeking*

Information, Expressing and Finding out Attitudes, Socializing, Deciding On and Managing the Course of Action, Assuring and Repairing Communication and *Structuring Discourse.* However, for this study, rather than assuming that any C level functions would fit into these categories, which were deliberately selected to reflect the needs of specific learners, an alternative set of functions was sought that could highlight the differences between levels and that might draw attention to areas that the Threshold categories do not encompass.

Following our review of the literature on communicative functions in the CEFR, Wilkins' (1976) lists were used as a basis for the functional comparison between levels. The Wilkins categories, although not intended to be exhaustive, provide the most comprehensive lists of function words associated with the Council of Europe scheme, not being limited to a set of communicative needs in the way that the T-series specifications are. They therefore seemed to offer the most useful available point of reference for identifying differences in functionality between the B and C levels.

Wilkins' (1976) functions are organised hierarchically into three levels. The six major categories or 'macro-functions' (argument, emotional relations, judgement and evaluation, personal emotions, rational enquiry and exposition, suasion) are subdivided into a number of intermediate functions and each of these is further divided into 'micro-functions'.

Key differences between levels were sought through comparison of the reference list of functions from Wilkins (1976) and the lists of functions and activities in the meta-documents at the B2 and C levels. After eliminating duplicated statements and filtering out homonyms of the listed function words (e.g. 'report' used to describe a text type) lists were derived of:

1. Function words shared between Wilkins (1976) and the lists of functions and activities at the B2 and C levels.
2. Function words unique to the C levels and not appearing in the B2 level listings.
3. Function words appearing at the B2 level and not appearing at C1 or C2.

Of the 258 micro-function words listed by Wilkins (1976) 75 (just under 30%) appeared in our database of functions and activities. The following of Wilkins' (1976) functions occur only at the C level in our lists; intermediate functional categories (where applicable) are given in parentheses.

judgement and evaluation:	assess (valuation); approbation (approval)
suasion:	advocate (inducement); threaten (prediction)
argument:	inform (asserted information); advocate (asserted information)
rational enquiry and exposition:	proposition; justification; conclusion
personal emotions:	annoyance (negative); irritation (negative)

Table 19 Wilkins' (1976) lists of functions compared with the Can Do statements and functions listed at the B2 and C levels in the database of materials

Category 1	Category 2	Function word	Occurring at B2 level	Occurring at C levels
judgement and evaluation	valuation	assess		✓
		appreciate	✓	✓
		rank	✓	
	approval	approbation		✓
		praise	✓	✓
	disapproval	blame	✓	
		complain	✓	✓
suasion	inducement	persuade	✓	✓
		suggest	✓	
		advise	✓	✓
		recommend	✓	✓
		advocate		✓
	prediction	warn	✓	✓
		threaten		✓
		predict	✓	✓
		invite	✓	✓
	tolerance	permit	✓	
argument	asserted information	tell	✓	✓
		inform		✓
		report	✓	✓
		assert	✓	
		state	✓	✓
		emphasise	✓	✓
		argue	✓	✓
		advocate		✓
		protest	✓	

Table 19 Continued

Category 1	Category 2	Function word	Occurring at B2 level	Occurring at C levels
argument	sought information	request	✓	✓
		question	✓	✓
		ask	✓	✓
	denied information	negate	✓	
		refuse	✓	
		decline	✓	
		protest	✓	
		describe	✓	✓
	agreement	confirm	✓	✓
		support	✓	✓
	disagreement	disagree	✓	✓
rational enquiry and exposition	rational enquiry and exposition	deduction	✓	
		proposition		✓
		hypothesis	✓	
		justification	✓	✓
		conclusion	✓	✓
		demonstration	✓	✓
		condition	✓	
		consequence	✓	
		inference	✓	✓
		interpretation	✓	✓
		explanation	✓	✓
		illustration	✓	
		reason	✓	
		classification	✓	
		comparison	✓	✓
		contrast	✓	✓
		generalisation	✓	

Table 19 Continued

Category 1	Category 2	Function word	Occurring at B2 level	Occurring at C levels
personal emotions	positive	pleasure	✓	✓
		satisfaction	✓	
		contentment	✓	
		surprise	✓	
	negative	dissatisfaction	✓	
		annoyance		✓
		irritation		✓
		anxiety	✓	
		disappointment	✓	✓
		bewilderment	✓	
		anger	✓	
emotional relations	greetings	welcome	✓	✓
		greeting	✓	
	sympathy	regret	✓	✓
		condolence	✓	✓
		sympathy	✓	✓
		comparison	✓	✓
	gratitude	acknowledgement	✓	✓
		thanks	✓	✓
	flattery	compliment	✓	
	hostility	indifference	✓	

No clear pattern emerges that would indicate that C level learners are able to access functions that are not available to B2 learners. Over 80% of the function words used to describe the C levels are also found at B2 (which covers all of Wilkins' macro and intermediate functional categories). Function words that are unique to the C levels are distributed across categories and would not seem to indicate substantive differences between the levels. Taking the example of the function word *inform*, synonyms such as *tell* or *give information* are found at B2 and below: the appearance of *inform* at the C levels may only represent a stylistic choice rather than any real gain in functionality. One might also question, for example, whether *irritation* and *annoyance* at the C levels represent anything more than synonyms for *dissatisfaction*, which occurs at B2.

There is little evidence of criterial differences between B2 and C1 to be found in the listings of functions that learners are able to carry out – the performance element of the descriptions. Might criterial differences rather be located in the other elements of the objective: the task conditions under which the functions are performed? Or in the criteria by which learner performance might be judged – the qualities of the performance?

2. *Are there differences between levels expressed through performance conditions and criteria?*

Although there is little difference in the function words appearing at B2 and at the C levels, criterial differences might be communicated through the modification of function words in descriptors appearing at the different levels: modification expressing how well learners might be expected or required to perform and relevant restrictions or conditions on their performance. Therefore, in addition to identifying function words appearing at the B2 and C level in the database of materials, attention was given to performance conditions and quality indicators in the collected descriptions. In exploring conditions and criteria as well as performance, an approach was sought that could highlight a range of potentially criterial features that might help users to distinguish one level from another. For this purpose a keywords analysis seemed a promising approach.

Keywords analysis involves comparing the text or corpus that is the focus for analysis with a reference corpus. The KeyWords Extractor accessible online as part of the Compleat Lexical Tutor (Cobb 2007) was employed to carry out the analysis. The program 'determines the defining lexis in a specialized corpus, by comparing frequency per word to frequency in a reference corpus' (www.lextutor.ca/keywords/). This entails computing a *keyness factor* for each word in the focal text – the comparative frequency of a word in the text (number of occurrences of the word per thousand words) relative to its frequency in a reference corpus (KeyWords extractor uses the Brown corpus as a default). The greater the keyness factor for a word, the more *key* that word is said to be in defining the topic of the text (Cobb 2007, Compleat Lexical Tutor online). Among the words with the highest keyness factor for Mary Shelley's *Frankenstein*, for example are *fiend, monster, lifeless, madness* and *solitude*, clearly reflecting the topic and themes of the novel.

In our analysis (Table 20), the individual word with the highest keyness factor at both the C and B2 levels was *texts*. At B2 the keyness factor for *texts* was 945.00: i.e. allowing for the relative size of the two corpora, it occurs 945 times more often in our database of B2 statements than in the Brown corpus.

Table 20 Top 20 keywords from the C and B2 levels (ranked by keyness factor)

Rank	Keyness factor	C1/C2 keywords:	Keyness factor	B2 keywords:
1	1503.00	texts	938.75	texts
2	429.50	finer	433.00	topics
3	411.50	contexts	291.00	appropriately
4	365.00	discourse	270.50	punctuation
5	304.00	edit	259.33	summarise
6	304.00	lexical	223.30	discourse
7	286.30	topics	221.78	topic
8	250.67	summarise	194.50	user
9	232.50	colloquial	193.08	expressing
10	214.75	grammatical	186.00	contexts
11	214.67	presentations	169.25	spelling
12	214.67	narratives	158.00	viewpoints
13	214.50	punctuation	155.60	clarification
14	200.40	appropriately	154.57	comprehension
15	197.00	integrating	152.25	grammar
16	197.00	genre	152.17	responding
17	179.00	slang	152.00	confirming
18	175.00	topic	152.00	orally
19	170.00	inferences	146.67	presentations
20	168.20	unfamiliar	145.00	speakers

In fact, it occurs 153 times in our B2 database (which contains 24,167 words in total) compared with four times in the Brown corpus of 1 million words. At C1/C2 the keyness factor for *texts* was even higher at 1582.75.

The lists of keywords offer some indication of criterial differences in functionality. There is, as one might expect, a good deal in common between the two lists. In addition to *texts, appropriately, discourse, contexts, summarise, topic/topics, presentations and punctuation* occur on both. Other words like *grammatical* and *lexical* that are among the 20 words with the highest keyness factors in the C level list also feature among the top 30 on the B2 list (grammatical has the 24th highest keyness value on the B2 list – 126.75 – and lexical the 29th – 118.50). Words such as *vocabulary*, *describe* and *formal* were also among those with keyness factors greater than 100 on both lists.

In contrast *finer* (with collocates such as *identify; differentiate; convey; express – subtleties; points of detail; points of attitude; shades of meaning*) does not occur at all in the B2 statements. *Colloquial* (with *idioms; highly – colloquial – expressions; speech; language*) does occur, but not as a key word – a learner at ALTE level 3 (B2) is said to be able to 'understand what is said in a personal letter, even where colloquial language is used'.

Genre (keyness of 50.05 at B2), *edit* (50.50), *inferences* (67.75), *unfamiliar* (84.60), and *integrating* (29.00) all have very much higher keyness values at C1 than at B2 as do *evaluate* (165.15 – 49.46), *unpredictable* (161.00 – 34.00), *confidently* (143.00 – 50.50), *formality* (143.00 – 50.50), *critically* (128.00 – 20.20) and *complex* (106.97 – 36.08).

The first of these, *genre*, has implications for the nature of the performance being described – the '*what*' in van Ek's (1986) terms. In the statements, *genre* is generally used to indicate types of texts fulfilling different social purposes. It either refers to the input that learners are able to process (reception activities) or to the nature of the texts that they are able to produce (production activities) in both speech and writing.

We can use the database of materials to explore how the word *genre* is used in statements describing both productive and receptive activities at the B2 and C levels. In production activities, *genre* is generally used in the context of satisfying expectations for an appropriate form in texts produced for specified purposes. At B2(+) on the CEFR *Creative Writing* scale, learners 'can write clear, detailed descriptions of real or imaginary events and experiences, marking the relationship between ideas in clear connected text, and following established conventions of the *genre* concerned'. At Level 4 of the HKCEE, 'an appropriate tone and style is used in familiar tasks, and the features of familiar *genres* of writing are used correctly'. This contrasts with Level 5 of the HKCEE: 'An awareness is shown of features of various *genres* of writing, including occasional stylistic features' and with C2 on the *Creative Writing* scale: 'Can write clear, smoothly flowing, and fully engrossing stories and descriptions of experience in a style appropriate to the *genre* adopted'. Appropriate style and awareness of audience are often mentioned in these C level statements alongside genre. The Kherson State University 4th year syllabus requires the learner to 'produce detailed, well-structured and developed descriptions in the style appropriate to the intended reader and *genre* adopted'; at CLB Benchmark 11, the learner 'conveys the persuasive message with adequate sense of audience, formality and *genre*; language, format and content of letter are appropriate and relevant to occasion, intent and social context/relationship.' At CLB Benchmark 12, when writing 'sales or marketing letters', the learner 'presents text as a coherent whole, with all the parts required by the *genre*'. At the C levels learners are expected to be able to adapt their production according to genre and to have a repertoire of styles to accomplish this, while B2 level learners appear to be restricted to the conventions of a more limited range of genres they might be required to produce.

The word *genre* is not used in relation to reception in statements at B2 level. At the C levels, a number of references are made to *literary genres*. At C2 for written reception, the Swiss *ELP* suggests that learners will 'understand contemporary and classical literary texts of different *genres* (poetry, prose, drama)'. The CERCLES portfolio model, designed for university students, goes further at C2: 'critically appraise classical as well as contemporary literary texts in different *genres*'. The Indiana ESOL standards *Advanced (Level 4)* require learners to 'explain the purpose of literary subgenres (e.g., satire, parody, allegory, pastoral) from poetry, plays, novels, short stories, or essays'. In reception as in production, the C levels seem to be marked by a greater awareness of the implications of linguistic choices on the nature of the communication.

Expanding on this keywords approach, words with a keyness factor of 10 or more were selected for further analysis (i.e. words that occurred 10 times more frequently in either the B2 or C level lists than in the Brown corpus). The results for the B2 level were compared with those for the C levels. First keywords were identified that appeared at the C levels but had no counterpart at the B2 level. Two further lists of keywords were then generated: those occurring only in the B2 level lists and keywords occurring both at the B2 and at the C levels.

In Table 20 both *topic* and *topics* are identified as keywords, but in the comparison between the levels it was preferable not to differentiate between similar words like these (or topical, topicality etc.). It was preferable therefore to carry out our comparisons at the level of word family (groups of words related by form and meaning) rather than individual words.

Having identified keywords, we generated concordance tables for each (see Table 21), including in these the tables for all words of the same word family – the concordance tables for the word *familiar* would include such variants as *unfamiliar, familiarise etc.* Concordance tables show the contexts in which each keyword appears, so highlighting relevant task conditions or qualitative differences in the expected performance of learners across levels.

Like genre, the word *texts* (which has the highest keyness factor at both the C and B2 levels) has implications for the nature of the performance required of learners. At both B2 and the C levels, *texts* often collocates with *read,*

Table 21 Extract from concordance table for the word texts at B2 level

I can write clear and detailed	**TEXTS**	compositions, reports or texts of presentations
Understand lengthy	**TEXTS**	containing complex instructions or explanations
s clearly legible and with typewritten and printed	**TEXTS**	containing some errors and less clear typography
senting ideas and information in a variety of oral	**TEXTS**	
in writing: emphasis on printed or word processed	**TEXTS**	
Explain why people may interpret the meaning of	**TEXTS**	differently
Read specialized	**TEXTS**	efficiently.
in writing emphasis in hand or type written	**TEXTS**	
can scan	**TEXTS**	for relevant information.
g which topic familiarity is very prominent. These	**TEXTS**	frequently involve description and narration in
tions and summaries taking notes and writing short	**TEXTS**	
Understand	**TEXTS**	in different styles and purposes with a large d
I can write summaries of scientific	**TEXTS**	in my field for use at a later date.
from different parts of a text, or from different	**TEXTS**	in order to fulfil a specific task.

write, understand, different, complex, information, ideas, language, meaning and *range*. However, there are common collocates that are much more closely associated with *texts* at the C levels than at B2 and that are therefore suggestive of important distinctions between the levels. Referring to productive use, these include *structured* (which also collocates with *clearly* and *well*), [*smoothly*] *flowing* and *area* (subject area; area of speciality; of study; of expertise – including references both to texts within a learner's expertise and to texts beyond his or her area of study or speciality). In relation to written reception, *evaluate* (critically) and *literary* more commonly occur at the C levels. Words that more commonly collocate with *texts* at B2 include *simple* (which occurs as part of the phrase *simple and complex* – *simple* on its own being associated with the lower levels) and *topics* (*range of; variety of; concrete and abstract; familiar and unfamiliar; complex*).

The range of text types envisaged for the C levels across schemes includes, among others, the following:

for learner reception:
serious newspapers; editorials; magazines; professional literature written for the well-educated reader; journals; textbooks; printed regulations; instructions; factual publications; general reports and technical material in professional fields; scientific texts; reports; websites; instruction manuals; complex instructional texts; complex forms; graphic displays; specialised articles; classical as well as contemporary literary works; experimental avant-garde prose; novels; short stories; poems; plays; publicity brochures; policy statements; general legal documents; correspondence; formal letters; radio news reports; TV, speeches, talks; lectures; debates; discussions; conversations etc.

for learner production and interaction:
articles; (academic) essays; (lab) reports; study projects; learning logs; short research papers; outlines; summaries; abstracts; charts; tables; graphs; comments on literary extracts; narratives; (complex) newspaper articles, reviews; biographies; CVs; job-related texts; position papers; private letters; social and business correspondence; (business/official) reports; faxes/memos/emails; press/news/media releases and public relations materials; notes/minutes/ records of complex meetings; technical material in professional fields; conversations; discussions; debates; presentations; speeches; lectures; conferences; negotiations; briefings etc.

These lists serve to elaborate the 'wide range of lengthy, complex texts' specified in the CEFR descriptors at C1 and illustrate a tendency towards academic and professional uses of language at the C levels, generally implying cognitively demanding subject matter. They do not, however, show a clear break with the B2 level (for which even more types of text are listed).

Of those listed above, only poems, journals, legal, classical, avant-garde and experimental texts are exclusively mentioned at the C levels.

In the following paragraphs, we explore in greater detail statements at each level that include the word *texts*. This illustrates how bringing statements together can help us to build up a fuller picture of activities involving text, of relevant restrictions or performance conditions and of the qualities of the texts that can be produced or accessed at each level.

Turning first to the scales for production activities, here *texts* most often refers to written (rather than spoken) output. At B2 the CEFR suggests that a learner 'can write clear, detailed texts on a variety of subjects related to his/her field of interest, synthesising and evaluating information and arguments from a number of sources'. The Swiss *ELP* supplements the CEFR statement by suggesting that such 'clear, detailed' production is to be expected in a range of text types: 'compositions, reports or texts of presentations'. The Bergen Can Do project suggests that B2 learners will write 'long, detailed texts that are clearly organised'.

At C1 on the Overall Written Production scale, learner texts are not only 'clear', but 'well-structured', concern 'complex subjects' and involve 'underlining the relevant salient issues, expanding and supporting points of view at some length with subsidiary points, reasons and relevant examples, and rounding off with an appropriate conclusion'. At C2 they are 'smoothly flowing' and have an 'effective style and a logical structure which helps the reader to find significant points.' The Swiss ELP at C1 refers to linguistic (grammatical and lexical) and sociolinguistic competences. Texts produced by learners 'show a high degree of grammatical correctness' and vary 'vocabulary and style according to the addressee, the kind of text and the topic'. The *Coherence and Cohesion* scale of the CEFR places the following statement at C2: 'Can create coherent and cohesive text making full and appropriate use of a variety of organisational patterns and a wide range of cohesive devices.' The *Mastery* level on the International ESOL tests also points to textual organisation: learners 'structure texts logically using linguistic markers to enable the reader to understand significant points'. The Canadian Language Benchmarks (CLB) suggest the types of text that learners should be able to produce at this level: at *Benchmark 10* learners 'can write formal texts needed for complex routine tasks in many demanding contexts of language use (business/work, academic, social)'. The CLB also refer to CEFR macrofunctions (or micro-activities): 'Can write complex original formal texts to inform, recommend, critique/evaluate ideas and information, present and debate complex arguments, or to persuade a mostly unfamiliar audience' (CLB *Benchmark 11*). Processes of textual monitoring and revision, aspects of strategic competence in the CEFR, are another feature in the CLB: at *Benchmark 12*, a learner is able to 'revise and edit all aspects of texts, using own resources. Evaluate, revise and edit information texts for public use'.

In reception, learners at B2 can read to extract a sufficiently full and detailed understanding of a text to produce a summary. In a statement from the *Processing Text* scale, they 'can summarize a wide range of factual and imaginative texts, commenting on and discussing contrasting points of view and the main themes'. At Canadian *Benchmark 9*, the learner can 'write summaries or summary reports of longer texts' and we are told that an adequate summary at this level 'conveys essential information to the reader (e.g., conclusions, decisions, actions to be taken and policy statements in minutes); reduces the information to main points with accurate supporting details, with no major factual omissions or errors; presents information with only minor errors in grammar, vocabulary, spelling and punctuation; document layout/ format.'

Texts accessible to B2 learners 'contain a broad range of grammatical structures' (International ESOL *Communicator*) and include 'longer more specialised sources' (International ESOL *Communicator*). They may include 'simple short stories, news items, bibliographical information, social notices, personal correspondence, routinized business letters and simple technical material written for the general reader' (ACTFL *Advanced*). Such texts 'have a reasonably clear structure, both conceptually and formally; the information contained in them is offered explicitly, or requires only a moderate amount of interpretation and inferencing; their understanding does not require close familiarity with a particular foreign culture; they are produced in an accessible form' (Van Ek and Trim 2001:11).

B2 learners are able to read strategically using expeditious or careful approaches as appropriate. The CEFR *Overall Reading Comprehension* scale states that learners 'can read with a large degree of independence, adapting style and speed of reading to different texts and purposes, and using appropriate reference sources'. They are also able to 'scan quickly through long and complex texts on a variety of topics to locate specific information or decide if closer study is worthwhile' (*Reading for Orientation*). They read to 'obtain necessary information, to make an outline, and to summarize the main points' (Japan MEXT *Upper Secondary*); to bring together information from different parts of a text; or to combine information across texts to complete tasks: 'Obtain information for key work/business tasks by locating and integrating several pieces of information in complex prose texts and formatted texts' (CLB *Benchmark 9*). They 'understand the relative importance of ideas' (TOEFL Can Do). Related to sociolinguistic and pragmatic competences, they are sensitive to reader stance – 'Can identify writer's bias and the purpose/function of text' (CLB *Benchmark 9*) – and to register – 'understand the features of register in texts including those conveying emotion or dispute' (International ESOL *Communicator*). Example reading tasks for CLB at this level include 'Read and summarize a 3–5 page article from a trade or professional journal in your field' or 'Read and explain instructions on how to stop smoking, how to deal with stress, how to look after children's dental care routine' (Pawlikowska-Smith 2002).

At the C levels, the CEFR *Global scale* affirms that learners can 'understand a wide range of demanding, longer texts, and recognise implicit meaning'. The International ESOL *Expert* level uses the same statement, but specifies that the texts may be 'both written and spoken'. On the *Overall Reading Comprehension* scale at C1, learners 'Can understand in detail lengthy, complex texts, whether or not they relate to his/her own area of speciality', but this is on condition that 'he/she can reread difficult sections'. Learners 'trace, summarize and evaluate the development of arguments in complex expository or argumentative texts (e.g., in a rational inquiry paper or in a problem-solution paper)' (CLB *Benchmark 10*). At C2, 'long and complex texts' continue to feature, but the C2 descriptor refers to 'a wide range of' these, with no mention of opportunities for rereading. The nature of this 'wide range' is suggested by the International ESOL *Mastery* level: 'Understand with ease virtually all types of authentic written texts of different purposes and style and those dense in complex structures.' The ACTFL *Guidelines* offer more specific textual features indicative of the Superior level: 'Superior-level texts feature hypotheses, argumentation and supported opinions and include grammatical patterns and vocabulary ordinarily encountered in academic/professional reading.' The CERCLES model at C2 has 'complex, technical or highly specialized texts to meet . . . academic or professional purposes', while the ELC portfolio model (C2), also aimed at higher education, points to topic familiarity: 'lengthy and complex scientific texts, whether or not they relate to [the learner's] own field'.

Sensitivity to implicit meanings, or 'hidden value judgements' (Swiss ELP *C2*), are frequently mentioned in C level statements. At C2 (CEFR *Overall Reading Comprehension*), the learner is able to appreciate 'subtle distinctions of style and implicit as well as explicit meaning'. At International ESOL *Expert* level, test takers 'recognise implicit meaning' while the ILR *4 Advanced Professional* is 'able to "read beyond the lines" (that is, to understand the full ramifications of texts as they are situated in the wider cultural, political, or social environment)' and at *4+* (*Advanced Professional, Plus*) learners have a 'strong sensitivity to sociolinguistic and cultural references' when listening. At STANAG *Level 4 (Full Professional)*, learners 'understand almost all cultural references and can relate a specific text to other written materials within the culture'. In the WIDA Consortium Standards at *Level 5: Bridging*, learners are able to 'apply author's perspective in literary text to other contexts'. At CLB *Benchmark 10*, the learner 'sometimes encounters difficulty interpreting low-frequency idioms and cultural references', but such problems are not encountered at *Benchmark 12* and at ALTE *Level 5*, learners can 'get the point of jokes or allusions with cultural content'. At the B2 level, learners may 'understand cultural references in scientifically oriented discourse' (Lebanon

Second Secondary), but these may also be a cause of difficulty: 'May not fully understand some cultural references, proverbs, and allusions, as well as implications of nuances and idioms' (STANAG *Level 3 (Minimum Professional)*); 'Often has difficulty with interpreting verbal humour, low-frequency idioms and cultural references' (CLB, *Benchmark 9*).

HKCEE *Level 5* addresses another potential source of difficulty that might differentiate C level learners: rate of speech in spoken reception. At *Level 5*, a 'range of both familiar and unfamiliar spoken text types are understood when delivered at a near-natural speed', while the *Level 4* learner understands texts delivered at 'moderate speed'. However, elsewhere (in the Irish ELP or International ESOL at *Communicator Level*) the B2 learner is able to understand at 'normal speed'. This is clearly defined in *Vantage*: 'Speech can be understood at normal conversational speed (c 150 words per minute) with the normal degree of phonetic reduction and using the regional or national accents in current use by educated speakers of Standard English of a particular regional or national accents in current use by educated speakers of Standard English of a particular regional or national provenance (but free from dialectal features of grammar and lexicon)'. *Vantage* Level learners are able to 'deal with' 'clearly legible' handwriting and with print that is 'less clear': 'faded smudged or using a wide variety of fonts'. At ILR *4+ (Advanced Professional Proficiency, Plus)*, learners have 'little difficulty in reading less than fully legible handwriting'.

The differences in the statements suggest that texts produced by C level learners are more coherent, more cohesive and more adequate to fulfil professional or academic requirements. In reception activities there is a level of engagement with input texts at the C levels that is less apparent at B2 and an ability to follow more complex texts; particularly those that include more cultural allusions and colloquial, idiomatic or specialised language. At B2 and at the C levels, learners *read, understand* (main ideas and relevant details), *scan, locate and understand details, extract details, get the gist, follow, summarise, combine* and *reorganise*, but a C level performance appears to involve a more evaluative, critical reading.

The treatment of *texts* in the International ESOL examinations exemplifies the way in which many scales approach functional progression. At (B2) *Communicator* level, test takers 'understand the way meaning is built up in a range of texts'; at (C1) *Expert* level they 'understand the different ways in which meaning is built up in a range of texts of varying complexity' and at (C2) *Mastery* level, they 'understand the different ways in which meaning is built up in abstract, structurally or linguistically complex texts'. This suggests a set of features with implications for criteriality – abstractness, generic diversity, organisational complexity; linguistic complexity – but offers no elaboration or exemplification that helps the user to distinguish, if such is intended, between 'texts', 'texts of varying complexity' and 'complex texts'.

In attempting to summarise scales like these, we may face similar restrictions more generally. We can identify features of interest and can see, for example that C level learners are able to evaluate as well as understand and summarise a wider range of less familiar and more demanding texts, but have only limited evidence for where the lines are being drawn between (among other features) general and specialist topics, explicit and implicit information, straightforward and subtle messages, concrete and abstract ideas, simple and complex language, major and minor errors, sympathetic and hostile audiences, or indeed between a wide and narrow range of text types. Within institutions, understanding of such distinctions can be built up through exemplification, discussion and moderation: as generally happens when teachers begin work in new settings or when examiners are inducted into the use of a rating scale. The challenge for English Profile is to find a means of extending such a process, and the shared understanding that can result, across institutions and across borders.

Activities in Can Do statements

Words like *text* and *genre* point to the products that learners are expected to bring into being or to process in order to achieve communication. Generating concordance tables for *texts* elicits information on the qualities of the texts that learners at each level are expected to produce or contend with – e.g. *lengthy, complex, literary, well-structured, precise* – performance conditions and the activities involved – e.g. *scan, understand, present, compose*. Another perspective is provided by exploring the database through words that describe activities more directly – e.g. *read, listen, write, speak* and their synonyms. Again, these should also elicit data on performance (*what* is said/written/listened to/read) relevant indicators of quality and performance conditions.

In the following section, we consider the word *write*. This occurs as a keyword at both the B2 and C levels with keyness values of 43.72 and 49.63 respectively. In this section, our concern will be with written production and interaction and so we exclude its use in references to written reception. In relation to performance, criteria and condition, the aim is to discover what learners at each level can write, how well they are expected to write and under what conditions.

We have already seen, in the section above, the range of written text types that writers are expected to be able to produce at the C levels and that this does not clearly distinguish the *proficient* user from the *independent*: the C levels from B2. What then are the qualities that writing is expected to have at the B2 level, and how does this compare with C level writing? In the following paragraphs, through the appearance of *write* in the database, the qualities of learner writing are considered from the viewpoint of linguistic, sociolinguistic and pragmatic competences as conceived in the CEFR and in relation to contextual variables that might impact on performance.

In terms of linguistic competences, we learn that at B2 learners are expected to be able to use 'a range of complex structures' (Sabanci University Syllabus *Upper Intermediate*) or a 'mix of simple and complex sentence forms' (IELTS *Band 6*) with 'increasing accuracy' (TOEIC *Advanced Working Proficiency –785–900*) in texts 'at least several paragraphs in length' (ACTFL *Advanced*). Learners are able to use 'correct punctuation in formal and informal writing to enhance meaning' (International ESOL *Communicator*) and can 'use correct grammar vocabulary, spelling and punctuation' (TOEFL Can Do), or at least 'mostly correct grammar'. The 'few mistakes in spelling and punctuation' (HKCEE *Level 4*) 'do not impede communication' (IELTS *Band 6*).

There are restrictions on accuracy, however. In Cambridge FCE or at ALTE Level 3, test takers have 'a limited range of expression (vocabulary, grammatical structures)'. At ACTFL *Advanced High* learners are 'strong in either grammar or vocabulary, but not in both'. At International ESOL *Communicator* level, test takers 'control grammar to communicate effectively, although errors may occur when complex structures are attempted' and at ILR *3 (General Professional Proficiency)* there are 'somewhat more frequent errors in low frequency complex structures'. Time pressures may also cause learners to be inaccurate and they may rely on 'more common words and structures' (Bergen Can Do B2) to convey meaning. Because of these limitations, texts at this level 'may resemble literal translations from the native language' (ACTFL *Advanced*).

At the C levels, output is more consistently accurate and uses a 'range of complex structures' (International ESOL *Expert*). There are few grammatical errors, 'even when complex structures are employed' (International ESOL *Expert*). Learners 'use clauses, phrases, mechanics of writing, and parallel structure to consistently vary grammatical forms' (Indiana ESOL standards *Fluent English Proficient Level 5*). Language is either 'without non-native errors' (ILR *5 Functionally Native Proficiency*) or 'such errors as occur will not prevent understanding of the message' (Cambridge CAE): they do not 'cause miscommunication' (ACTFL *Superior*), although even with a 'broad lexical repertoire' some 'circumlocution' (Swiss ELP C1) may be needed. The learner produces only 'rare errors in spelling and/or word formation', 'skilfully uses uncommon lexical items', and 'uses idiomatic expressions appropriately and naturally' (International ESOL *Expert*), but even at C1 level there may still be 'occasional inaccuracies in word choice and collocation' (IELTS Band 8): 'errors in phrases, collocations and idiom use still occur' (CLB *Benchmark 10*).

In relation to sociolinguistic competences, learners at B2 are able to 'adjust style for intended audience' (Indiana ESOL standards *Intermediate*

Level 3) which may be 'academic' or 'impersonal' (Sabanci University Syllabus *Upper Intermediate*) with 'formal or informal register' (Inside Out *Upper Intermediate*), making 'appropriate use of register and conventions' (CERCLES B2). The repertoire may be limited to 'a few prose styles pertinent to professional/educational needs' (ILR *3+ General Professional Proficiency, Plus*), and these styles may be identifiably 'non-native' (STANAG 6001 *Level 3 Minimum Professional*). Even so style is 'appropriate to the occasion' (STANAG 6001 *Level 3 Minimum Professional*) and 'audience context and purpose' are considered (PNG Curriculum *Level 4*). The learner has the ability to 'adjust register in familiar contexts to suit purpose and readership' (International ESOL *Communicator*). However, there are restrictions on this ability to 'tailor language to suit audience' (ILR *3+ General Professional Proficiency, Plus*): 'Weaknesses may be in poor control of low frequency complex structures, vocabulary or the ability to express subtleties and nuances.'

The C level learner draws on 'a very wide range of stylistic devices' (ILR *5 Functionally Native Proficiency*) to compose texts in 'a variety of prose styles' (STANAG 6001 *Level 4 Full Professional*) with a 'length, format and style appropriate to purpose, content and audience' (International ESOL *Expert*) or even 'fully appropriate to purpose and target readership' (*Mastery*) as well as to 'genre' (Swiss ELP C2). The register is more or less formal, 'depending on the purpose and the reader' (TOEFL Can Do). The resulting text may be 'tactful' (International ESOL *Expert*) or 'persuasive' (CLB *Benchmark 11*). The ability to shape texts to audience is thought to develop through the higher levels; even at ACTFL *Superior* level, the learner 'still may not tailor writing precisely to a variety of purposes and/or readers'

Considering pragmatic competences, at B2, learner writing achieves 'significant precision' (ACTFL *Advanced High*) so that it is 'easily readable' (Swiss ELP B2) or 'understandable to natives not used to the writing of non-natives' (ACTFL *Advanced*). It is 'clear' (UK Adult ESOL Core Curriculum *Level 1*), coherent and cohesive (Singapore syllabus *Secondary Four/Five*), and 'connected' (International ESOL *Communicator*): a 'sense of organisation (rhetorical structure) is emerging' (ACTFL *Advanced*). Cohesive devices are used 'effectively' (IELTS Band 6) and include 'pronouns' (ACTFL Advanced), but 'cohesion between sentences may be faulty or mechanical' (IELTS Band 6). A 'lack of variety in organizational patterns or in variety of cohesive devices' may cause organisation to suffer (ILR *3+ General Professional Proficiency, Plus*). There is an impression of 'reasonable ease' (ILR *3 General Professional Proficiency*) or even of 'considerable ease' (STANAG 6001 *Level 3 Minimum Professional*) where the writing concerns the learner's familiar 'special fields of competence', and 'concrete aspects' of these topics (ACTFL *Advanced High*).

At the C levels, the writing is again 'clear', but also 'explicit', 'user-friendly'

(Swiss ELP C1) and 'informative' (ILR *5 Functionally Native Proficiency*) so that it is 'adequate to express all his/her experiences' (ILR *4 Advanced Professional Proficiency*), 'clearly communicating ideas, impressions, feelings and opinions' and 'emphasising important points' (International ESOL *Expert*). The learner is able to 'use appropriate indicators in discourse (e.g. introducing an idea, developing an idea showing transition to another idea, concluding an idea, emphasising a point, indicating the main or important information, explaining or clarifying a point)' (Kherson University 4th Year syllabus). At the ACTFL *Superior* level 'underlying organization, such as chronological ordering, logical ordering, cause and effect, comparison, and thematic development is strongly evident, although not thoroughly executed and/or not totally reflecting target language patterns.' Among the cohesive devices available to writers are 'ellipses, parallelisms and subordinates' (ILR *4 Advanced Professional Proficiency*). Writing appears 'fluent', 'smoothly flowing' and the 'message can be followed throughout' (ALTE Level 4).

At B2, learners may write on 'familiar topics from everyday life' and 'topics relevant to some social, professional, and educational situations' (*Eiken* Can Do *Pre-Grade 1*); 'a wide range of subjects from a variety of personal, social, educational and working contexts' (London Tests of English *Level 3*); 'complex topics (which may include economics, culture, science, and technology) as well as his/her professional field' (STANAG 6001 *Level 3 Minimum Professional*); 'the concrete aspects of topics relating to particular interests and special fields of competence' (ACTFL *Advanced High*); 'about a lot of different themes . . . even if themes are not very familiar' (Bergen Can Do B2) and they may write to carry out 'complex routine tasks in some demanding contexts of language use (business/work, academic or social)' (CLB *Benchmark 9*).

Purposes for writing at B2 include, for example, 'to fulfil a range of functions for practical purposes' and 'describing real or imaginary people or events' (International ESOL *Communicator*); 'evaluating, expressing opinions, hypothesizing, justifying, persuading, prioritising, summarising, comparing and contrasting, advising, apologising, correcting, describing, explaining, recommending and suggesting' (Cambridge ILEC); 'arguing your case for and against'; 'applying for a job' (Headway *Upper Intermediate*); 'conveying degrees of emotion and highlighting the personal significance of events' (ELC B2); reviewing books, films or TV series (face2face *Upper Intermediate*); making notes or records of lectures, meetings or telephone calls; 'argumentation, analysis, hypothesis, and extensive explanation, narration, and description' (STANAG 6001 *Level 3 Minimum Professional*); 'to find satisfactory accommodation' (ALTE *Level 3*); 'to express thanks, state acceptance and acknowledgement in a business/academic environment'; 'to request and to respond to requests for information, directions, service/product, clarification, permission'; 'to present information and state a position on a previously researched topic' (CLB *Benchmark 9*); and to 'describe and narrate personal experiences' (ACTFL *Advanced High*).

B2 writing is addressed to friends, clients and 'mostly familiar and some-times unfamiliar readers' (CLB *Benchmark 9*). Examples of tasks at CLB *Benchmark 9* include, among others, the following: 'Write a letter to immi-gration officials to inquire how to sponsor someone. Write lab reports in a required format. Write summaries of readings, book and article reports. Synthesize a half hour meeting into 2 pages of notes or minutes' (Pawlikowska-Smith 2002:26). The GEPT Upper Intermediate specifications recommend the (B2) *Upper Intermediate* level for those using English in roles such as, 'business professionals; secretaries; engineers; research assistants; airline flight attendants; airline pilots; air traffic controllers; customs officials; tour guides; foreign affairs police; news media personnel; information man-agement personnel'.

At the C levels, writing is successful even when tasks are comparatively unfamiliar and cognitively demanding: 'Can prepare highly effective written communication in a variety of prose styles, even in unfamiliar general or professional-specialist areas' (STANAG 6001 *Level 4 Full Professional*). Topics may include 'social issues of a general nature' (ILR *4 Advanced Professional Proficiency*) 'complex or abstract subjects' (International ESOL *Mastery*) or even 'any subject' (ALTE *Level 4*) and be 'in areas of special interest or in special fields' (ACTFL *Superior*). Learners carry out 'complex non-routine tasks in demanding contexts of language use (business/work, academic)' (CLB *Benchmark 11*).

Purposes for writing include 'to persuade others and to elaborate on abstract concepts'; 'all professional purposes including the representa-tion of an official policy or point of view' (STANAG 6001 *Level 4 Full Professional*); 'to fulfil a wide range of functions including those requiring a tactful approach' (International ESOL *Expert*); 'emotional, allusive and joking usage' (CERCLES, C1); to 'speculate and hypothesize about causal and logical relationships between facts, phenomena, events' (CLB *Benchmark 11*). At the highest levels, 'texts are often for public consumption and for various purposes: reporting, projecting, evaluating, promoting, expounding an argument, or appealing to an unfamiliar audience' (CLB *Benchmark 12*).

Writing often serves to summarise other texts: 'summaries of magazine and newspaper articles concerning contemporary social issues (e.g. editorials and feature articles)'; 'notes to record the main points raised during lectures and meetings' (Eiken Can Do *Grade 1*); 'summaries of general/professional topics' (GEPT *Advanced*); 'summarize information from various sources (e.g., radio, TV or newspapers) in paragraph form' (WIDA *Level 4Expanding*); 'summaries of and comments on literary extracts' (Kherson State University *4th year Syllabus*); 'summarize a text so that it is appropriate to a given com-municative situation or to a predefined framework' (KPG). Notes taken from lectures will be 'of reasonable use for essay or revision purposes' (ALTE *Level 4*). Although there are many references in the scales to a 'target readership', 'intended audience' or similar, the nature of these audiences is rarely made explicit. CLB *Benchmark 10* suggests 'familiar and unfamiliar audiences' and *Benchmark 12* has texts for 'public consumption'. At C2, according to the ELC portfolio, learners may write 'with a view to being published', but texts written by learners at TOEIC *General Professional Proficiency (905–990)* and intended for publication will 'still require review'.

Examples of writing tasks at CLB *Benchmark 11* include, among others, 'Write critiques of scientific journal articles. Write thesis/research proposals. Develop a marketing/informational brochure. Write an extensive, formal, analytical incident/accident report' (Pawlikowska-Smith 2002:26). The GEPT specification recommends the *Advanced* level for, 'high-level business professionals; negotiators in business and government; English language teachers; researchers; translators; foreign affairs officials; international news personnel.'

Function words in the Can Do statements

In addition to approaching the database from the perspective of inputs/ outputs (*texts*) and activities (*write*), a third perspective is provided by function words, which cut across activities and may relate to processes as well as products. One word that describes a function and that occurs as a keyword, and so might exemplify this approach to the data, is *argue*. 'Argument' is one of Wilkins' (1976) macrofunctions, and 'arguments' occurs as a keyword both at B2 (with a keyness value of 76.67) and at the C levels (97.8).

At the B2 level in the (spoken production) *Sustained Monologue* scale of the CEFR, learners are said to be able to 'construct a chain of reasoned argument' or to 'develop an argument systematically with appropriate highlighting of significant points, and relevant supporting detail.' In the (written production) *Reports and Essays* scale they 'can synthesise information and arguments from a number of sources'. They can *present* an argument, *developing* or *elaborating* it with 'reasons for and against' or with 'details and examples' (Sabanci University Syllabus *Upper Intermediate*), 'weighing pros and cons' (CERCLES B2). Learners can 'argue for [a] point of view in detail' (Bergen Can Do B2); produce 'essay-length argumentation' (STANAG 6001 *Level 3 Minimum Professional*) by 'linking ideas logically and expanding and supporting . . . points with appropriate examples' (Ireland ELP B2), or 'emphasising decisive points and including supporting details' (Swiss ELP B2): 'Express his/her overall opinion on an issue or problem and support it with logical and concisely expressed arguments' (KPG). However, argument is a feature that distinguishes B2 from B1 and ability may still be limited: learners 'present arguments to a limited extent' (Cambridge ILEC), may depend on a *familiar topic* and have a 'limited range of expression (vocabulary, grammatical structures)'(Cambridge FCE).

In interaction, in the CEFR scale for *Informal Discussion (with Friends)*, B2 learners 'present and respond to complex lines of argument'. 'I can account for and sustain my opinion in discussion by providing relevant explanations, arguments and comments' (CERCLES B2). The Swedish ELP model is more concrete: 'I can cope with a job interview, i.e. introduce myself, present my qualifications and experience and argue convincingly about my suitability' (Sweden ELP B2). At ALTE *Level 3*, learners 'can argue/ complain effectively about most problem areas that are likely to occur'. *Argue* in these statements, as in those for spoken production, would seem to be used more in the sense of giving reasons or citing evidence in support of a proposition, but there are also references to argument in the sense of exchanging diverging views: 'I can argue against someone and defend my position' (Straightforward *Upper Intermediate*), or, alternatively, at International ESOL *Communicator* level, 'concede a point or argument, demur'.

In reception at B2 on the *Overall Listening Comprehension* scale, learners 'follow extended speech and complex lines of argument provided the topic is reasonably familiar, and the direction of the talk is sign-posted by explicit markers'. There is a scale for *Reading for Information and Argument* in the CEFR. At B2 on this scale learners 'can understand articles and reports concerned with contemporary problems in which the writers adopt particular stances or viewpoints': the Irish ELP suggests as examples 'arts reviews, political commentary'. Topic familiarity and overt organisation are features of a number of statements: 'follow clearly structured extended speech and more complex argument when familiar with the topic' (International ESOL *Communicator*); 'follow the argument of a clearly organized talk if the topic is familiar' (Sabanci University Syllabus *Upper Intermediate*); 'the development of an argument may be followed if straightforward' (HKCEE Level 4 Reading). The Singapore School Syllabus (*Secondary Four/Five*) suggests that discourse competence will be required: 'use knowledge of cohesive devices and text organisation e.g. knowing the structure of an argument leads a reader to expect a stand taken, evidence to support the stand and a re-statement of the stand'. The International ESOL *Communicator* level stresses linguistic competence: 'understand ideas, arguments and descriptions expressed through complex sentence forms'.

Consistent with the CEFR references to 'synthesising and evaluating information and arguments from a number of sources', a number of statements at this level suggest integration of receptive and productive skills in summarising and responding to a case: 'I can summarize information and arguments from various written sources and reproduce them orally' (ELC B2); 'Respond critically to an argument' (Lebanon Second Secondary); 'recognize well-structured, simple ideas and arguments and produce persuasive writing with detailed sentences and paragraphs' (Indiana ESOL standards Intermediate Level 3).

At C1, on the *Reports and Essays* scale of the CEFR, the learner 'can produce clear, smoothly flowing, complex reports, articles or essays which present a case, or give critical appreciation of proposals or literary works'. Arguments should be *coherent, well* or *consistently supported* and *developed*. They may be more intricate than at B2: 'integrating sub-themes, developing particular points and rounding off with an appropriate conclusion' (CERCLES C1). A learner is able to 'argue his/her case effectively, justifying, if necessary, a need for service' (ALTE Level 4). The constraints on expression and topic at B2 are relaxed and the learner is expected to be able to use a 'wide range of complex grammatical structures' (International ESOL *Expert*), shaping their production to generate *effective* arguments that *highlight important points*: to 'present and support arguments well' (ALTE *Level 5 Writing*) so that they may 'persuade a mostly unfamiliar audience' (CLB *Benchmark 11*). In short, 'good control of a full range of structures, spelling or non-alphabetic symbol production, and a wide general vocabulary allow the writer to hypothesize and present arguments or points of view accurately and effectively' (ACTFL *Superior*).

In the CEFR *Self-Assessment Grid* (*Spoken Production*) at C2, arguments are not only 'clear' and 'smoothly flowing', but also in a 'style appropriate to the context'. At International ESOL *Mastery* level, they are 'cogent and smoothly flowing' and in the London Tests at *Level 4*, they are 'complex, detailed, developed and qualified' and may take the form (in writing) of 'complex formal letters and formal reports, leaflets and brochures, discursive essays, articles, reviews'. At Level 5, test takers' written work will 'reflect original thought and creative ideas and include information, qualified opinions, arguments and conclusions on a variety of topics related to daily, academic and professional life' and (in addition to 'discursive essays') can take the form of 'complex newspaper articles and reviews; biographies, CVs and notes for a speech'.

In both production and interaction, account is taken of contrasting points of view: both 'justifying an argument' and 'challenging arguments and opinions' (Trinity GESE *Advanced stage: Grade 11*). In interaction at C1, the learner can 'answer complex lines of counter argument fluently, spontaneously and appropriately'. (CEFR *Formal Discussion and Meetings* scale); should be 'prepared to defend a point of view and develop an argument further'; or 'evaluate and challenge statements and arguments made by the examiner' (Trinity GESE *Advanced stage: Grade 11*); 'present arguments and counter-arguments about one's own opinion or that of someone else' (KPG C1) and to 'make and respond to hypothetical arguments' (London Tests *Level 4*). At ALTE *Level 5* for *Listening/Speaking*, learners 'can rebut counter-arguments', and at Straightforward *Advanced*, groups are able to 'argue for and against an opinion in order to come to a [collective] decision'. However, even at ACTFL *Advanced High*, learners may attempt to avoid argument tasks 'by resorting to simplification through the use of description or narration in place of argument or hypothesis'. By C2, in the *Formal Discussion and Meetings* scale, the learner is able to 'put an articulate and persuasive argument' and is 'at no disadvantage to native speakers'. At this level, as a mark of communicative success, learners should be able to 'get a concession from the other party through logical argumentation' (CLB *Benchmark 11*).

Receptively, learners at the C levels have the ability to follow *subtle, complex* and *inexplicit* arguments including those found in 'a serious newspaper' (Cambridge CAE) or 'discussion programme' (ALTE *Level 4*). In the Swiss ELP at C1, learners are able to read 'complex reports, analyses and commentaries where opinions, viewpoints and connections are discussed'. At B2 the topic may need to be *familiar*, but this is not the case at the C levels. Learners can 'understand and summarize a speaker's main argument' (Straightforward *Advanced: Listening*) and 'recognise specific details, arguments and implications of complex topics in the spoken discourse' (London Tests of English *Level 4*). However, even at C1, there are references to restrictions: at ALTE Level 4, learners 'follow discussion and argument with only occasional need for clarification' – although they are able to draw on 'good compensation strategies to overcome inadequacies' (Cambridge CAE).

Learners are able both to summarize and to evaluate arguments: 'trace, summarize and evaluate the development of arguments in complex expository or argumentative texts (e.g., in a rational inquiry paper or in a problem-solution paper)'; 'analyze the arguments presented in literary works to determine credibility and authority of characters' (Indiana ESOL standards *Fluent English Proficient*); 'summarize and evaluate the main differences in the argumentation [of two articles/essays on the same topic]'; 'distinguish a proposition from its argument'; 'identify logical relations and organization in text' and identify 'fallacies in arguments' (CLB *Benchmark 10*); 'the development of a point of view or argument is followed, and the reasons are fully understood' (HKCEE *Level 5 Reading*).

At C2, distinguishing features include the abstract nature of the arguments and the ease with which they are grasped. Here learners 'follow abstract argumentation, for example the balancing of alternatives and the drawing of a conclusion' (ALTE *Level 5 Listening/Speaking*); 'understand abstract concepts and argumentation' (ALTE Level 5 Reading); 'identify and reconstruct with ease the main points, secondary ideas, critical details and implications, and arguments' (London Tests of English Level 5). At this level, arguments can be followed even when not explicitly signalled or structured: 'understand the main points, arguments, inferences, changes in register and emphasis in extended, complex and sometimes unstructured speech' (Trinity GESE

Advanced stage: Grade 10, 11 & 12); 'follow a complex argument even when it is not clearly structured'; 'understand ideas, arguments and descriptions regardless of their structure and considerable complexity' (International ESOL *Mastery*).

Conclusions

The lack of consistency in the terminology used in the CEFR is compounded in a study of this nature that brings together materials from very diverse sources. The collected materials provide less clarity concerning performance conditions and criteria than might be hoped. However, the analysis has suggested that it is possible to abstract a broad, and reasonably coherent, set of claims about the distinctive features of C level performance that could be refined, enhanced and summarised in a new set of Can Do statements. The claim of these new statements to represent the C1 and C2 levels and their relative status can be tested against the perceptions of educators and the analyses of learner language as the English Profile develops.

Overall, differences in the conditions for language use envisaged in the statements we collected are much more often focused on the social than the physical. In spoken reception, rapid speech, accent and dialect may be sources of difficulty even at the C1 level (although distorted sound does not prevent comprehension of announcements or phone calls); but it is notable that time pressures are given little attention (appearing only in examination related statements). Interlocutors may be hostile or confrontational rather than sympathetic; the learner is expected to recognise and take account of status and social distance and to be able to adapt to an unfamiliar audience. In written production and reception, learners are more sensitive to the conventions of a variety of genres. Topics are also important: C level learners are apparently able to move beyond their own fields of interest in a way that B2 learners may not.

When considering quality indicators, sociolinguistic and pragmatic competences would seem to be more criterial in identifying 'proficient' (i.e. C1/C2 level) users than linguistic competences. Grammar is generally accurate, pronunciation clear and vocabulary wide ranging, although phrasing may be a basis for distinguishing more able speakers. Greater fluency is accompanied by an increased ability to structure written production and extended monologues. Precision, subtlety, connotation and nuance become available to the C level learner together with a greater appreciation for and control of colloquialisms and idioms. At C2, learners are aware of the rhetorical functions of metaphor, ambiguity and symbolism.

Domain, and learners' (sociolinguistic and pragmatic) ability to manage the implications of the personal, professional, educational and public contexts, appears to be central to the C level and will have implications for how linguistic exponents of the specified functional and notional categories can be presented. There is a need to exemplify the kinds of sophistication and subtlety with which C level learners are said to be able to select appropriate forms from a repertoire of options.

One criticism of the CEFR has been that there is not enough in the illustrative scales that relates to young learners (at lower secondary or below) or migrant learners of languages. The schemes we have collected to date do include some intended for migrant learners of English (the UK Adult ESOL core curriculum and CLB 2000), and so might help to address the second of these gaps, but we did not find material that addressed learners younger than 16. As is apparent from our analysis, complex language of the kind associated with the C levels is most often used to address complex subjects and questions have been raised about whether it is as much linguistic as cognitive complexity that is required to carry out activities at the higher levels; cognitive complexity that younger learners cannot be expected to have acquired.

In relation to this issue, the distinction made in the CEFR between interaction and production in spoken and written language appears particularly important to the C levels. In productive language use – which North (2007a) reminds us is associated with cognitive academic language proficiency (CALP) (Cummins 1979) and formal, planned uses of language – accuracy, complexity and precision are of more central importance; in interactive language or basic interpersonal communication skills (BICS) it is idiomaticity, fluency and sensitivity to social context that come to the fore.

Can Do statements at the C levels of the CEFR have proved the most difficult to scale (North 2000) and this raises the possibility that the Can Do approach is better suited to the clear-cut activities described at the lower levels. It is certainly more straightforward to make the constrained judgement about whether a learner is able to 'introduce him/herself and others and . . . ask and answer questions about personal details' than to decide whether he/she 'can use language flexibly and effectively for social, academic and professional purposes' with all that this assumes about the range of contexts within which the learner uses and encounters language, and the level of judgement required in interpreting 'use language', 'flexibly' and 'effectively'.

It is an often-voiced criticism of outcomes-based assessment schemes that as activities become more complex and distinctions between success and failure more nuanced, the value of the Can Do approach may begin to break down. Of course, this is an empirical issue and the scalability of the Can Do statements that emerge from the process can be established through trialling. However, there is a risk when calibrating descriptors that the highest levels of the scale will be overstated. Statements that learners can use language with consummate skill for any purpose under any conditions will inevitably rise to the top of the scale, but may not represent a realistic objective for even the most gifted.

As discussed above, functional categories in themselves do not offer sufficient detail to define the C levels. It would however also be helpful to carry out a more detailed investigation of some of the material included in this study not only at the level of the metadocuments used here, but also analysing the content of the textbooks and test materials to which they relate. This would help us to cast more light on how the functions described are operationalised by course and test providers.

On this basis, it should be possible to draft a set of functional categories that define the salient features of the C levels with respect to communicative functions. As the CEFR makes clear, devising descriptors, whether on the basis of judgement or empirical data, is not the end of the development process. The descriptions must subsequently be:

- tested and calibrated against the perceptions of language educators in contexts where the English Profile may be used
- revised on the basis of feedback and matched to finer-grained descriptions of level (C1, C2)
- integrated with notions, situational contexts and themes
- tested against and contextualised by grammatical exponents using evidence gathered from naturalistic settings, the classroom and the examination hall in parallel with English Profile research.

This chapter has outlined the process of identifying criterial differences as expressed in currently operational schemes used in English language education around the world. The picture that this provides of the ways in which higher levels of English language learning are conceived enables us to begin the fully empirical stage of specifying criterial C level functional uses of language for English Profile, informed through our research by the perspectives of the educators who have prepared, refined and used these schemes.

4 Progression in learner input

In Chapter 2 it was suggested that the descriptions of the C1 and C2 levels for English Profile would benefit from a re-evaluation and expansion of the design of CEFR Can Do statements and from elaboration of the terms being used therein. Chapter 3 reported on work directed primarily towards the first of these goals and this chapter reports on work directed towards the second. Specifically, a study is presented involving preliminary work towards characterising input texts for Reading in terms of the CEFR levels.

In Chapter 3, the word 'texts' emerged as a defining keyword in descriptions of language learning at higher levels. Texts are functional units in the sense that producing, interpreting and contributing to texts represent a large part of what learners do through language: texts are concrete expressions of language activities. In attempting to identify distinctive features of performance at different levels, it may therefore be particularly helpful to investigate the features of the texts that learners engage with. We have seen that level differentiation in Can Do statements is often expressed in comparative terms: more or less familiar/complex/abstract/specialised etc. In this chapter we begin to explore how some of these differentiating features may be quantified in relation to texts. This provides an empirical basis for further elaborating the CEFR Can Do statements, helping to make the distinctions more concrete and more explicit for users.

Meeting a demand from users, the Council of Europe has provided resources in several European languages (including English) exemplifying materials that target, and recordings of learner performance that represent communicative language ability at the various CEFR levels. These are accompanied by explanatory commentaries, test statistics or both. In addition, collaborative projects such as WebCEF (www.webcef.eu) and CEFtrain (www.helsinki.fi/project/ceftrain) have emerged as further sources of exemplification to assist users in interpreting the levels. The English Profile work of Hawkins and Filipović (2012) and of Capel (2010) is beginning to provide us with more detailed empirical evidence relating to the language that learners use to produce different kinds of texts. This chapter begins the work of analysing texts that learners at different levels of the CEFR are expected to understand.

Task description grids developed by the Dutch CEFR Grid group (Alderson et al 2004) (for Reading/Listening) and by the Association of Language Testers in Europe (ALTE 2005) (for Speaking/Writing) also represent attempts to operationalise criterial features that might help users to locate input texts and elicitation tasks in relation to the CEFR levels. Although these grids serve to support a process of specification, capturing salient features of task design, like the lists and tables in Chapter 5 of the CEFR itself, they do not explain how the features being recorded might serve to determine the level of the task in question.

As a first step and as an illustration of the process of quantifying criterial differences in input texts, this chapter is concerned with written reception – Reading – and specifically with the kinds of written input that learners might be expected to understand at the B2, C1 and C2 levels. Of course, as discussed in Chapter 3, different levels of 'understanding' of a text are possible. Here this is taken to mean a detailed understanding of propositional content of the kind required by most tests of English language learning reading comprehension and in intensive in-class English language learning reading activities. It is acknowledged, as discussed, for example, in Chapter 2 above, that a full account of the CEFR levels will require attention to the cognitive processes involved in reading and to social context as well as to textual input.

A similar approach to that adopted in this chapter could be taken to the spoken language and to interactive and productive language use: indeed the work reported here for reception parallels the work of English Profile partners in tracing the grammatical and lexical features of learner production. In common with other English Profile projects (see Hawkins and Filipović 2012, Capel 2010) this strand of research begins with materials from University of Cambridge ESOL Examinations and Cambridge University Press, but over time, increasing quantities of material from other sources will be incorporated and findings refined accordingly.

What makes an English text difficult for L2 readers?

Chapter 3 discussed the keyword *texts* and its uses in Can Do statements at the B2 and proficient user (C1/C2) levels. We have seen that there is little evidence in the collected Can Do statements of progression in the types of text that learners read beyond the B2 level, but that certain characteristics of texts may make them less accessible to any but the highest level learners. Such texts may, for example, be characterised as 'abstract, structurally complex or highly colloquial:' (Council of Europe 2001:69); 'dense in complex structures', (International ESOL Mastery), 'technical or highly specialized' (CERCLES) in content, or inexplicit in structure and meaning.

Khalifa and Weir (2009) detail the progression through the CEFR levels as it is operationalised through the input texts used in the Cambridge Main Suite of examinations (KET, PET, FCE, CAE, CPE). Their findings are summarised in Table 22 below. They locate some evidence for progression in the

Table 22 Functions in Main Suite Reading papers (based on Khalifa and Weir 2009:116-117)

Exam	Overview of nature of functions	Exemplification (based on analysis of one set of examination papers*)
KET (A2)	Basic functions relating to personal information, everyday activities and social interaction, expressed in writing in a straightforward way	• advising • warning • informing • describing activities • requesting and responding to requests • asking for and giving information • asking for and expressing preference • describing people and their lives • defining • expressing likes and dislikes
PET (B1)	As for KET, plus: • slightly more demanding understanding of functions is required in terms of: 　(a) length 　(b) text type 　(c) language complexity and 　(d) complexity of exponents chosen.	• expressing likes and dislikes • describing experiences • stating rules and regulations • describing people • describing places • describing an organisation • giving instructions • giving factual information
FCE (B2)	As for PET, plus: • more demanding appreciation of functions is required in terms of: 　(a) variety of context 　(b) text type and 　(c) language complexity. Candidates at this level are expected to be able not only to survive in an English-speaking environment but also to appreciate a degree of complexity and subtlety in functional use.	• describing people • describing places in a literary way • describing experiences and events • narrating • describing objects • giving opinions
CAE (C1)	As for FCE, plus: • some more demanding functional appreciation required in terms of: 　(a) variety of context 　(b) text type and 　(c) language complexity. Candidates at this level need to have an appreciation of register differences between different functional exponents. They should have an increasing awareness of how functions can be expressed in a range of stylistically differentiated ways.	• giving precise information • describing places in a literary way • presenting a reasoned argument • describing a situation in an entertaining way • narrating • giving an opinion in an entertaining way • describing people in an entertaining way • summarising • giving opinions

Table 22 Continued

Exam	Overview of nature of functions	Exemplification (based on analysis of one set of examination papers*)
CPE (C2)	As for CAE, plus: • some more demanding functional appreciation required in terms of: (a) variety of context (b) text type, and (c) language complexity. Candidates at this level need to have a deep appreciation of the full range of functional exponents. They should be able to appreciate language used in a sophisticated way for the full range of personal, literary and academic functions.	• giving precise information • comparing and contrasting • commenting on change • giving an opinion • describing a person's work in a literary style • criticising • describing a process • reviewing a work of art • praising • summarising

*Source: Examination handbooks (KET 2005, PET 2005, FCE 2007, CAE 2008, CPE 2005)

language functions in the texts used at the different levels. For example, they find some argumentative texts and tasks involving conative elements (appealing to the reader or exhorting them to act) at FCE (B2), but note that these are more common and appear more demanding at CAE (C1). However, in relation to functional progression, echoing the principles of the T-series (see Chapter 2), they conclude that 'on the whole it could be said that it is the lexical and grammatical resources rather than function which are more significant in determining level'. This is because 'it is the exponents used to express function that become more complex rather than the functions themselves' (p.118). This chapter pursues this line of inquiry, seeking measurable features of input texts (including, but not limited to grammatical and lexical features) that might clearly locate them at one or other of the CEFR levels.

Attempts to measure and control the difficulty of reading material in English have a long history, dating back at least to Thorndike (1921): *The Teachers Word Book* comprised a core vocabulary list of 10,000 frequently occurring words that Thorndike suggested should be prioritised in teaching or used to produce texts that would be more accessible to school children. Since that time a wide range of different measures have been developed to estimate readability. The Flesch-Kincaid Grade Level and Flesch Reading Ease measures (both available through Microsoft Word), are among the better known. Although these have proved helpful in estimating readability, including for L2 learners of English (Greenfield 2004), they have been widely criticised. They have not generally been developed with the L2 reader in mind and tend in any case to rely on surface level features of text (the Flesch-Kincaid Grade Level, for example, is based on word and sentence lengths).

Empirically based theories of L2 reading have suggested a considerably wider range of features that might influence the difficulty of input texts for L2 readers of English and a selection of these are set out in Table 23. There is a good deal of agreement between the listed authors on potentially criterial features and there is empirical evidence from studies such as Freedle and Kostin (1993) and Fortus, Conat and Fund (1998) that at least some characteristics in addition to word and sentence length do have an impact on the difficulty of reading comprehension tests. Recent advances in computational linguistics have raised the possibility of developing more comprehensive measures of readability, better reflective of the range of cognitive abilities involved (Crossley, Greenfield and McNamara 2008).

In this chapter we apply automated text analysis tools to measure the occurrence of a range of text characteristics in texts from English language materials targeted at different CEFR levels. The characteristics are selected on the basis of Khalifa and Weir (2009), which synthesises earlier work and provides a more explicit categorisation of the features that are used in the CEFR to differentiate between adjacent levels: features such as 'complexity' and 'abstractness'.

Readability formulas are typically developed through linear regression analysis to produce a single equation that will allow users to predict the readability of a text for learners at different levels of ability. The Flesch-Kincaid formula, for example, is based on the grade levels of the US school system and the same formula is employed at the elementary level as at the high school and college levels. Although it might be possible to adopt or develop a similar formula to estimate the CEFR level of a given text, a key objective of the English Profile is to identify the distinctive criterial features that will discriminate most effectively between neighbouring CEFR levels. The features that best differentiate between B2 and C1 may not be the same as those that differentiate between C1 and C2. Rather than using linear regression, separate discriminant function analyses were employed to investigate which characteristics might serve to differentiate most effectively between texts targeting English language learners at the B2 and C1 levels and between texts targeting C1 and C2.

The input texts

The texts were taken from three types of source. The first category was made up of texts taken from test forms published by Cambridge ESOL, Cambridge University Press (CUP), City and Guilds and Pearson Language Tests covering the Cambridge Main Suite tests – KET (A2), PET (B1), FCE (B2), CAE (C1) and CPE (C2), the Pearson Test of English (General) at Level 3 (B2), Level 4 (C1) and Level 5 (C2) and the City and Guilds International ESOL tests at Communicator (B2), Expert (C1) and Mastery (C2) levels. The

Table 23 Language testing frameworks for the description of text characteristics

Freedle and Kostin (1993)	Bachman et al (1995)	Fortus et al (1998)	Enright et al (2000)	Alderson et al (2006)	Khalifa and Weir (2009)
Prediction of reading comprehension item difficulty	*Comparison of test batteries*	*Prediction of reading comprehension item difficulty*	*Framework for reading comprehension test development*	*Instrument for developing tests of reading comprehension based on the CEFR*	*Framework for the validation of tests of reading comprehension*
Text variables Negations Referentials Rhetorical organisers Fronted structures a) cleft structures b) marked topics c) combinations of a) or b) with co-ordinators Vocabulary incidence of multi-syllabic words Sentence length Paragraph length Number of paragraphs Abstractness/concreteness of text Passage length	**Nature of language** **Length** **Propositional content** Vocabulary frequency, specialisation Degree of contextualisation embedded/reduced Distribution of new information compact/diffuse Type of information concrete/abstract, positive/negative, factual/counterfactual Topic Genre **Organisational characteristics** Grammar	**Length of text** **Number of negations** **Number of referential markers** **Level of text vocabulary** **Level of grammatical complexity of text** **Level of abstractness** **Topic of text** Humanities/social sciences/sciences **Rhetorical structure** **Overall text difficulty**	**Grammatical/discourse features** Syntax Vocabulary Discourse features **Pragmatic/rhetorical features** Pragmatic features Exposition Argumentation/persuasion/evaluation Historical narration Rhetorical features Definition Illustration Classification Comparison/contrast Cause/effect Problem/solution Analysis **Linguistic variables** Vocabulary, syntactic complexity, transition markers (cohesion), antecedent reference,	**Text source** **Authenticity** Genuine/adapted or simplified/pedagogic **Discourse type** Mainly argumentative Mainly descriptive Mainly expository Mainly instructive Mainly narrative Mainly phatic **Domain** Personal Public Occupational Educational **Topic** **Nature of content** Only concrete – Mainly abstract **Text length in words** **Vocabulary** Only frequent vocabulary	**Text length** **Discourse mode** Genre Rhetorical task **Grammatical resources** Only simple sentences – Many complex sentences **Lexical resources** Common items – Very wide range of vocabulary **Nature of information** Concrete – Abstract **Content knowledge**

Text by item interaction variables
Location of relevant information
Lexical overlap between text and options

Cohesion
Rhetorical organisation
Pragmatic characteristics
Illocutionary force
Sociolinguistic characteristics

modality (adverbs of attitude), amount of text, amount of time allowed, distances across text when cycle or integration is involved, competing linguistic distractors in the text environment, cohesion determiners, grammatical relations as referents and cohesion

– Extended
Grammar
Only simple structures – Wide range of complex structures

texts from the examination boards were complete input texts used in papers testing Reading skills (the Cambridge ESOL 'Use of English' papers, which include extensive input texts, but focus on grammar and vocabulary knowledge, were not included). The texts were drawn from sample paper packs and handbooks published on the internet or from the CUP *Past Papers* series. The second type of source was English language textbooks. Texts employed in tasks focused on 'Reading' were sampled at intervals of approximately 20 pages from the following textbook series: *New Headway*, *New English File*, *Total English* and *New Inside Out*. The texts were taken from the *Upper Intermediate* and *Advanced* level books which are intended for B2 and C1 level learners respectively. No books in these series target the C2 level. The third source was graded extensive reading texts marketed for English language learners. Extracts of approximately 500 words each were taken from books in the Cambridge University Press *Cambridge English Readers* series at Level 5 (B2) and Level 6 (C1/C2). The intention is for the English Profile to build up this resource over time into a substantial collection of input texts representing the range of CEFR levels as operationalised in a wide variety of settings.

This initial study is concerned with extensive continuous prose at the B2 level and above and focuses on criterial differences between the B and C levels and between C1 and C2. A summary of the texts collected to date is presented in Table 24. In order to provide for a comparison with the lower levels a small number of texts were included to represent A2 and B1 (12 at A2, 11 at B1). These A2 and B1 texts were all taken from the KET and PET examinations in the Cambridge ESOL suite. At the A1 level, learners are assumed to have only a very restricted ability to process continuous prose beyond the sentence and so no texts were collected representing the A1 level. There were 98 texts at B2 level, 104 at C1 and 73 at C2. To date 298 texts have been collected to represent levels A2 to C2 of the CEFR. It is a limitation of the project that, at this early stage, the collection is weighted towards the B2 and C1 levels and towards Cambridge ESOL test material. As the English Profile progresses, the sets of texts representing each level will be expanded, embracing a wider range of sources.

Table 24   Texts included in analyses by source

Target CEFR level	A2	B1	B2	C1	C2
Test: City & Guilds (International ESOL)	0	0	15	14	15
Test: Cambridge ESOL (KET, PET, FCE, CAE, CPE)	12	11	48	49	53
Test: Pearson Test of English (General)	0	0	8	12	5
Textbook: *New Headway*	0	0	4	7	0
Textbook: *Inside Out*	0	0	6	6	0
Textbook: *New English File*	0	0	6	5	0
Textbook: *Total English*	0	0	6	6	0
Extensive Reader: *Cambridge English Readers*	0	0	5	5	0
Total (298 texts)	12	11	98	104	73

The analysis tools

Three software tools were used to analyse the texts in the collection. These included *Coh-metrix*, *Wordsmith Tools* and *RANGE*. Descriptive statistics for the number of words, sentences and paragraphs in each text are displayed in Table 25.

Table 25 Texts included in analyses: descriptive statistics

Target CEFR level	N	Words		Sentences		Paragraphs	
		Mean	*St. Dev.*	*Mean*	*St. Dev.*	*Mean*	*St. Dev.*
A2	12	128.08	56.54	7.48	2.44	1.92	.90
B1	11	351.64	143.33	16.73	7.44	5.82	3.12
B2	98	523.83	185.52	21.11	9.96	7.53	4.53
C1	104	581.55	284.27	25.53	13.75	7.54	4.51
C2	73	369.77	323.48	14.12	12.92	4.47	4.79

Coh-metrix (McNamara, Louwerse, Cai & Graesser 2005) is a computational tool, freely available online for research purposes, that generates indices on a range of text characteristics under the headings of a) readability indices (including Flesch Reading Ease and Flesch-Kincaid Grade Level); b) general word and text information (including word counts, word frequency measures and indices of word concreteness and hypernymy); c) syntax indices (including consistency of sentence structure, occurrence of grammatical constituents, connectives and logical operators); d) referential and semantic indices (including referencing and latent semantic analysis); and e) situation model dimensions (causal, intentional, temporal and spatial). An overview of the indices provided and links to more comprehensive information can be found on the Coh-metrix home page (http://cohmetrix.memphis.edu).

Wordsmith Tools is a commercially available suite of computational tools developed by Scott (2006) for analysing texts from a lexical perspective and for developing corpora. This study employed the *Wordlist* tool to generate statistics on each text including the average length of words (in characters), the type: token ratio (see the Analyses section below), and standardised sentence and paragraph lengths. Further information on Wordsmith Tools can be accessed at Scott's home page (http://www.lexically.net/).

RANGE (Heatley, Nation & Coxhead 2002) is a vocabulary profiler that can be used to find the coverage of a text by selected word lists. This study used the 14 word lists developed by Nation for use with RANGE, based on the frequency of occurrence of words in the British National Corpus (BNC), a corpus of 100 million words of mainly (90%) written text designed to represent a wide cross-section of British English. Further information and a copy of the current version of the software can be downloaded from Nation's home page at Victoria University (www.victoria.ac.nz/lals/staff/paul-nation).

Analyses

The objective of the study was to develop formulas, based on the concept of criterial differences, capable of distinguishing between texts at the B2, C1 and C2 levels. As a statistical technique that is used to determine which linear variables can be used to distinguish between two or more categories, discriminant function analysis is well-suited to this purpose. It is used here to determine which text characteristics could be used to discriminate between texts in English language learning materials targeting learners at the B2 and at the C1 levels and between those targeting the C1 and C2 levels.

Initially, a total of 60 indices based on the three automated text analysis tools (*Coh-metrix*, *Wordsmith Tools* and *RANGE*) were considered, addressing the range of characteristics listed by Khalifa and Weir (2009). However, such a large number of variables is unlikely to produce a satisfactorily generalisable discriminant function. A preliminary analysis of variance was therefore used to screen out variables that would be unlikely to contribute to prediction. Only variables that produced a significant effect at $p<.05$, indicating substantive differences between the texts at the relevant levels, were retained for the subsequent analysis. To provide a test of the generalisability of the analysis, approximately 40% of the texts were held back from each analysis for use as a testing set and the remaining 60% of the texts were used in developing the predictive model.

The following section provides a brief overview of the significant features in relation to Khalifa and Weir's (2009) categories, and introduces the indices used to address them. For comparison, two readability indices are also discussed: Flesch-Kincaid Grade Level, which is based on word and sentence lengths, and Coh-metrix L2, which takes account of textual cohesion.

Text characteristics

Lexical and syntactic resources

A number of researchers and commentators (see for example Alderson 1996; Nuttall 1996) have identified potential sources of difficulty arising from the linguistic characteristics of a text. They suggest that structural, lexical, and conceptual difficulty strongly influence the ease with which a text can be read.

Vocabulary restrictions are often used as a means of simplifying English language learning Reading texts. Cambridge ESOL publishes word lists that are used to restrict the vocabulary load of KET (A2) – around 1,250 words – and PET (B1) – around 2,850 words. The Cambridge English Lexicon (Hindmarsh 1980) – a list of over 4,000 words based on word frequencies and EFL practice – has been used to guide the vocabulary used in FCE (B2). The *Cambridge English Readers* employ a restricted vocabulary of 800 words at level 2 (A2); 1,300 words at level 3 (B1); 1,900 words at level 4 (B1+); 2,800 words at level 5 (B2) and 3,800 words at level 6 (C1/C2). One of the purposes of the English Profile Wordlists (Capel 2010) is to better ground such lists in the vocabulary actually used by learners. Evidence from the Cambridge Learner Corpus (CLC) (see Chapter 1) suggests that on this basis the lists at the lower levels can reasonably be expanded: the English Profile list at A2 has over 20% more words than the KET word list (Capel 2010). Readers should note that *English Profile Wordlists (EPW)* was a working title for the project, now replaced by *English Vocabulary Profile*. This reflects the scope of the final interactive online resource, which offers far more than lists of words. The *English Vocabulary Profile* describes what vocabulary learners of English know at each CEFR level, covering the individual meanings of words, as well as phrases and phrasal verbs.

The emergence of computer-assisted analysis of extensive language corpora has facilitated the use of frequency-based word lists to explore the lexical features of texts. Khalifa and Weir (2009) describe a lexical analysis carried out by Schmitt on behalf of Cambridge ESOL to investigate the differences between input texts used in the Cambridge Main Suite examinations. This revealed a clear progression from KET (A2) to CAE (C1) in terms of the proportions of high-frequency and low-frequency vocabulary and of sub-technical academic vocabulary (words that are infrequent in general texts, but that occur relatively frequently in academic text across disciplines). However, no significant differences were found in vocabulary frequency between texts used in CAE (C1) and CPE (C2).

Where Schmitt (in the unpublished study cited in Khalifa and Weir 2009) compared the occurrence of *tokens*, or the number of individual words in a text (including repeated words), this analysis compares the proportions of different *types*: unique words. If the word 'book' occurred three times in a text, this would count as three tokens, but one type. Counts based on tokens may misrepresent the difference in the range of words that a learner would need to understand when reading relatively longer texts. A small number of words (many of them function words such as determiners, prepositions and auxiliaries) can account for a large proportion of each text: the most common word in this collection – 'the' – alone accounts for over 5% of all the tokens and the most common 25 words cover 32.3%. The ratio of types to tokens is affected by the length of a text: all else being equal, lengthier texts usually involve more repetition. Texts targeting lower levels are generally shorter than those targeting higher levels. In this collection, the type-token ratio (TTR, expressed as a percentage) is 64.7% at A2 compared with 52.2% at B2. The advantage of counting types is that repeated words are not counted more than once, thus giving a more accurate picture of the range of vocabulary required to access a text.

Five word-frequency level indices were investigated for this study. These were based on lists that accompany the RANGE programme (Heatley et al 2002) representing the percentage of types in a text that can be found in the

1 to 1,000 (*1K*); 1,001 to 2,000 (*2K*); 2,001 to 3,000 (*3K*) and 3,001 to 14,000 (*4 to 14K*) most frequent word families in the BNC. A word family is a set of words that are related in form and meaning to a *headword*. In the 1K list, the headword 'accept' is associated with the following family members: acceptability; acceptable; acceptably; unacceptable; acceptance; accepted; accepting; accepts; unacceptably. Each set of 1,000 word families covers a very much larger set of types: the 1K list of the 1,000 most frequent word families from the BNC includes 6,019 different types.

This approach to counting words makes a number of questionable assumptions about the relative difficulty of words. Unlike the English Profile Wordlists, it fails to take account of differences in word sense, is incapable of distinguishing effectively between homonyms, fails to consider multi-word expressions and makes the questionable assumption that knowledge of one word gives access to the meaning of all members of the word family. However, it has been widely used in vocabulary research as it does seem to provide a valid estimate of the vocabulary load represented by a text for English language learners.

In addition to the 14 frequency-based lists, two further lists were considered: *Off-list words*, covering words such as 'alchemical' and 'chiropractic' that do not appear on any of the 14 BNC frequency lists, and *Names*, representing all of the proper nouns occurring in the texts that do not appear on the BNC frequency lists. Some proper nouns, like 'England' and 'America', are sufficiently frequent in the BNC to appear on the 1K list and so do not appear on the *Names* list, but 'Oxford' and 'Cambridge' are examples of words that are less frequent in the BNC, do not appear on any of the 14 BNC frequency lists and so are included on the *Names* list.

Figure 4 BNC word frequency levels by target CEFR level

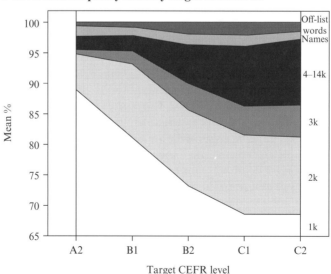

In Figure 4, there is a clear downward trend in the proportion of very frequent (1K) vocabulary (types) in texts from A2 (mean = 88.98%, standard deviation = 5.48%) to C1 (mean = 68.12%, standard deviation = 7.76%), but there is little difference between C1 and C2 (mean = 68.56%, standard deviation = 7.45%). In fact the proportion of types at the 1K, 2K and 3K levels is very similar at the C1 and C2 levels (the mean coverage of the first three word lists is 86.31% at C1 and 86.46% at C2), suggesting that word frequency counts may not discriminate as well between texts targeting C1 and C2 as between those targeting lower levels. Indeed no significant differences were revealed between C1 and C2 texts on any lexical feature by the analysis of variance and so none was used in the discriminant function analysis for these levels.

As word length is also associated with propositional complexity, in addition to the word frequency data, word length indices were also considered for the analysis. Three word length indices yielded significant differences between texts targeting B2 and C1: the average number of syllables per word, the proportion of long words in a text (long words being those containing six or more letters) and the proportion of short words in a text (words containing four letters or fewer).

Table 26 ANOVA: B2/C1 lexical measures

	B2 Mean	(N = 59) St. Dev.	C1 Mean	(N = 62) St. Dev.	F (1,119)	Sig.
Infrequent words: 4K to 14K	6.27	3.06	9.83	3.81	31.838	.000
Frequent words: 1K	73.16	6.50	68.12	7.76	14.932	.000
Proportion of long words in text: words of 6 letters or more	.27	.05	.32	.06	23.066	.000
Proportion of short words in text: words of 4 letters or fewer	.61	.06	.57	.06	18.140	.000
Average Syllables per Word	1.45	.11	1.56	.15	19.608	.000

The average length of words in the texts increases with level: the proportion of long words increases and the proportion of short words decreases (although the latter are always in the majority). It is notable in Figure 5(b) that there is little difference between the B1 and B2 texts in terms of word length (B1 mean = 1.45, standard deviation = .097; B2 mean = 1.45, standard deviation = .11).

In the widely used Flesch-Kincaid Grade Level formula, average word length is combined with average sentence length to produce a readability index that is easy to compute. Average sentence length – Figure 6(a) – increased in

Figure 5 Lexical measures by target CEFR level

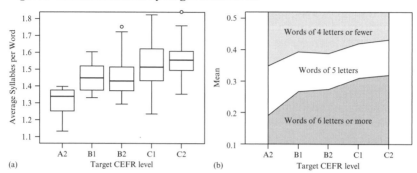

(a) Target CEFR level   (b) Target CEFR level

Figure 6 Average Words per Sentence and Flesch-Kincaid Grade Level by target CEFR level

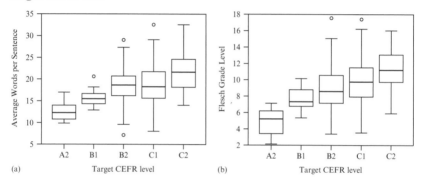

(a) Target CEFR level   (b) Target CEFR level

line with CEFR level, rising with progression through the levels from a mean of 12.46 words at A2 to 21.49 words per sentence at C2. From the B2 level, with the mean for the C1 texts (18.97) being slightly lower than for B2 (20.08), this difference was not significant.

The Flesch-Kincaid Grade Level index is intended to reflect the grade level in the US school system at which learners would be able to access the text in question. For example, a child of 9 or 10 in an American elementary school would generally be expected to understand a text estimated to be at Grade 4. As shown in Figure 6(b), the Flesch-Kincaid Grade Level of the texts rose in line with progression through the CEFR. Means for each CEFR level place most A2 texts between Grades 4 and 6 (A2 mean = 4.83, standard deviation = 1.60), B1 texts between Grades 7 and 8 (B1 mean = 7.69, standard deviation = 1.66), B2 between Grades 8 and 10 (B2 mean = 8.86, standard deviation = 2.46), C1 between Grades 9 and 11 (C1 mean = 9.93, standard deviation = 2.87) and C2 between Grades 10 and 12 (C2 mean =

11.14, standard deviation = 2.47). It is notable that, on the Flesch-Kincaid measure at least, few of the texts targeted at C2 would be classified as 'college level' (i.e. typically requiring more than a high school level of education). It is noteworthy that this finding appears entirely inconsistent with the CEFR *Overall Reading Comprehension* Can Do statement for C2: 'Can understand and interpret critically virtually all forms of the written language including abstract, structurally complex, or highly colloquial literary and non-literary writings' (Council of Europe 2001:69) or with the avant-garde literary works, journal articles and legal contracts identified with C2 in our database of Can Do statements.

As well as controlling the range of vocabulary employed in materials for learners at different levels, most English language learning materials, at least those developed for use with lower level learners, also aim to restrict the syntactic complexity of input texts. Cambridge ESOL and CUP both offer guidance in this area. 'Language Specifications' are published in the handbooks for KET (A2) and PET (B1) (see www.CambridgeESOL.org). The CUP *Cambridge English Readers* offers a *Teachers' Guide* with a chart setting out grammatical structures that may be encountered at each level (Cambridge University Press 1999). This introduces 'Future perfect', 'Future continuous' and various passive and modal structures at Level 5 (targeted at B2 level learners), but has no grammatical restrictions at Level 6 (targeted at C1 and C2).

The analysis of variance for B2 and C1 produced three significant results for measures of syntactic complexity. These included noun phrase incidence, personal pronoun incidence and mean number of modifiers per noun phrase (Table 27). Significantly higher means were found for C1 than for C2 for the incidence of personal pronouns (C1 mean = 87.71, standard deviation = 35.87; C2 mean = 66.55, standard deviation = 31.63). The mean for the average number of words per sentence (see Table 28) was significantly lower for C1 than for C2 (C1 mean = 18.97, standard deviation = 4.55; C2 mean = 21.49, standard deviation = 4.43).

Table 27 ANOVA: B2/C1 syntax measures

	B2 Mean	(N = 59) St. Dev.	C1 Mean	(N = 62) St. Dev.	F (1,119)	Sig.
Noun phrase incidence score (per thousand words)	285.78	22.53	272.58	17.18	13.225	.000
Personal pronoun incidence score	87.71	35.87	66.55	31.63	11.873	.001
Mean number of modifiers per noun phrase	.81	.21	.91	.19	7.343	.008

Table 28 ANOVA: C1/C2 syntax measures

	C1 Mean	(N = 60) St. Dev.	C2 Mean	(N = 47) St. Dev.	F (1,105)	Sig.
Average words per sentence	18.97	4.55	21.49	4.43	8.285	.005
Personal pronoun incidence score	72.69	38.78	58.45	28.81	4.425	.038
Sentence syntax similarity, all, across paragraphs	.09	.02	.07	.02	17.014	.000
Sentence syntax similarity, sentence all, within paragraphs	.10	.03	.08	.02	14.877	.000
Sentence syntax similarity, adjacent	.10	.03	.08	.02	11.136	.001

Figure 7 Syntax measures by target CEFR level

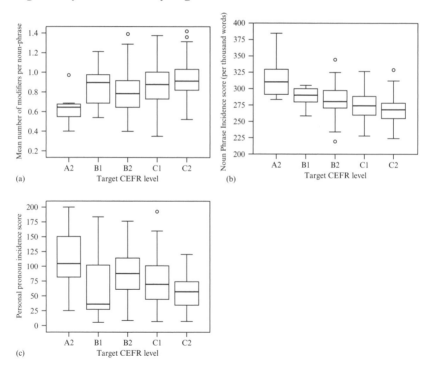

The results for these indices showed longer sentences (Figure 6) and increasing numbers of modifiers in noun phrases in texts targeting higher levels. The mean number of modifiers per noun phrase – see Figure 7a – represents the average of the number of words (adjectives, adverbs, or determiners) that modify the head noun in each noun phrase in a text. The noun phrase 'the famous blue book' has three modifiers: 'the', 'famous' and 'blue'. Larger numbers of modifiers are associated with more complex texts. With progression through the CEFR levels, the proportion of personal pronouns in the texts fell (Figure 7c). This is consistent with a greater complexity and sophistication of language in the higher level texts as lengthier phrases become more frequent. Again the B1 level appears discrepant: potentially an interesting finding. As this level is represented in these analyses by just 11 texts drawn from a single examination, the inconsistent results may stem from inadequate sampling (a limitation that needs to be kept in mind in relation to everything that is said here about A2 and B1). This is a question that will be pursued further as the collection of texts develops and the lower levels are more fully represented.

Figure 8 Sentence syntax similarity by target CEFR level

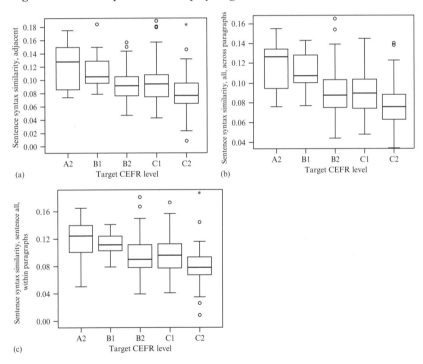

Three measures are offered in Coh-metrix that represent the degree of consistency in the syntax employed across parts of a text. These measures compare syntactic trees generated by an automated parser: sentence syntax similarity, adjacent (C1 mean = 1.0, standard deviation = .03; C2 mean = .08, standard deviation = .02); sentence syntax similarity, all, across paragraphs

(C1 mean = .10, standard deviation = .03; C2 mean = .08, standard deviation = .02); and sentence syntax similarity, sentence all, within paragraphs (C1 mean = .09, standard deviation = .02; C2 mean = .07, standard deviation = .02). It is assumed that a text will be easier for learners to process if the syntactic patterns are relatively uniform throughout. The repeated use of parallel constructions is often used as a form of simplification or syllabus grading in English language learning texts. The lower values on these indices observed in the texts targeting the higher CEFR levels suggest greater grammatical and conceptual complexity.

Discourse characteristics

The coherence of texts appears to make an important contribution to the readability of English language learning texts and is not well captured by the traditional formulas. Koda (2005) cites a number of studies reporting the positive effects of improved text structure and the benefits of explicit training in coherence on comprehension and memory. Freedle (1997) finds that texts subjectively judged to be high in coherence are associated with easier 'main idea' reading comprehension items. It has been argued that explicit cohesive devices help in establishing textual coherence (Goldman & Rakestraw 2000) and their absence inhibits the recall of texts, being symptomatic of a less successful mental representation (Ehrlich 1991).

Crossley, Greenfield and McNamara (2008) have developed a readability formula that takes account of features of textual coherence including syntactic similarity across sentences and lexical cohesion as represented by the proportion of content words in common across sentences. In their study, this formula, the *Cohmetrix L2 Index*, proved more successful than Flesch-Kincaid and indices proposed by Bormuth (1969) and Brown (1997) at predicting readability (as operationalised by scores on a suite of cloze tests).

Figure 9 Coh-metrix L2 index by target CEFR level

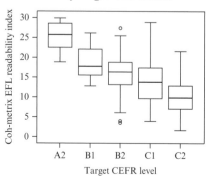

Scores are reported on a scale of 0 to 30, with 30 representing the easiest texts for English language learner readers.

The Coh-metrix L2 index, like the Flesch-Kincaid Grade Level with which it correlates at $r = -.686$ on this data, shows a clear progression by level (Figure 9). In common with other lexical and syntactic measures, it differentiates most clearly between the A2 and B1 texts.

Of the 10 separate Coh-metrix measures addressing cohesion, only one was indicative of significant differences between texts targeting B2 and those targeting C1: *anaphor reference, all distances, unweighted* (Table 29, Figure 10). This is the proportion of anaphoric references in a text that refer back to a constituent up to five sentences earlier. As can be seen in Figure 10, there is generally a modest reduction in the size of this index with progression through the levels. Again the B1 level (mean = .21, standard deviation = .19) is atypical as it has a lower mean than the B2 level (mean = .28, standard deviation = .19) and is closer to C1 (mean =.19, standard deviation = .14). The pattern of progression suggests that there is proportionally less use of anaphoric references in texts presented at higher levels than at lower levels, although there is substantial variation across texts at all levels.

Table 29 ANOVA: B2/C1 anaphor reference

	B2 Mean	(N = 59) St. Dev.	C1 Mean	(N = 62) St. Dev.	F (1,119)	Sig.
Anaphor reference, all distances, unweighted	.28	.19	.19	.14	9.503	.003

Figure 10 Cohesion measures by target CEFR level

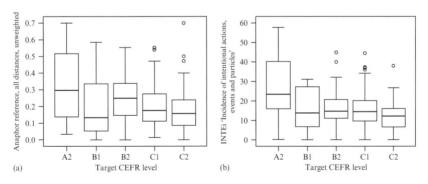

Between texts targeting C1 and those targeting C2 (Table 30) there was a significant difference for intentional cohesion – for the incidence of

Table 30 ANOVA: C1/C2 intentional cohesion

	C1 Mean	(N = 60) St. Dev.	C2 Mean	(N = 47) St. Dev.	F (1,105)	Sig.
Incidence of intentional actions, events and particles	15.33	9.20	11.87	8.49	3.980	.049

intentional actions, events and particles. Intentional cohesion is a concept that derives from text comprehension research. High intentional cohesion occurs in 'texts that refer to animate protagonists who perform actions in pursuit of goals, as in the case of simple stories and other forms of narrative'. Low intentional cohesion is associated with texts that 'describe events that are not goal directed and not executed by animate agents (e.g. mechanisms that cause volcanoes)'. Hence, 'the higher the incidence of intentional actions in a text, the more the text is assumed to convey goal-driven content' (Coh-metrix, n.d. online).

The analysis of variance revealed a significantly higher mean for C1 than for C2 (C1 mean = 15.33, standard deviation = 9.20; C2 mean = 11.87, standard deviation = 8.49). Thus it appears that in our collection, the C2 texts are less likely to be goal driven than the C1.

Nature of information

When the propositions in a text are more abstract, this may divert the reader's cognitive resources from language processing and so make it more difficult to understand. Abstract information often also entails a degree of linguistic complexity that may further stretch the L2 reader's resources. Coh-metrix includes a range of indices concerned with the degree of concreteness or abstractness of the words in a text, based on the MRC Psycholinguistics Database (Coltheart 1981) and hypernym relations based on WordNet (Fellbaum 1998), but the analysis of variance failed to reveal significant differences between texts targeting B2 and texts targeting C1 on any of these indices.

There was a significant difference between C1 and C2 for the average minimum concreteness value of the content words in sentences. With progression through the levels (Figure 11), there was a substantial fall in the concreteness minimum between A2 (mean = 206.50, standard deviation = 18.48), followed by a plateau to B1 (mean = 174.82, standard deviation = 21.75), followed by a plateau from B1 to C1 (C1 mean = 178.00, standard deviation = 18.93) with a significant increase at C2 (mean = 186.47, standard deviation = 20.59), although the mean concreteness value for C2 (mean = 378.48, standard deviation = 27.10) was not significantly different to C1 (383.54, standard

Table 31 ANOVA: C1/C2 for concreteness of content words

	C1 Mean	(N = 60) St. Dev.	C2 Mean	(N = 47) St. Dev.	F (1,105)	Sig.
Concreteness, minimum in sentence for content words	178.00	18.93	186.47	20.59	4.883	.029

Figure 11 Concreteness of content words by target CEFR level

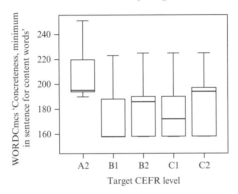

deviation = 24.69). Nonetheless, this does suggest, contrary to the CEFR, that the content of these C2 texts is somewhat less abstract than the C1 texts.

Content knowledge

Nuttall (1996) puts forward the widely held view that, all else being equal, the greater a reader's knowledge of the topic of a text, the easier it should be to process. In the socio-cognitive framework proposed by Weir (2005b) the relationship between the candidate's pre-existing knowledge and the propositional content of a text will affect the way it is processed.

Tan (1990) and Clapham (1996) both investigated the effect of topic familiarity on test taker performance without finding a substantial impact on reading test scores. Clapham concluded that readers would only benefit from a familiar topic when the text reached a certain level of subject specificity. She also found evidence of a 'threshold effect'. Learners below a certain level of ability as measured by a grammar test were unable to use their subject knowledge to compensate for lack of language ability. Above the threshold, a higher level of language ability seemed to help to overcome lack of subject knowledge. Only learners scoring within a relatively narrow range on the grammar test seemed to benefit from having reading texts within their academic subject area.

Studies such as Steffensen, Joag-Dev and Anderson (1979), Chihara, Sakurai and Oller (1989) and Sasaki (2000) have provided evidence that cultural knowledge can play an important role in text comprehension. In these studies, certain culturally loaded words – proper nouns, words describing institutions and words that reflected unfamiliar cultural practices - were changed into words that would be more familiar for the participants. For example in Chihara et al's (1989) and Sasaki's (2000) studies, which used the same texts, *Joe* was changed to *Hiroshi*, *state* to *prefecture* and a mother *hugged* rather than *kissed* her son because these changes were felt to reflect a Japanese rather than an American cultural context for the narrative. The adapted texts produced higher cloze test scores.

Clearly both subject and cultural specificity are difficult to operationalise adequately because both would seem to depend as much on variation between readers as variation between texts. However, it may be assumed that texts with a high proportion of proper nouns are likely to refer to culturally specific phenomena that may be less familiar to some readers while those with a high proportion of low frequency words are likely to be relatively technical in content. As noted above, no significant differences on these measures were found between the texts targeting B2 and those targeting C1.

The following nine indices emerged from the analysis of variance as potentially predictive of differences between B2 and C1:

Higher at B2 than C1

1. Frequent words: 1K.
2. Proportion of short words in text: words of four letters or fewer.
3. Noun Phrase Incidence Score (per thousand words).
4. Personal pronoun incidence score.
5. Anaphor reference, all distances, unweighted.

Higher at C1 than B2

6. Infrequent words: 4K to 14K.
7. Proportion of long words in text: words of six letters or more.
8. Average syllables per word.
9. Mean number of modifiers per noun phrase.

An assumption of discriminant function analysis is that variables used in prediction should not be highly correlated with each other. Table 32 and Table 33 show the correlations between the selected variables at the B2/C1 and C1/C2 levels. Where correlations between variables were greater than .7, the variable with the lower univariate effect size was excluded. On this basis, six of the nine variables were eliminated and the following three were retained for the B2/C1 analysis:

Table 32 Correlations between predictor variables: B2/C1

	1	2	3	4	5	6	7	8	9
1. Infrequent words: 4K to 14K									
2. Frequent words: 1K	−.851								
3. Proportion of long words in text: words of 6 letters or more	.420	−.506							
4. Proportion of short words in text: words of 4 letters or fewer	−.486	.564	−.942						
5. Average syllables per word'	.431	−.448	.912	−.856					
6. Phrase Incidence Score (per thousand words)	−.294	.259	−.372	.414	−.379				
7. Personal pronoun incidence score	−.473	.558	−.688	.750	−.643	.561			
8. Mean number of modifiers per noun phrase	.505	−.605	.617	−.652	.613	−.580	−.750		
9. Anaphor reference, all distances, unweighted	−.372	.511	−.594	.624	−.516	.372	.769	−.612	

Table 33 Correlations between predictor variables: C1/C2

	1	2	3	4	5	6	7
1. Personal pronoun incidence score							
2. Average words per sentence'	−.460						
3. Incidence of intentional actions, events and particles	.492	−.478					
4. Sentence syntax similarity, adjacent	.334	−.613	.361				
5. Sentence syntax similarity, all, across paragraphs	.357	−.662	.428	.900			
6. Sentence syntax similarity, sentence all, within paragraphs	.359	−.629	.446	.902	.931		
7. Concreteness, minimum in sentence for content words	−.090	.110	.051	−.120	−.100	.036	

1. Infrequent words: 4K to 14K.

2. Proportion of short words in text: words of four letters or fewer.

3. Noun Phrase Incidence Score (per thousand words).

Removing two of the three sentence structure similarity variables, which were all highly correlated with each other (Table 33), the following five variables were retained for the C1/C2 analysis:

Higher at C1 than C2

1. Sentence syntax similarity, sentence all, within paragraphs.

2. Personal pronoun incidence score.

3. Incidence of intentional actions, events, and particles.

Higher at C2 than C1

4. Average words per sentence.

5. Concreteness, minimum in sentence for content words.

In the next phase of the study, discriminant function analysis was used to identify the combination of variables best able to discriminate between texts targeting the B2 or C1 levels. It was clear from the preliminary analyses that the *Cambridge Readers* series texts, being intended for fluent unsupported reading, were, according to the metrics employed, considerably easier to read than the textbooks and test materials (mean scores on the Flesch-Kincaid Grade Level, for example, were 4.54 for Level 5/B2 and 5.39 for Level 6/C1). The decision was therefore taken to exclude these 10 texts from the discriminant function analysis.

The first bivariate discriminant function analysis was conducted with the CEFR level (B2 or C1) as the dependent variable. In order to find the most efficient prediction model, a stepwise model was adopted using Wilks' lambda to evaluate the contribution of each variable to prediction. On this basis, the number of predictor variables might be further reduced and the level of prediction improved. In this case, all three predictor variables were retained as this model achieved the greatest prediction accuracy.

Fisher's classification function coefficients for each variable are shown in Table 34. Multiplying the scores for a text on the relevant variables by these coefficients and subtracting the constant gives the probability that the text should be classified as B2 or as C1. Classification of the text is based on the comparison between these two probabilities: if the probability of a B2 classification is higher than for a C1 classification, the text is predicted to target B2.

The accuracy of the classification can be shown by tabulating the degree of correspondence between the predicted levels and those actually targeted in the source materials. Table 35a shows the number of texts that were correctly assigned to their target level (the numbers in bold type) and the

Table 34 Fisher's classification function coefficients: B2/C1

Variable	B2	C1
Proportion of short words in text: words of 4 letters or fewer	161.302	154.801
Infrequent words: 4K or less	1.683	1.942
DENSNP 'Noun Phrase Incidence Score (per thousand words)'	0.659	0.637
(Constant)	−149.180	−141.355

Table 35 Classification accuracy: B2/C1

a)

		Predicted level	
		B2	**C1**
Model building set	B2	**40**	16
	C1	16	**44**
Testing set	B2	**26**	11
	C1	14	**25**

b)

		precision	recall	F
Model	B2	.71	.71	.71
	C1	.73	.73	.73
Testing	B2	.65	.70	.68
	C1	.69	.64	.67

number of incorrect predictions. The proportion of predictions that proved to be correct is expressed by the 'precision' figure in Table 35b and the proportion of texts targeting each level that were correctly identified by the model is represented by 'recall'. The F figure is a weighted average of the two. Overall, 71% of the predictions were accurate for the model building set and 67% for the testing set. This compares with a 60% level of accuracy using the Coh-metrix L2 index or 59% using the Flesch-Kincaid Grade Level as the basis for prediction. Figure 12 plots the distribution of the estimated classification probabilities in relation to the CEFR levels actually targeted by the texts.

Calculating discriminant scores for each text allows us to plot differences between the texts employed in the different source materials as an indication of how consistent this is across materials (Figure 13). In Figure 13, scores above 0 represent a C1 classification and scores below represent B2. Across most of the materials, there is a progression in difficulty between B2 and C1, although on this metric (as on the Flesch-Kincaid Grade Levels and Coh-metrix L2 readability index) the texts targeting the C1 level sampled from the Pearson Tests of English appear to be easier than those targeting B2: all eight of the Level 3 (B2) texts were classified as C1, while six of the 12 Level 4 (C1) texts were classified as B2.

The second bivariate discriminant function analysis was conducted with

Figure 12 Classification probabilities: B2/C1

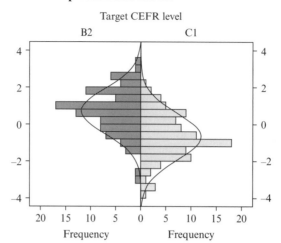

Figure 13 Discriminant scores by text source: B2/C1

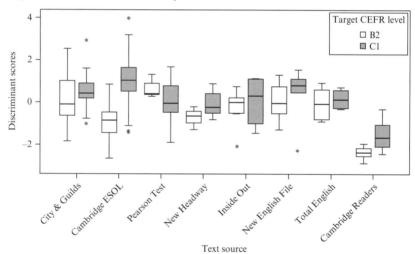

CEFR level (C1 or C2) as the dependent variable. Again a stepwise model was adopted using Wilks' lambda to evaluate the contribution of each of the five candidate variables to prediction. On this basis, the number of predictor variables was reduced from five to two, although the level of prediction improved. The two predictor variables were sentence syntax similarity and minimum concreteness of content words across sentences (Table 36).

Following the same procedures for the C1/C2 contrast shows an overall accuracy of prediction of 70% on the model building and 74% on the testing

Table 36 Fisher's classification function coefficients: C1/C2

Variable	C1	C2
Sentence syntax similarity, all, across paragraphs	176.575	133.379
Concreteness, minimum in sentence for content words	.457	.490
Constant	−48.835	−51.292

Table 37 Classification accuracy: C1/C2

a)

		Predicted level	
		C1	C2
Model building set	C1	43	17
	C2	15	32
Testing set	C1	37	7
	C2	11	15

b)

		precision	recall	F
Model	C1	.74	.72	.73
	C2	.65	.68	.67
Testing	C1	.77	.84	.80
	C2	.68	.58	.63

set. This compares with 63% accuracy of prediction for both the Flesch-Kincaid Grade Level and the Coh-metrix L2 index.

Plotting the discriminant scores (Figure 15) shows consistency across the test providers in interpreting the C1–C2 distinction. Scores above 0 on this scale should be interpreted as a prediction that the text targets the C1 level; those below zero represent a prediction of C2. Seventy per cent of the Cambridge ESOL texts, 76% of the Pearson Test texts and 56% of the City and Guilds texts were predicted to be at the targeted level.

Figure 14 Classification probabilities: C1/C2

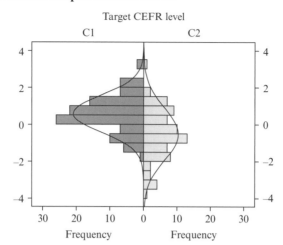

Figure 15 Discriminant scores by text source: C1/C2

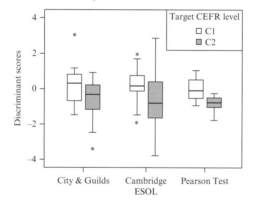

Conclusions

The initial evidence supplied by the study described in this chapter suggests that it should be possible to identify criterial features of English language learning input texts that will help users to estimate text difficulty in relation to the CEFR. The study suggests that it may be possible to discriminate most effectively between texts targeting the different CEFR levels by employing distinct measures at each level boundary. Word frequency discriminates well between texts targeting B2 and C1, but it is not effective at discriminating between C1 and C2. On the other hand, the cohesion and word concreteness measures that discriminate effectively between C1 and C2 are not as helpful in distinguishing B2 from C1.

A wider range of materials now needs to be incorporated into the collection, the predictive models further tested against these and refined as necessary. It is possible that the models developed on the basis of the current collection reflect idiosyncrasies in the way in which level distinctions are operationalised in the sources. A more broadly representative sample of English language learning texts is to be preferred. With rapid development in computational linguistics, it may also be possible to develop new text analysis tools that are more sensitive to text characteristics of interest. The tools we have used offer better measurement of syntax and vocabulary than they do of discourse features and it may be possible to improve on the levels of prediction by taking fuller account of features such as text genre.

If the analysis suggests scope for greater consistency between texts used in different source materials, it should also be borne in mind that this study has investigated text characteristics in isolation without considering the tasks that readers are asked to perform or the conditions that apply: both key issues for future English Profile research. Further expansion of the collection of English language learning texts is needed to establish how consistent the interpretations of levels may be across a wider range of settings. It also remains to be established whether the characteristics that predict the targeting of an English language learning text also predict the difficulty that learners will actually experience in reading it: another question that will need to be taken up in future English Profile research.

In spite of its limitations, the study has raised issues that deserve further investigation. Firstly, why is it that vocabulary measures appear to be important in classifying texts at the B2/C1 interface, but syntax appears to be more so at C1/C2? Hawkins and Filipović (2012) have found that most of the syntax features they identify in learner writing are observable in learner text at the B2 level, but that lexical diversity and increases in production at the C levels. In these input texts, in contrast, there is scant evidence of increasing lexical diversity beyond C1, but syntactic diversity does appear to be criterial. The greater complexity of the grammar in these input texts may reflect the increasing mastery of grammatical features reflected in the falling error rates at the C levels observed in the CLC data by Hawkins and Filipović.

Secondly, on the preliminary evidence provided by the investigations described in this chapter, the texts used to indicate whether a learner is at the highest, C2, level of the CEFR do not seem to represent 'practically all forms of written language' as set out in the C2 level Can Do descriptor for Overall Reading Comprehension (Council of Europe 2001:69). Indeed, the readability indices and vocabulary frequency measures for C2 texts are consistent with those found for serious newspapers or magazines rather than with the more esoteric text types suggested in our analysis of Can Do statements. This could be taken to suggest that perhaps the texts in these materials do not truly reflect the highest levels of the CEFR. On the other hand, for all three test providers, there does seem to be a measurable difference between the texts that they judge to be suitable for C1 and C2 test takers.

This raises interesting questions about the status of the CEFR scales. Should we simply use such evidence to refine our interpretation of the Can Do descriptors – e.g. interpreting 'practically all forms of the written language' and 'manuals, specialised articles and literary works' to represent a degree of readability extending as far as texts found at the serious end of the news media spectrum? Or does the evidence question the validity of the C2 tests? If so, how do we account for the apparent consensus around the kinds of text that C2 test takers are expected to 'understand and interpret'? Is there a measurable level of L2 reading ability to be found between C1 and C2? Might evidence of this kind be taken to contradict the CEFR and the all-encompassing wording of the C2 descriptors: evidence that the descriptors are an overstatement of what might realistically be expected at C2? Is there necessarily a difference in the degree of measurement sensitivity that can be achieved in ranking Can Do descriptions and in tests of Reading comprehension? Such questions will need to be resolved as the CEFR and the English Profile continue to develop.

Section 3
Connections in the English Profile

5 Proposing a Can Do model for the English Profile

Based on the theoretical background outlined in Section 1 and on the emerging findings reported in Chapters 3 and 4, this chapter offers suggestions for additional Can Do statements for the higher levels of the CEFR that illustrate the levels in functional terms, like the Can Do statements of the CEFR, but that are also more detailed and so are more *generative*. By generative, I mean that they should provide enough information to guide users in carrying out a variety of purposes. They should offer sufficient detail to inform materials writers and test developers (who need to operationalise the general CEFR framework through specific, contextualized tasks); but they should also support briefer summary statements that might communicate suitably general information to others, such as the users of test results (who need brief, consolidated summaries of outcomes). The statements should also serve as a link between these different purposes: users should be able to trace the ways in which the elements of the framework are interpreted and represented in the specific demands made of learners in using language to carry out a task.

The chapter suggests how these Can Do statements might be elaborated and exemplified in ways that are meaningful for users and how a process of mutual validation might be introduced to support the CEFR goal of shared standards.

Chapter 3 explored how English language educators have conceived of levels of functional language ability and how they have used differences between learners to construct systems of levels for a range of purposes including sequencing instruction and making judgements about learner proficiency. It was noted that, in the absence of empirical evidence, certain assumptions about how learners progress from level to level often have to be made. In Chapter 4, we have seen how concepts such as text difficulty might be quantified to provide more concrete and generalisable definitions of the CEFR levels for written reception while other strands of the English Profile programme are generating evidence about the nature of learner production (Hawkins and Filipović 2012) and the range of vocabulary that learners know (Capel 2010). This chapter brings these strands together to suggest how the system of functional Can Do statements for the English Profile might be developed to meet the needs of diverse groups of users working with different populations of learners at different stages of education.

It was argued in Chapter 2 that, in order to be meaningful, Can Do statements should incorporate the three elements of classic educational objectives: performance, condition and criterion. Inclusion of all three elements should inform the three key categories of audience identified by Alderson (1991): the assessor (who judges performance and whose main concern is therefore the criterion), the constructor (who creates learning or testing tasks and whose main concern is therefore the condition) and the user (who interprets results and so needs a readily accessible summary of the performance). The English Profile functional Can Do descriptions should provide a common source that will allow for the generation of statements capable of satisfying the needs of each of these groups.

Unfortunately, shared sets of descriptions are not enough to guarantee shared standards. Current methodologies for relating tests to the CEFR advocated in the Council of Europe Manual (2009) appear to rest on the assumption that diverse groups of language specialists will, if they carefully follow sound standard setting procedures, interpret the tables of Can Do statements in similar ways. However, experience with standard setting methodologies (Cizek and Bunch 2007) suggests that different panels of experts (even when using the same methods) may arrive at quite different recommendations on the test score that best represents an adequate performance. In the face of the diversity inherent in international language learning, as Jones (2009) has rightly argued, 'our default expectation must be that different countries' interpretations will be culturally determined (in a broad sense) and therefore may differ' (p.37). The experience of developing the *Breakthrough* specification bears this out. Trim (2009) relates how, when working with groups of educators from a range of European countries, 'it became clear from different specimen descriptions that very different interpretations of words like "simple", "basic", "familiar", etc. were possible' (p.6).

For this reason, both assessors and constructors will need more than Can Do statements to inform their work. The provision of sets of scales to assessors is, by itself, unlikely to result in sufficiently consistent or systematic interpretations to support valid and reliable score interpretations. Assessors usually build (or are inducted into) a collective understanding of the levels of performance represented in a scale by observing benchmarked sample performances, by discussing their relationship to the scale descriptors and through training and practice. Constructors such as materials writers and test item writers work to a design brief or to test specifications. These specifications set out detailed requirements for tasks that will reflect the nature of language use by the target population. As with assessors, more is involved for constructors than a personal reading of scale descriptors. Understanding of the kinds of tasks that are most likely to be appropriate for a particular purpose is built up through engagement with the brief, through discussion with the client or with colleagues and through trialling of materials with learners in the targeted groups. The third key stakeholder group – the users, who might be employers, academic institutions, government agencies etc. – although usually less directly involved with learning and testing materials, may also benefit from experience of interpreting and using scores and reports, and from seeing benchmark performances to enrich their interpretation of the results they receive.

The coherence of the levels found within educational systems is therefore not guaranteed by a shared set of scales, but depends additionally on the availability and accessibility of (and willingness of participants to engage with) other sources of support as well as measures directed at quality assurance (such as the monitoring of rater agreement or the systematic trialling of teaching materials). Some support processes may be more formal and fixed – further elaboration of Can Do statements providing clarification; glosses of key terms; benchmark samples with commentaries explaining how these relate to the statements; training and standardisation sessions – others are less formal and more fluid – opportunities for sharing and discussing interpretations in formal meetings and informal exchanges with colleagues; experience with tasks that are currently used to operationalise the levels. Ultimately, it is not perhaps so much the products – Can Do statements and scales – that define levels of language ability as the practices that grow up around them. To the extent that distinct communities each arrive at separate interpretations, the coherence of the scheme will be diminished. In addition to publishing scales and support materials, the English Profile will therefore need to further develop the support that it offers to the community of users by providing additional detailed guidance, a forum for discussion and debate and suitable processes for ensuring consistent interpretations.

This chapter is concerned with the development of a set of Can Do statements that might serve as a bridge between the general, language-independent statements of the CEFR and more detailed English language reference level descriptions. In the next chapter suggestions are made on how the English Profile can present a more integrated system of interrelated materials as an interactive resource for English language educators.

As discussed in Chapter 2, statements of objectives need to steer a careful path between over-specification and vagueness or over-abstraction. Wilkins and Trim perceived at the outset of the original Council of Europe Unit/ Credit project that basing language learning objectives around specific tasks leaves 'no rational basis for the distinction between what is learnt for use in any situation and what is learnt for use in one particular situation' (Trim 2009:7). If objectives are stated at the level of detail required of test or task specifications there is a risk that learning will take on the worst aspects of test preparation: training tactically focused on fulfilling the demands of the specified task. On the other hand, the objectives enshrined in the grammar based pedagogy of the traditional Modern Languages classroom are too abstract because they largely fail to relate theories of usage (the linguistic system) to practical use (achieving effective communication).

The CEFR itself, most explicitly in the concise description of language use and learning on page 9 of the English version (and quoted by Trim in the Preface to this volume), suggests that language use involves the following elements:

communicative language competences	language activities	tasks
conditions and constraints	language processes	texts
contexts	strategies	themes
domains		

Figure 16 suggests one way of depicting or mapping out how these elements relate to each other. Performance of a task involves strategic decisions on the part of the language user about the nature of the task, the resources at his or her disposal and the best way to deploy these resources to accomplish the task. Language activities are the functional means by which the learner is able to meet the demands of the task – employing communicative language competences in 'processing (receptively and/or productively) one or more texts' (Council of Europe 2001:10) to do so.

Figure 16 CEFR model of language use (Council of Europe 2001:9)

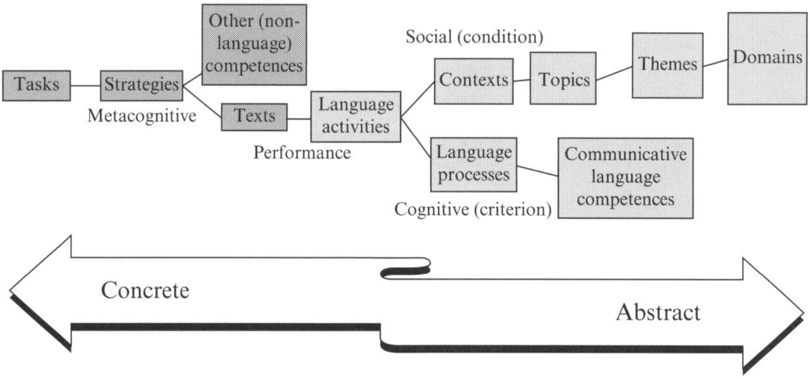

In general, orienting statements towards competences and domains of use (Figure 16) involves greater abstraction while statements focused on tasks are inevitably more concrete and closely specified. Contexts for language use (involving themes or topics and social and physical conditions) can be identified with Mager's (1962) condition, while criterion clearly implies competences and the ease or automaticity of (cognitive) processing. Performance (as language use rather than task accomplishment) is, in the CEFR, represented by language activities and by the types of text that are produced or received by the learner.

Although it is central to the CEFR, the elements of this model are not consistently or comprehensively specified in each of the Can Do statements or in the *Activities – Strategies – Competence*s scales presented in Chapters 4 and 5 of the CEFR. We saw in Chapter 2 that some elements receive a mention in statements at one level, but not at another. For example, 'sometimes at one level (B1) something is said about vocabulary in texts, while at lower or higher levels nothing is said about vocabulary' (Alderson et al 2004). No indication is given in the CEFR as to whether such omissions are related to the salience or criteriality of the element at the levels concerned.

Where the CEFR Can Do statements do provide guidance, constellations of features are inevitably treated as more or less fixed units. For example, in the scale for Overall Reading Comprehension (p.69) at A2 level learners understand 'short, simple texts on familiar matters of a concrete type which consist of high frequency everyday or job-related language' while at C1 they can read 'lengthy, complex texts' that may or may not relate to 'his/her own area of speciality'. This leaves open the question of which of the features making up the descriptions – length, concreteness, frequency – is most salient. As a consequence it also begs questions about how one should estimate the level of a text that does not readily fit the given descriptions: a lengthy, but *simple* text or a short, simple text on *unfamiliar* matters, for example.

Following the approach outlined in Chapter 4 of this volume, it may be possible to develop a probabilistic model of language use in which different scales, (based on different elements of the model) interrelate to generate predictions about learner performance. Contextual features such as the time available for reading might interact with the linguistic features of a text and relevant aspects of the learner's competences (see Chapter 4 above) to allow us to better predict, for example, the likelihood that a given learner would be able to understand the gist of the text or reconstruct it in detail under given conditions. We might, pursuing the example, find that given sufficient time, a learner with a C1 level of lexico-grammatical competence (language competence scales) who has completed secondary education and has a modest familiarity with health-related topics (topic familiarity scale) would have a better than 80% chance of understanding the gist of a clearly printed, short article from a popular science magazine on health issues that uses a wide range of vocabulary and moderately complex syntax (based on scales of relevant text features), while another learner with a similar profile, but with a much more limited knowledge of the topic might have a substantially lower chance of understanding the gist of the same text under the same conditions. Of course, given the complexity and inherent unpredictability of linguistic systems, the prospect of such a comprehensive model remains remote, but this kind of multi-dimensional triangulation is the ultimate goal of those involved in test and task construction and of CEFR-related projects such as the Dutch Constructs Group (Alderson et al 2004, 2006) and ALTE grid (ALTE 2005) initiatives described above in Chapter 4. Much of the work of the English Profile is directed at identifying and calibrating the component features of a system of this kind: more/less complex syntax, structured discourse, frequent lexis, L1 interference etc.

Between the CEFR statements, which have proved meaningful and therefore scalable for language teachers, and the level of detail that may be required by users of English Profile, an intermediate stage seems to be required: one that directs the user towards more detailed information on the key features impacting on the likely level of difficulty of a given task. This stage involves the collation of elements from the calibrated statements as they relate to the categories of the CEFR model.

The Dutch CEFR Construct Project (Alderson et al 2004, 2006) attempts something of this kind as a preliminary step towards 'an instrument that contains test-relevant linguistic, psycholinguistic, and sociolinguistic as well as pragmatic criteria for text and task selection at different CEFR levels' (Alderson et al 2006:7). Building on the experience of the DIALANG project (Alderson & Huhta 2005), it brings together statements from the CEFR scales, deploying a template or 'frame' to capture and compare features across levels. The frames for Reading (Alderson et al 2004, Appendix 1, pp. 33–35) are not based directly on the CEFR language use model, but have categories derived from analysis of the Can Do statements. They include the following six features:

1. Operation

    a verb characterising aspects of the nature of comprehension:
    understand, recognise, locate, infer etc.

2. What

    the object of the operation – what is to be understood or recognised etc. 'in terms of the meaning of a text, the language of the text, and so on' (Alderson et al 2006:9) – e.g. 'specific details'; 'implicit meanings'; 'subtleties of style'

3. Source texts

    the kinds of text on which learners at a given level are said to be able to carry out the specified operations characterised in terms of genre or text type – 'newspaper articles'; 'personal letters'; 'descriptions'; 'instructions' – and/or of a variety of text characteristics such as 'straightforward'; clearly written'; 'lengthy'; 'highly specialised'

4. Text features

    linguistic features of texts and tasks that previous research had indicated as relevant to defining difficulty including familiarity of content, frequency of vocabulary and (again) text length

5. Strategies

> reading strategies include rereading sections of text and varying reading speed according to purpose and text type; but the group found that strategies 'could not easily be distinguished by level' (Alderson et al 2004:12)

6. Conditions and limitations

> this was said to contain 'an unprincipled mix of different aspects of comprehension' (Alderson et al 2004:12). Elements placed into this category included 'well enough to correspond regularly with a pen friend'; 'difficulty with less common phrases and idioms and with terminology'; and 'occasional use of dictionary'

The frames are completed using elements extracted directly from the CEFR scales so that the 'operations' listed for B2 in the frame for reading are verbs used in CEFR Can Do statements to describe reading comprehension at the B2 level: *understand, scan, monitor, obtain, select, evaluate, locate* and *identify*. Because the CEFR Can Do statements do not consistently provide information on all six of the features identified, many of the cells in the frame are, of necessity, left blank. For reading, of the eight operations at B2, only two are accompanied by text in all related cells of the frame; *conditions and limitations* are only found at B1, B2 and C1.

Through this work, in addition to the numerous empty cells, the group identified a number of further obstacles to deriving test specifications from the CEFR including a lack of definition and inconsistencies in the terminology used between Can Do statements at different levels (see Chapter 2 above). Among the issues identified, features appearing at one level of the CEFR might not be mentioned at another; definitions for key terms like *simple* or *frequent* were lacking; sometimes it was unclear whether a term used in one statement was synonymous with a term used in another.

These gaps and inconsistencies moved the Dutch CEFR constructs group away from their initial CEFR-based frames towards an investigation of test materials that had been previously assigned to a CEFR level (Alderson et al 2006). They derived from these a more detailed classification system or 'grid' for the specification of test items. However, the detailed grids for Reading and Listening (like the similar classification grids developed by ALTE for Speaking and Writing) do not directly inform decisions about text and task level. Initial estimation of task difficulty is based on a detailed analysis, assisted by the grids, and comparison of the outcomes of this analysis with the CEFR scales. Empirical confirmation (or disconfirmation) of this initial estimate comes from the performance of learners of 'known' ability.

Unfortunately, knowing the ability of the learners in relation to the CEFR requires a validated measurement instrument, leaving the researcher in a catch-22 situation. Where texts or tasks (or learner performances or Can Do statements) are assigned to a CEFR level on the basis of rater judgement and analysis of the text or task (or performance characteristics or descriptor) is then used to define the level, this inevitably invites an accusation of circularity. This is also an issue for the English Profile: the Cambridge Learner Corpus based investigation of levels for English Profile assigns learners to a level on the basis of their performance and the performances are then used as the basis for identifying the characteristics of language at that level.

Such circularity is partly an inevitable feature of any process of refinement. The analyses employed in the Grid projects and in the English Profile programme are directed towards a fuller, more elaborated picture of currently operational levels and are based on more extensive sources of data than their operational equivalents. This should in turn help to improve the consistency of judgement in operational applications. Provided that the sources of data are sufficiently diverse to represent a consensus interpretation of the levels, results should serve to better ground that consensus in relation to theory and to empirical evidence. Importantly, it should also lead to the formulation of more clearly stated, falsifiable claims about the nature of the levels which can be tested against the experiences of learners, teachers and the users of assessment results. The CEFR levels are not a closed system, but are, as Alderson et al (2006) note, open to external validation.

In the case of Can Do statements and functional descriptors, many (although by no means all) of the descriptors included in the English Profile collection (see Chapter 3) are derived from, or are influenced by the CEFR. Many different schemes have defined their levels according to the CEFR descriptions. As statements are adapted to meet the needs of different users, elements are repeated and so may appear to be more 'key' than others. Identifying these elements can provide insights into which are most robust and which seem to require clarification, as well as providing potentially helpful wording for the updated descriptors. In addition, as descriptors are taken up in different schemes, examples and other forms of elaboration are often added, serving to clarify the ways in which the statements are being interpreted.

The English Profile approach differs from that taken by the Dutch Grid (Alderson et al 2004) and ALTE Grid (ALTE 2005) developments in a number of ways. First, the categories for the proposed Can Do frame are not restricted to those available in the CEFR and are not simply derived from a content analysis of the Can Do statements in the collection, but are based on the CEFR theoretical model. Secondly, the content of the proposed statements is not restricted to the wording of CEFR descriptors, but looks beyond the CEFR to current practice in English language education more generally. This project sets out to populate the equivalent of the 'frames' by additionally interrogating functionally oriented English language learning objectives other than the CEFR. Where gaps or omissions remain, descriptions can be proposed, refined and added to the scheme to fill these.

Because the resulting Can Do statements are not drawn directly from the CEFR, a process of validation is needed to ensure that they reflect the CEFR levels as understood by language experts and by potential users. The draft statements presented here have been reviewed by over 200 English Profile partner members at seminar events and have been made available for public review and discussion on the English Profile website. Following further review and revision, a process of calibration will eventually allow these new statements to be integrated with the CEFR scheme.

The intended outcome is a set of clear and falsifiable propositions representing a consensus view of the probable relative difficulty of certain language activities performed in English to a defined standard, under given conditions. Where possible, the reliance on expert judgement is reduced and more objective measures are introduced to help users to define criterial parameters more consistently. For this purpose, a set of categories or Can Do elements is now proposed that draws on current practice, is based on the CEFR model and so might serve to more fully characterise the levels, while allowing scope for more detailed specification, elaboration and exemplification according to local needs.

The component elements proposed here for Can Do statements, which are based on the functions strand of English Profile research – and draw particularly on the collection of descriptors discussed in Chapter 3 – include the following:

Activity: Can . . .	The social act (function) or related sequence of acts (activity) that the learner might be expected to accomplish by means of the language
Theme/ Topic: Concerned with . . .	The themes, topics and settings in relation to which the learner might be expected to perform. In the CEFR, applicable themes are grouped under the four domains: educational, public, professional and personal
Input text: Based on . . .	The nature of the text that the learner might be required to process as a basis for their own contribution or to demonstrate their comprehension
Output text: Producing . . .	The nature of the text that the learner might be expected to produce or participate in producing to demonstrate (a

	specified degree of) understanding or to accomplish a task
Qualities: How well?	The qualities that the learner would be expected to demonstrate in carrying out language activities. For production, these qualities are grouped under the CEFR headings of Linguistic, Pragmatic, Sociolinguistic and Strategic competences
Restrictions: Provided that . . .	Physical or social conditions and constraints under which the learner would be expected to perform

Can Do statements that include all of these elements are intended to serve a pivotal role, linking the general statements of the CEFR to more detailed and technical definitions of the levels, as required for the English Profile. In one direction, they can be simplified to help in the process of devising new Can Do statements based on the CEFR to inform different audiences such as the task developers, assessors and users involved in a specific language learning initiative and concerned with the different informational needs envisaged by Alderson (1991). In another direction, because they address all the elements of the CEFR model, they provide a starting point for further elaboration through grids of criterial features, glosses, commentaries, sample tasks and sample performances. This process of elaboration is considered in the next chapter.

The illustrative descriptors in Appendix C employ elements, categorised according to the CEFR model, from the collection of descriptors discussed in Chapter 3 as well as innovations based on other strands of English Profile research. They are intended to fill a mediating role between the broad descriptions provided in the CEFR and the specific requirements of contextualised English language educational applications.

To exemplify the approach adopted, the following paragraphs provide a brief discussion of one Can Do descriptor: the first of the descriptors listed for *Spoken Interaction* in Appendix C. The first element of this Can Do statement, describing a functional language activity, is, '*can account for and sustain his/her opinions*'. Giving and justifying opinions is a common activity found in B2 and C level statements in many of the schemes analysed in Chapter 3 above and is associated with the academic and professional applications of English language learning that are often linked to the C levels. In these contexts, learners may need, in the course of a discussion or consultation, to be able to give opinions on issues arising in an academic discipline or on matters of specialist professional expertise, hence their opinions will be '*concerned with complex technical/abstract topics*'. In interaction, spoken input and output are in a dynamic relationship: the speaker responds to and elicits responses from other participants and co-operates with them to sustain an interaction. In such settings, language users often discuss a topic on the basis of additional input from, for example, case notes, reports or lectures, but these sources are not a prerequisite for discussion and may in any case be too diverse to specify in a general Can Do statement of this kind. For these reasons the '*Input: based on*' element of the statement is left unfilled and the '*Output text: producing*' element consists of the '*spoken interaction/ discussion*' to which the speaker contributes.

A key element of the statement concerns the quality of the performance, the 'how well' element or criteria for success. In the statements in Appendix C, this element is linked to the categories of communicative language competences in the CEFR (Council of Europe 2001, Chapter 5): linguistic competences; sociolinguistic competences and pragmatic competences. For different activities, concerned with different domains and topics, different aspects of the learner's competences are likely to prove more criterial.

In the case of accounting for and sustaining opinions, pragmatic competences are likely to be particularly important as, to be effective, speakers need to ensure that '*contributions are relevant and are integrated into the flow of the discourse*'. In accordance with the CEFR, learners may support the coherence of their contributions by '*using linking words*' or the '*repetition of words used by other participants*'. Another element derived from our collection of C level Can Do statements – '*providing relevant explanations, arguments and comments*' –also seems to be regarded as particularly pertinent in such contexts.

Linguistic qualities are also indispensable to successful discussion. It is essential, for example, that the speaker should be '*readily comprehensible*', and speakers will be more effective if intonation is used in a way that '*supports meaning*' – by, for example, adding emphasis to underline important points. Reflecting the importance of sociolinguistic considerations in conceptions of higher level language use, the speaker will also need to '*use a range of grammatical forms and vocabulary appropriate to the audience, topic and social context*' in order to convey their ideas effectively to other participants and in a style that takes account of the social relationships between speakers: '*formal*', '*informal*' or '*colloquial*' according to the context.

This proposed statement, still in draft form at this stage and as yet uncalibrated, brings together a description of performance – a language activity – broadly contextualised in relation to topic types and accompanied by criteria for judging communicative success. It is not claimed that such statements can, without further elaboration, provide a basis for the generation of numbers of fully equivalent tasks, but they should help to inform task development and the production of illustrative material: to extend the shared understanding of levels that the CEFR promotes.

This chapter has explored an alternative approach to operationalising the CEFR model of (functional) communicative language competences, casting this in the form of Can Do statements that incorporate performance, condition and criterion. The following chapter sets out how the English Profile can offer an interactive structure through which specific instances of educational practice can be guided by and related to the wider context represented by the CEFR, encouraging users to build and develop their shared understanding of the nature and limits of a common set of descriptive levels.

6 Navigating the English Profile

This volume has shown how *functions* and *activities*, as they have emerged from the Council of Europe and related work, embody an applied linguistics perspective on communicative language ability, drawing on and adapting theoretical perspectives from speech act theory, sociolinguistics and elsewhere. Section 1 explained how functions and activities are units of analysis that provide a link between the abstractions of linguistic description and the practical, context-bound tasks that learners will need to use language to accomplish. Given the role that functions and activities play in reconciling the more theoretical linguistic categories with the empirical practices of the classroom or examination hall, it is surprising that they have received relatively little focused attention from applied linguists.

There is a particular need for further consideration and elaboration of the role of *activities* in the CEFR model. One concern is that the binary distinction between productive and interactive activities is not well supported in the literature. A scale ranging from more chiefly productive to chiefly interactive activities would be a more adequate representation. The fuzziness of the distinction is well illustrated in the CEFR scales. In the *Spoken Production* scale for *Addressing Audiences*, level distinctions are made on the basis of how well the speaker interacts with the audience by responding to questions. In the *Spoken Interaction* scales for *Informal Discussion (with friends)* and *Formal Discussion and Meetings*, learners at B2 level can '*present complex lines of argument convincingly*' (Council of Europe 2001:77–78). It is not clear that the activity of 'presenting' an argument here is substantially different from '*develop an argument systematically*' in the *Spoken Production: Sustained Monologue (putting a case)* scale (Council of Europe 2001:59). The relationship between activities and other more familiar (if disputed) terms such as *discourse type*, *genre* and *text type* also needs to be more clearly elaborated.

By describing performance in terms of activities and by addressing the range of categories included in the CEFR theoretical model, it is envisaged that the Can Do statements presented in draft form in Appendix C and discussed in Chapter 5 will play a pivotal role in a flexible descriptive system for the English Profile. The CEFR (Council of Europe 2001:40) introduces such a system through the concept of an 'information pyramid' for the user, explained in the following terms:

> The user is presented with an information pyramid and can get an overview, a clear perspective, by considering the top layer of the hierarchy (here the 'global' scale). More detail can be presented – ad infinitum – by going down layers of the system, but at any one point, what is being looked at is confined to one or two screens – or pieces of paper. In this way complexity can be presented without blinding people with irrelevant detail, or simplifying to the point of banality. Detail is there – if it is required.

Although in the CEFR, the 'top layer' of the pyramid is the global scale and the 'detail' refers to the illustrative sub-scales, I would argue that this conception should be revised. The Can Do statements are all underspecified in the CEFR and providing more sub-scales does not fully satisfy the information needs of task developers or assessors: it has emerged that it is not more reconfigurations of the same Can Do statements, but additional details relating to performance criteria and contextual parameters that users most need.

As yet, no such information pyramid (which seems to be envisaged in the CEFR as a set of hyperlinked electronic resources) has been operationalised for English as a single coherent scheme, although elements have been emerging as the 'CEFR toolkit' of grids, user manuals and sample materials expands. As affirmed above, the English Profile, as it generates more CEFR-related detail, offers an opportunity to address this gap. As the English Profile progresses, each layer of the overall system should be integrated, to the extent possible, to provide complementary information, lending substance to the reference level descriptions.

This chapter considers how different elements of the English Profile programme can be brought together with existing resources to create such a system. The information pyramid should allow users to approach the descriptions from the perspective of any of the categories of the CEFR model captured in the Can Do frames described in Chapter 5 to obtain the level of detail required.

Earlier chapters have indicated that meeting the needs and expectations of users will involve the provision of a number of informational layers made up of components such as the following:

1. Illustrative Can Do statements presented in the most general terms for the user.

2. Generative Can Do statements: frames setting out how the elements of the CEFR model may interact in shaping the difficulty of defined language activities and tasks.

3. Grids of criterial features: lists of features that impact on the difficulty of the relevant language activities and estimates of how these might affect level estimates.

4. Glosses: definitions and elaborations of key words used in the reference level descriptions.

5. Commentaries: discussions of how the components of the reference level descriptions might be interpreted in relation to specified tasks.

6. Sample tasks: examples of (receptive and productive) tasks that learners at different levels might be expected to carry out, with commentary explaining how these relate to the criterial features.

7. Sample performances: examples of learner performance – recordings or scripts – illustrating the interpretation of the level descriptions.

It is becoming clear from the experience with the CEFR that a scheme of this kind cannot be expected to succeed as a static representation of English language education. It must be flexible and open to challenge, encourage debate and reflection and allow for regular revision. The English Profile will need to provide a suitable forum for these processes with ongoing systems of management and support. This provision is already beginning to take shape with the development of the English Profile website and online forum.

In accordance with the approach outlined in the CEFR, the relative difficulty of the multiple means of realising language activities must be considered both from a social perspective and from a cognitive perspective. A given activity involves, as we have seen, the activation of (cognitive) language processes, the 'many-to-many' (Hawkins & Filipović 2012) relationship between form and function opening a wide variety of choices to the user. Processing occurs 'in relation to [social] themes, in specific domains' (Council of Europe 2001:9) which introduce sets of constraints on these choices. Only by understanding the interaction between the cognitive and the social does it become possible to get an adequate fix (for objective-setting, teaching and testing purposes) on the relative demands of language learning tasks.

Chapter 4 presented some of the ways in which the characteristics of input texts can be pursued to more clearly define level differences. The work of Hawkins and Filipović (2012) based on the Cambridge Learner Corpus (CLC) shows how concrete indicators of features such as grammatical and semantic complexity and associated errors can be established from learners' writing. They suggest how criterial features in grammar and lexis can be linked with criterial features of language functions. From the user perspective, it is helpful to trace the language processes brought into play by a given task.

In the CEFR, we are presented with lists of different skills that may be engaged in processing the language needed to carry out a task (Figure 17). Language processing models, like Weir's (2005b) socio-cognitive model, suggest that different tasks will call on the learner's language skills to differing degrees and in different combinations. Communicative purpose, affected by contextual variables, impacts on the nature of the processing that occurs.

Figure 17 Language processes in the CEFR (Council of Europe 2001:90–92)

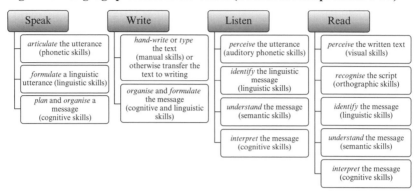

Shaw and Weir (2007) and Khalifa and Weir (2009) identify the higher levels of the CEFR with an increasing role for the semantic and cognitive skills, while perception, recognition and linguistic skills become more automatic with progression through the CEFR.

When reading a text, higher level learners are able to process the input more quickly (committing fewer cognitive resources to recognition and linguistic processing). In arriving with relative ease at an understanding of the message of the text, such learners have sufficient resources in reserve to be able to interpret and evaluate this message in relation to their prior knowledge or to the content of other texts. Learners with more limited competence may recognise the language and even understand it linguistically, but this requires so much of their cognitive resource that without additional support they may struggle to form a coherent representation of the text as a whole.

All else being equal, tasks that require retrieval of individual words (such as expeditious local reading or scanning tasks) are likely to prove easier than tasks requiring understanding of individual sentences (careful local reading). These in turn are likely to prove easier than tasks that require a detailed understanding of a text as a whole (careful global reading) or those that require integration of information from multiple texts (Khalifa & Weir, 2009). From this point of view, it should be possible to identify the language processing demands made by different tasks and to estimate the potential impact of these demands on the learner.

Taking a socio-contextual category, it is equally possible to approach the description from the standpoint of topics and themes, navigating through the information pyramid from the more general information provided in the CEFR to access layers of increasing detail. In the figures that follow, the boxes that are shaped as arrows indicate that this is a strand to be explored further in the following sections; just as a hypertext link is followed in navigating from one screen to the next. Figure 19 and Figure 20 expand on the personal domain in Figure 18. Figure 21 expands on Figure 20.

In the CEFR, each domain is associated with certain themes or 'topics which are the subjects of discourse, conversation, reflection or composition'

Figure 18 Domains in the CEFR (Council of Europe 2001:45)

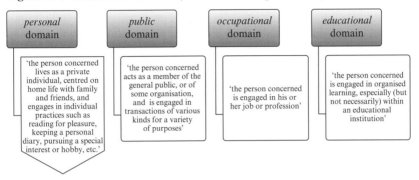

(Council of Europe 2001 p.51). For each domain, these themes are organised around seven categories: *locations, institutions, persons, objects, events, operations* and *texts*. The personal domain, following the strand we have taken as an example, has the following (Figure 19 and Figure 20):

Moving beyond the CEFR, each theme might be pursued further to produce a set of topic-related 'specific notions.' Both the T-series vocabulary

Figure 19 Locations, institutions and persons in the personal domain in the CEFR (Council of Europe 2001:48–49)

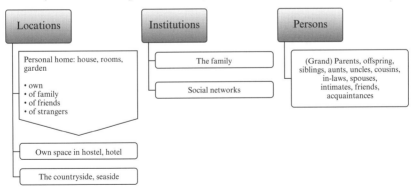

lists and the English Profile Wordlists (Capel 2010) can be explored through semantic categories (as well as from different perspectives). The system of

Figure 20 Objects, events, operations and texts in the personal domain in the CEFR (Council of Europe 2001:48–49)

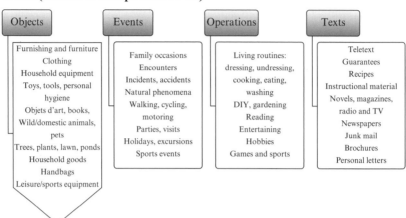

categorisation used in the English Profile lists differs both from that used in the T-series and from that used in the CEFR, but it would certainly improve the coherence of the overall scheme for the CEFR user if the systems of classification could be reconciled.

The English Profile Wordlists (Capel 2010) provide a guide to common words and phrases that learners of English might typically be expected to know at different CEFR levels. Individual meanings of each word or phrase on the lists are assigned a level between A1 and B2 on the CEFR scale. The appropriate level for each word sense is determined with reference to the CLC and evidence of use from other sources, such as examination word lists and classroom materials. Because of the differences of classification mentioned above, it is not possible to pursue the *house/home* theme from the CEFR directly into the EP Wordlists, but the Wordlist theme of 'buildings' is closely related and identifies the following words at each CEFR level (note that the lists for the C levels are still in development).

As illustrated by the entry for *door* in Figure 21, the Wordlists are supported by lexicographic information, including a simple definition, dictionary examples and, where available, a learner example taken from the Cambridge Learner Corpus. Wherever possible, learner examples are chosen at the same CEFR level, though the relatively small amount of data at A1 does not always allow this.

By attributing a CEFR level to each sense of a word or phrase, the English Profile Wordlists provide detailed analysis for syllabus designers, examination setters and other language teaching professionals in the areas of polysemous words, phrases and collocations, phrasal verbs, word families and (for the C levels in development) idioms. Further information on the Wordlists can be found on the English Profile website (www.english profile.org).

Just as the user may navigate from the CEFR domains via themes and topics to listings of specific words associated with each of the CEFR levels (Figure 21), links can also be made between the CEFR and the T-series specifications, although again there is scope for making these more direct and explicit for the user. The theme of *personal house/home* in the CEFR is reflected in the *house and home, environment* theme in *Vantage* (van Ek and Trim 2001:74). This theme introduces a number of related Can Do statements involving tasks based around the function of *describing* (Figure 22).

The grammatical resources that learners might be expected to draw on in realising these tasks can be traced in the listing of functions and linguistic exponents. *Describing* is linked in the T-series with *identifying* and *reporting* under the functional heading of *imparting and seeking information* (van Ek and Trim 2001:29). Examples of grammatical exponents, exemplifying the progression in these for the functions of *identifying (and specifying)* and *(stating and) reporting* are shown in Table 38 for the *Breakthrough* (A2) and *Vantage* (B2 and above) levels.

The work of Hawkins and Filipović (2012), informed by the Cambridge Learner Corpus (CLC), serves as a check on the progression in general notions and associated grammatical patterns mooted in the T-series. They note the importance of lexical triggers for grammatical patterns, but with this proviso generally find the T-series predictions are borne out by evidence from the learner data:

> Some of [van Ek and Trim's] proposed properties for *Waystage,* *Threshold* and *Vantage* matched our searches perfectly. For example, reflexive and emphatic pronouns (myself, etc) are indeed present at B1, and appear to be transitional for, i.e. acquired at, this level. So are indefinite determiners used for frequency or measure such as once a day or two pounds a kilo (Hawkins and Filipović 2012).

On the other hand, some discrepancies have emerged. 'Subject-to-Subject Raising' (e.g. *John is likely to pass the exam*) is a pattern in which the subject of the subordinate clause (*John* in the example) has been 'raised' out of the subordinate clause and placed into the subject position of the main clause. Here *John* is the logical subject of *passing the exam* and it is this event, rather than *John* himself, that is claimed to be *likely* (Hawkins & Filipović 2012 Chapter 7). Van Ek and Trim (1991) introduce such patterns in the Threshold level (B1) specification, but the learner data from the CLC suggested that it is more closely associated with B2. However, this example also highlights the important role played by lexical triggers. It was found that 'simpler and more frequent verbs appear in this frame at B1 (e.g. *seems* as in Monika seems to be

Figure 21 English Profile Wordlist entries for 'Buildings' (www.englishprofile. org)

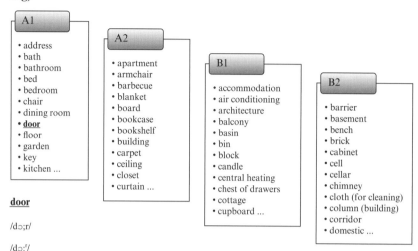

door

/dɔ;r/

/dɔːʳ/

> NOUN [C]

door ◀)) /dɔːʳ/   Outline view

► NOUN [C]

A1 a flat object, often fixed at one edge, that is used to close the entrance of something such as a room or building, or the entrance itself
Dictionary examples:
*the **front** door*
*the **back** door*
a car door
a sliding door
*The door **to** his bedroom was locked.*
*We could hear someone knocking **at/on** the door.*
*Could you **open/close/shut** the door, please?*
*She asked me to **answer** the door.*

> • **Learner example:**
> *There is a garden [outside the] back door but [it] isn't big.*
> *Skills for Life (Entry 1); A1; Thai*

behind closed doors

C2 privately and not in public
Dictionary example:
Most of the deals were done behind closed doors.

> • **Learner example:**
> *Decisions which affect the whole world are made behind closed doors and are top secret.*
> *Certificate of Proficiency in English; C2; Russian*

Figure 22 The theme of house, home and environment in *Vantage* (van Ek and Trim 2001:123–125)

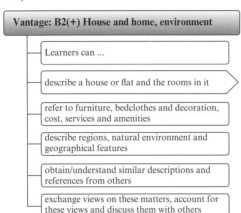

[a] good, intelligent teacher)' while the verb 'chance' (*I chanced to know about your competition*) was only found in raising constructions at C1 (Hawkins and Filipović 2012).

An advantage of this corpus-based approach is that it allows the researchers to trace typical errors made by learners at each CEFR level, taking into account intervening variables such as the first language of the learner. As this work progresses, incorporating more evidence from the spoken language and from non-test settings, the T-series can be revisited and updated in the light of the available data.

While it is already possible to pursue domains, themes and topics in the ways outlined above, the contribution of the English Profile will be to bring together the available information in a more accessible and integrated form, to incorporate emerging findings and to provide a forum for debate on their implications.

To help build the consensus around the levels, it would no doubt be helpful for users to see additional material, such as more extended examples of learner production related to themes of this kind, and to share comments on how these relate to aspects of the level descriptions. The English Profile data collection process (Salamoura 2008) involves gathering performance data from learners carrying out a wide range of tasks under a wide variety of conditions. This could form the kernel of an extensive and constantly growing library of sample performances that might serve a range of purposes including familiarisation with the levels and the categories of description, communication between stakeholders working in different contexts and with

Table 38 *Identifying (and reporting)* in *Breakthrough* (Trim 2009:20) and *Vantage* (van Ek and Trim 2000,:29)

Breakthrough	Vantage
1.1 identifying (with pointing gesture)	**1.1 identifying and specifying** (with indicating gesture, e.g. pointing, nodding)
(an object) *this one, that one, these, those* (a person) *me, you, him, her, us, them*	(an object) *this (one)/that (one)/these/ those* (a person) *me/you/him/her/us/them* *the* (adj) *one* + adjunct phrase/relative clause
(where pointing impossible) (a person) *It + BE + me/you/him/her/ us/them.* (a person or object) *It + BE* + NP (noun phrase)	*It's me you/him/her/us/them/*NP Pronoun/NP + *BE* +NP
Examples This is the key. It is John's garden.	**Examples** The small one with the blue curtains. Her office is at the end of the corridor on your left. This is the largest bedroom in the house.
1.2 reporting (describing and narrating) declarative sentences within the learner's grammatical and lexical competences (**see 9.2.1**) N.B. This limitation applies wherever *declarative sentence* is specified.	**1.2 stating and reporting (describing, narrating)** (sequences of) declarative sentences NP+ say, think + complement clause NP+ ask/wonder + indirect question there + be +NP + adjunct
	Examples The train has left. He says the shop is shut. He asked where they were going. There is a bank on the corner. There is a cow in our garden eating the plants.

different populations of learners as well as supporting ongoing research into learner language.

Other elements in the CEFR model are not as well covered in existing materials as themes and topics and there is scope for more pioneering work. The 'conditions and constraints' (Figure 23) listed in the CEFR is one such area. These include *physical* and *social conditions* together with *time* and *other* (*financial* and *anxiety-producing*) *pressures*. While there is research available that addresses the impact of features such as preparation time or numbers of interlocutors on performance on certain kinds of task (typically test tasks in which these can be more easily controlled), this has served to indicate just how complex such issues can be (see for example Skehan and Foster 1997). More information on the impact of a range of contextual variables on performance is urgently needed and the English Profile should act as a spur to further research in this area.

The work now facing the English Profile thus includes three key areas of activity:

The first involves continuing basic research into the nature of criterial differences between learners at distinct levels of functional language ability. Taking the CEFR theoretical model as its point of departure, this research is directed towards identifying the criterial differences in the language that learners are able to produce or to process receptively under defined conditions. Both the scope of the research and the evidence base for this research will continue to expand and new insights into the nature of the levels will come into view.

Second, an accessible and practical information pyramid must:

a) be assembled, by bringing together the available material in a way that will facilitate the work of English language educators, and

b) be expanded and refined over time by incorporating emerging findings and insights from the research programme.

Third, the success of the programme will depend on effective dissemination and on the engagement of a multitude of partners. Co-operation and collaboration are cornerstones of the CEFR, but it is recognised that 'a major educational effort is needed to convert . . . diversity from a barrier to communication into a source of mutual enrichment and understanding' (Council of Europe 2001:2). The English Profile can promote diversity and mutual understanding by encouraging users to actively participate in advancing, questioning and exchanging ideas and by providing a welcoming space for this to happen.

Conclusions: functional progression

The Common European Framework of Reference takes a functional view of communicative language ability. The concern is with what learners can (or might wish to) *do* in making use of their linguistic resources as social actors. It might therefore be expected that progression through the levels could be expressed purely in terms of language functions: the learner can *greet* at A1, but cannot *predict* until he or she reaches B1. However, as discussed in Chapters 1 and 2, when reading the CEFR and related Council of Europe publications it is soon apparent that such a literal interpretation of functional progression is not tenable. The objectives are intended to provide learners with the widest possible functional repertoire based on even the most limited linguistic resources. When seeking assistance, the need is the same for the *Breakthrough* (A1) learner as it is for the *Vantage* (B2 and higher) learner, but where the *Breakthrough* learner might be restricted to learning 'Help!' or 'Can you help me, please?' (Trim 2009:8) the *Vantage* learner is working towards a wider range of linguistic resources to indicate different levels of politeness,

Figure 23 Conditions and constraints listed in the CEFR (Council of Europe 2001:46–7)

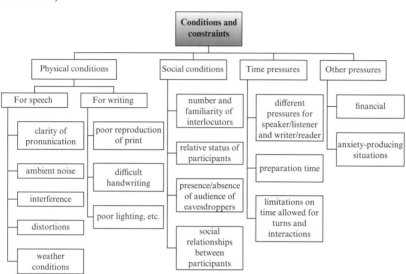

formality or urgency and this introduces new choices of expression: 'Could you help me, please?' 'Do you think you could give/lend me a hand?' (van Ek & Trim 2001:47). Illustrating how the CLC can offer a new perspective on the T-series, it is interesting to note that while 'give me a hand' is found in the CLC in the writing of B2 level learners, 'lend me a hand' is not found below C2.

In the T-series, with progression through the levels, the target functions generally remain the same; the pools of grammatical and lexical exponents expand (see also Hawkins and Filipović 2012, Chapter 9, for an illustration of lexico-grammatical progression from A1–C2). While there are some linguistic restrictions on the functions that can be expressed at the lower levels, these are limited in number. Hypothesising, for example, is associated with the B2 level (Council of Europe 2001:77), because it entails the use of complex syntax. However, as learners acquire a range of linguistic means to express them-selves, sociolinguistic and pragmatic considerations become increasingly prominent. At *Breakthrough*, the objective is simply to *express agreement with a statement*; at *Vantage* it is to *express strong agreement*, to *express reluctant agreement*, to *express reservations*, to *concede a point* or to *demur* (Appendix B). Another feature of this widening repertoire would seem to be the greater use of indirect functions at higher levels.

As learner language becomes more complex, so functions increasingly tend to be modified or combine together to form larger units. Paralleling the progression from isolated sentences and utterances to extended texts in the CEFR, there is a recognisable development from unconnected functions to coherent sequences of social acts: activities and genres. If there is little progression in the T-series in terms of functions, there is more to be found in macrofunctions or activities: exchanging information is particularly identified with A2; conversation, explanation and discussion with B1; argument and negotiation with B2; gaining the floor and sequencing ideas with C1. These areas will be focused on in future research as the English Profile expands in scope.

It was noted in Chapter 2 that there is potential for confusion in the CEFR concerning whether level distinctions can be made purely on the basis of qualitative criteria or whether contextual elements are also important. This can be seen very clearly in a comparison between the *self assessment grid* on pages 26 to 27 and the scale for *qualitative aspects of spoken language use* on pages 28 to 29. The *qualitative aspects* are presented in the form of a scale for rating learners that is independent of task. If a learner '*shows great flexibility reformulating ideas in differing linguistic forms to convey finer shades of meaning precisely*' he or she is rated as C2 for *Range*. If he or she '*uses some simple structures correctly, but still systematically makes basic mistakes*' the rating is B1 for *Accuracy*. The assumption appears to be that the same procedures can be used to establish that a learner is 'at' the A1 or A2 level as can be used to establish that they are at C2: the distinction lies in the quality of the performance. In the self-assessment grid, in contrast, the tasks and activities that learners engage in are given prominence. At A2, learners are able to communicate in '*simple and routine tasks*' and in '*very short social exchanges*' (p.27); at C2, they can '*present a clear, smoothly flowing description or argument*' (p.26). Here, C2 is functionally distinct from A2: learners at the higher level carry out tasks that are more demanding (both linguistically and cognitively). An A2 level task would not seem to provide an adequate basis for identifying a C2 level learner (and *vice versa*).

The English Profile recognises the intricacy of the relationships between form and function and the need to take task characteristics into account when considering learner language. Contextual variables such as the time available for processing, the relationships between interlocutors and the familiarity of the topic can have a strong impact on the language that learners are able to produce. Equally, the social nature of any task affects what linguistic performance might be considered minimally adequate. These are strong arguments in favour of extending our shared understanding of what the CEFR levels imply, taking conditions and criteria more fully into account. The draft Can Do statements in Appendix C are intended to begin this process and the recommendations on the information pyramid above suggest ways of carrying it forward.

A rich conception of level descriptions also implies recognition that there are limitations on the precision with which a broad, multi-purpose framework can be expected to represent shared standards. There is little reason to believe (and many reasons to doubt) that because two educational systems, tests or sets of materials are aligned to the same level of the framework, that they will be equivalent. An adequate account of the comparability between two measures of language ability can only be obtained through direct comparison between them in terms of construct, content, scoring and use – not on the basis that both make a well-supported claim to represent the same CEFR level.

One issue that is highlighted by the exploration of the C levels concerns the interpretation of C2 as the highest level of the scheme. It is explicitly the intention that C2 should represent a realistic target: not 'native-speaker or near native-speaker competence', but the language abilities of 'highly successful learners' (Council of Europe 2001:36). North (2007b) has begun to explore possible descriptions of D1 and D2 levels beyond C2 to represent the 'ambilingual proficiency' (Wilkins 1978) of language professionals and bilinguals. In spite of this, the textual analysis in Chapter 4 draws attention to the tendency (perhaps a by-product of the scaling method employed) for descriptors at the highest levels to portray an aspirational ideal of unconstrained ability. It is clear that in tests of reading skills targeting the C2 level, test takers do not have scope to demonstrate that they can 'read with ease virtually all forms of the written language' (p.69). It also seems questionable whether any language user could honestly endorse the statements that they have 'no difficulty in understanding any kind of spoken language' (however 'familiar with the accent' they may be) (p.66), that they can 'take part effortlessly in any conversation or discussion' (p.27) or even that they are able to give 'often memorable descriptions' (p.59). This raises questions about the extent to which any qualification can claim to represent the C2 level as currently characterised. It will be interesting to see whether new Can Do descriptors for English Profile can be calibrated at C2 level, but nonetheless represent attainable targets for learners.

In revisiting communicative language functions after almost 40 years, this volume has traced their provenance in the literature and in the Council of Europe projects and has found them now firmly established in language learning materials in use across the globe, often embedded in Can Do statements. They are evidently still highly valued by language educators because they so elegantly link learning materials to the fundamental communicative motivation for language learning. The social use of language has been fundamental to the Council of Europe modern languages projects since the first and reflects the priority given to language learners and their needs. The work of the English Profile is still in its earliest stages, but substantial empirical evidence is already emerging on features of the language that learners adjudged to perform at different levels of the framework are able to process and to produce. Full integration with the pedagogic imperatives of the CEFR will require detailed attention to the implications of these features for what learners are able to achieve with their linguistic resources.

It is worth stressing again that the work on the projects described here is ongoing and more is needed on language functions, activities and Can Do statements as well as on the linguistic competences addressed by Hawkins and Filipović (2012). The English Profile is already expanding into new territory with research into spoken production and interaction, but many areas of the communicative competence model informing the CEFR remain to be explored. In particular, the work described in this volume has pointed to the pivotal role played by *texts* in defining levels for educators. This implies a particular need for attention to discourse competence, where the 'bottom-up' – the microlevel elements of the lexico-grammar – intersects with the 'top-down' – the macrolevel elements of communicative intent and sociocultural context 'to express attitudes and messages, and to create texts' (Celce-Murcia, Dörnyei and Thurrell 1995:13).

Finally, the CEFR is regarded here as a shared resource that has to be adapted to suit the needs of users. Rather than simply accepting the CEFR as it stands as authoritative and attempting to 'implement' it for the English language, this volume has suggested ways in which the English Profile may profit by refining, supplementing and challenging the framework, perhaps contributing to its further development. Equally, it is suggested that the English Profile itself will succeed to the extent that it becomes a resource for the sharing of ideas and a site for informed debate and engagement. It is to be hoped that this book will encourage researchers and teachers to join the collective endeavour of English Profile, to engage in related research and to contribute to the development of useful tools to support English language learning.

References and further reading

Alderson, J C (1991) Bands and scores, in Alderson, J C and North, B J (Eds) *Language Testing in the 1990s: The Communicative Legacy,* London: Modern English Publications and The British Council, 71–86.

Alderson, J C (1996) The testing of reading, in Nuttall, C, *Teaching Reading in a Foreign Language,* London: Heinemann, 212–228.

Alderson, J C (2004) *Waystage and Threshold: Or Does the Emperor Have Any Clothes?,* Unpublished manuscript.

Alderson, J C (2007) The CEFR and the need for more research, *Modern Language Journal* 91(4), 659–663.

Alderson, J C (Ed.) (2002) *Common European Framework of Reference for Languages: Learning, Teaching, Assessment: Case Studies,* Strasbourg: Council of Europe.

Alderson, J C and North, B (Eds) (1991) *Language Testing In The 1990s,* London: Modern English Publications and the British Council.

Alderson, J C, Figueras, N, Kuijper, H, Nold, G, Takala, S and Tardieu, C (2004) *The Development of Specifications for Item Development and Classification within the Common European Framework of Reference for Languages: Learning, Teaching, Assessment: Reading and Listening, Final Report of the Dutch CEFR Construct Project,* Unpublished document.

Alderson, J C, Figueras, N, Kuijper, H, Nold, G, Takala, S, and Tardieu, C (2006) Analysing tests of reading and listening in relation to the Common European Framework of Reference: The experience of the Dutch CEFR Construct Project, *Language Assessment Quarterly* 3 (1), 3–30.

Alderson, J C and Huhta, A (2005) The development of a suite of computer based diagnosis tests based on the Common European Framework, *Language Testing* 22 (3), 301–320.

Alexander, L G (1967) *New Concept English,* London: Longman.

ALTE - Association of Language Testers in Europe (2005) *CEFR Grid for the Analysis of Speaking Tasks (report), Version 2.0, prepared by ALTE members,* retrieved 22 February 2009 from http://www.coe.int/T/DG4/Portfolio/documents/ALTE CEFR Speaking Grid OUTput51.pdf

American Council on the Teaching of Foreign Languages (1986) *ACTFL Proficiency Guidelines,* Hastings-on-Hudson: ACTFL.

Applied Linguistics (1983) Special Edition: Papers from the first colloquium of the Cross-Cultural Speech Act Realization Project (CCSARP), *Applied Linguistics* 4 (2).

Austin, J (1962) *How To Do Things With Words,* Oxford: Oxford University Press.

Bachman, L F (1990) *Fundamental Considerations in Language Testing,* Oxford: Oxford University Press.

Bachman, L F and Savignon, S (1986) The evaluation of communicative language proficiency: A Critique of the ACTFL Oral Interview, *Modern Language Journal* 70, 380–90.

Bachman, L F, Davidson, Ryan, K and Inn-Chull Choi (1995) *An Investigation*

Into The Comparability of Two Tests of English as a Foreign Language, Cambridge: Cambridge University Press.

Bachman, L F and Palmer, A S (1996). *Language Testing in Practice: Designing and Developing Useful Language Tests*, Oxford: Oxford University Press.

Baldiger, M, Müller, M and Schneider, G in Zusammenarbeit mit A Neff (1980) *Kontaktschwelle: Deutsch als Fremdsprache*, Berlin, Langenscheidt.

Bardovi-Harlig, K and Hartford, B S (1993b) Refining the DCT: Comparing open questionnaires and dialogue completion tasks, *Pragmatics and Language Learning* 4, 143–165.

Bardovi-Harlig, K (2001) Evaluating the empirical evidence: Grounds for instruction in pragmatics? In Rose, K and Kasper, G (Eds), *Pragmatics in Language Teaching*, Cambridge: Cambridge University Press, 13–32.

Bardovi-Harlig, K, and Hartford, B S (1993a) Learning the rules of academic talk: A longitudinal study of pragmatic development, *Studies in Second Language Acquisition* 15, 279–304.

Bardovi-Harlig, K and Hartford, B S (2005). Practical considerations, In Bardovi-Harlig, K and Hartford, B S (Eds), *Interlanguage pragmatics: Exploring institutional talk*, Mahwah, NJ: Erlbaum, 201–221.

Bausch, K, Christ, H and Königs, F and Krumm, H (Eds) (2002) *Der Gemeinsame Europäische Referenzrahmen für Sprachen in der Diskussion*, *Arbeitspapiere der 22*, Frühjahrskonferenz zur Erforschung des Fremdsprachenunterrichts, Tübingen: Gunter Narr.

Block, J H (Ed.) (1971) *Mastery Learning: Theory and Practice*, New York: Holt, Rinehart and Winston.

Bloom, B S (1968) Learning for mastery, *Evaluation Comment (UCLA-CSIEP)* 1(2), 1–12.

Bloomfield, L (1933) *Language*, New York: Holt, Rhinehart, Winston.

Blum-Kulka, S and Olshtain, E (1986) Too many words: Length of utterance and pragmatic failure, *Studies in Second Language Acquisition* 8, 47–61.

Blum-Kulka, S, Kasper, G and House, J (Eds) (1989) *Cross-Cultural Pragmatics: Requests and Apologies*, Norwood, NJ: Ablex.

Bonnet, G (2007) The CEFR and education policies in Europe, *Modern Language Journal* 91(4), 669–672.

Bormuth, J R (1969) *Development of readability analyses*, Final Report, Project No. 7–0052, Contract No. 1, OEC-3–7–070052–0326, Washington, DC: U.S. Office of Education.

Breen, M P and Candlin, C (1980) The essentials of a communicative curriculum in language teaching, *Applied Linguistics* 1 (2), 89–112.

Brindley, G (1998) Outcomes-based assessment and reporting in language learning programs: a review of the issues, *Language Testing* 15 (1), 45–85.

Brindley, G (2001) Implementing outcomes-based assessment: some examples and emerging insights, *Language Testing* 18 (4), 393–407.

Brown, H D (2007) *Teaching by Principles: An Interactive Approach to Language Pedagogy*, Pearson ESL.

Brown, J D (1997) An EFL readability index, *University of Hawaii Working Papers in English as a Second Language* 15 (2), 85–119.

Brown, P and Levinson, S (1987) *Politeness: Some Universals in Language Usage*, Cambridge: Cambridge University Press.

Brumfit, C J (Ed.) (1984) *General English Syllabus Design*, Oxford: Pergamon.

Bühler, K (1990) *Theory of Language: The Representational Function of Language*. Amsterdam, John Benjamins (First published 1934).

Bung, K, (1973) *The Specification of Objectives in a Language Learning System for Adults*, Strasbourg, Council of Europe.

Cambridge Assessment (2007) *Cambridge Assessment Annual Review 2005–2006*, available from http://www.cambridgeassessment.org.uk

Cambridge University Press (1999) *Cambridge English Readers Teachers Guide*, Cambridge: Cambridge University Press.

Canale, M (1983) From communicative competence to communicative language pedagogy, in Richards, J and Schmidt, R (Eds) *Language and Communication*, London: Longman.

Canale, M and Swain, M (1980) Theoretical bases of communicative approaches to second language teaching, *Applied Linguistics* 1(1), 1–47.

Candlin, C, Bruton, J, and Coleman, H (1980) *Dentist-patient communication skills*, University of Lancaster.

Capel, A (2010) A1–B2 vocabulary: insights and issues arising from the English Profile Wordlists project, *English Profile Journal* 1(1), e3.

Carroll, B J (1992) The ESU Framework, in North (Ed.) *Transparency and Coherence in Language Learning in Europe: Objectives, Assessment and Certification, proceedings of the intergovernmental Symposium held at Rüschlikon, November 1991*, Strasbourg: Council for Cultural Cooperation.

Carroll, B J and West, R (1989) *ESU Framework: performance scales for English language examinations*, Harlow: Longman.

Carroll, J B (1963) A model of school learning, *Teachers College Record* 64, 723–733.

Carroll, J B (1971) Problems of measurement related to the concept of learning for mastery, In Block, J H (Ed.) *Mastery Learning: Theory and Practice*, New York: Holt,Rinehart and Winston, 29–46.

Celce-Murcia, M, Dornyei, Z and Thurrell, S (1995) Communicative Competence: A pedagogically motivated model with content specifications, *Issues in Applied Linguistics* 6 (2), 5–35.

Chalhoub-Deville, M (1997) Theoretical models, assessment frameworks and test Construction, *Language Testing* 14 (1), 3–22.

Chiba, M (2002) *Learning To Request in a Second Language: Child Interlanguage Pragmatics*, Clevedon: Multilingual Matters.

Chihara, T, Sakurai, T, and Oller, J (1989). Background and culture as factors in EFL reading comprehension, *Language Testing* 6 (2), 143–151.

Cizek, G J and Bunch, M (2007) *Standard Setting: A Practitioner's Guide*, Newbury Park, CA: Sage.

Clapham, C (1996) *The development of IELTS: A Study in the Effect of Background Knowledge on Reading Comprehension*, Studies in Language Testing volume 6, Cambridge: Cambridge University Press.

Clark, J and Clifford, R (1988) The FSI/ILR/ACTFL Proficiency Scales and Testing Techniques: Development, Current Status, and Needed Research, *Studies in Second Language Acquisition* 10 (2), 129–147.

Cobb, T (2007) *The Compleat Lexical Tutor*, available from http://www.lextutor.ca

Coh-metrix (n.d. online) *Coh-Metrix version 2.0 indices*, retrieved from http://cohmetrix.memphis.edu, 4 September 2010.

Coltheart, M (1981) The MRC psycholinguistic database quarterly, *Journal of Experimental Psychology* 33A, 497–505.

Committee for Out-of-school Education and Cultural Development (1971) *Linguistic content, means of evaluation and their interaction in the teaching and learning of modern languages in adult education*, Report of a symposium organised at Rüschlikon, Switzerland, 3–7 May 1971, Strasbourg, Council of Europe.

Cook, G (1989) *Discourse*, Oxford: Oxford University Press.

Coste, D, Courtillon, J, Ferenczi, V, Martins-Baltar, M. and Pape, E (1976) *Un niveau-seuil*, Paris: Hatier.

Council of Europe (1970) *Recommendation 611: On permanent education in Europe*, Strasbourg: Parliamentary Assembly

Council of Europe (1973) *Permanent Education: The Basis and Essentials*, Strasbourg: Council for Cultural Cooperation.

Council of Europe (1982) Recommendation no. R(82)18 of the Committee of Ministers to member States concerning modern languages, in Girard, D and Trim, J LM (Eds) (1998) *Project no.12 'Learning and teaching modern languages for communication': Final Report of the Project Group (activities 1982-87)*, Strasbourg:Council of Europe.

Council of Europe (1988) *Learning and teaching modern languages for Communication*, final report of the Project Group, Strasbourg.

Council of Europe (1998) *Recommendation no. R(98)6 of the Committee of Ministers to member States concerning modem languages*, Strasbourg: Council of Europe.

Council of Europe (2001) *Common European Framework of Reference for Languages: Learning, Teaching, Assessment*, Cambridge: Cambridge University Press.

Council of Europe (2005) *Draft Guide for the Production of RLD: Version 2*, Strasbourg: Language Policy Division.

Council of Europe (2009) *Relating Language Examinations to the Common European Framework of Reference for Languages: Learning, Teaching, Assessment (CEFR): A Manual*, Strasbourg: Language Policy Division.

Council of Europe. (2009) *Relating Language Examinations to the Common European Framework of Reference*, Strasbourg: Council of Europe.

Crossey, M (2009) The role of micropolitics in multinational, high-stakes language assessment systems, in Alderson, J C (Ed.) *The Politics of Language Education: Individuals and Institutions*, Bristol: Multilingual Matters, 147–164.

Crossley, S A, Greenfield, J, and McNamara, D S (2008) Assessing text readability using cognitively based indices, *TESOL Quarterly* 42 (3), 475–493.

Crystal, D (2003) *English as a Global Language*, Cambridge: Cambridge University Press.

Cummins, J (1979) Cognitive/academic language proficiency, linguistic interdependence, the optimum age question and some other matters, *Working Papers on Bilingualism* 19, 121–129.

de Jong, J H A L (2004) *Comparing the psycholinguistic and the communicative paradigm of language proficiency*, presentation given at the international workshop Psycholinguistic and psychometric aspects of language assessment in the Common European Framework of Reference for Languages, 13–14 February, University of Amsterdam.

de Jong, J H A L (2009) *Unwarranted claims about CEF alignment of some international English language tests*, paper presented at the Sixth Annual Conference of EALTA, 5 June, Turku, Finland.

Dunlea, J and Matsudaira, T (2009) Investigating the relationship between the EIKEN tests and the CEFR, in Figueras, N and Noijons, J (Eds), *Linking to the CEFR levels: Research Perspectives*, Arnhem: CITO/EALTA.

Eckersley, C (1955) *Essential English for Foreign Students*, London: Longmans, Green & Co.

Ehrlich, M F (1991) The processing of cohesion devices in text comprehension, *Psychological Research* 53 (2), 169–174.

Ellis, R (1992) Learning to communicate in the classroom: A study of two learners' requests, *Studies in Second Language Acquisition* 14, 1–23.

Enright, M, Grabe, W, Koda, K, Mosenthal, P, Mulcahy-Ernt, P, & Schedl, M (2000) *TOEFL 2000 Reading Framework: A working paper*, TOEFL Monograph Series 17, Princeton, NJ: ETS.

Faucett, L (1933) *The Oxford English Course*, London: Oxford University Press.

Faucett, L, Palmer, H, Thorndike, West, M (1936) Interim report on vocabulary selection for the teaching of English as a Foreign Language, in Smith, R (Ed) (2003) *Teaching English as a Foreign Language,1912–1936: Pioneers of ELT*, London: King CELTE.

Feldt, L S, and Brennan, R L (1989) Reliability, in Linn, R L (Ed.), *Educational Measurement*, New York: Macmillan, 105–146.

Fellbaum, C (Ed.) (1998) *WordNet: An Electronic Lexical Database*, Cambridge, MA: MIT Press.

Figueras, N and Noijons, J (Eds) (2009) *Linking to the CEFR levels: Research Perspectives*, Arnhem: Cito/EALTA.

Firth, J (1957) *Papers in Linguistics 1934–1951*, London: Oxford University Press.

Flowerdew, J (1990) Problems of Speech Act Theory from an applied Perspective, *Language Learning* 40 (1), 79–105.

Fortus, R, Coriat, R, and Fund, S (1998) Prediction of item difficulty in the English subtest of Israel's inter-university psychometric entrance test, in Kunnan, A J (Ed.), *Validation in language assessment: Selected papers from the 17th Language Research Colloquium, Long Beach*, Mahwah, NJ: Lawrence Erlbaum, 61-87.

Freedle, R and Kostin, I (1993) *The prediction of TOEFL reading comprehension item difficulty for expository prose passages for three item types: Main idea, inference, and supporting idea items*, TOEFL Research Reports No. RR-93–44. Princeton, NJ: Educational Testing Service.

Fulcher, G and Davidson, F (2007) The Common European Framework of Reference (CEFR) and the design of language tests: A matter of effect, *Language Teacher* 40, 231–241.

Garfinkel, H (1974) On the Origins of the Term 'Ethnomethodology', in Turner, R (Ed.), *Ethnomethodology*, Penguin, 15–18.

Girard, D and Trim, J (Eds) (1998) *Project no.12 'Learning and teaching modern languages for communication'*, final report of the Project Group (activities 1982–87), Strasbourg, Council of Europe.

Glaboniat, M, Müller, M, Rusch, P, Schmitz, H, and Wertenschlag, L (2005) *Profile DeutschVersion 2.0. Levels A1 to C2*, Berlin: Langenscheidt.

Goffman, E (1974) *Frame Analysis*, Cambridge: Harvard University Press.

Golato, A (2003) Studying compliment responses: A comparison of DCTs and recordings of naturally occurring talk, *Applied Linguistics* 24 (1), 90–121.

Goldman, S R and Rakestraw, J A (2000) Structural aspects of constructing meaning from text, in Kamil, M L, Mosenthal, P B, Pearson, P D and Barr, R (Eds), *Handbook of Reading Research, Vol. II*, Mahwah, NJ: Erlbaum, 311-335.

Greenfield, J (2004) Readability Formulas for EFL, *JALT Journal* 26 (1), 5–24.

Grice, H (1975) Logic and conversation, in Cole, P and Morgan, J (Eds) *Syntax and Semantics, Vol 9: Pragmatics*. New York: Academic Press.

Halliday, M (1970) The form of a functional grammar, in Kress, G (Ed) (1976), *Halliday: System and Function in Language,* London: Oxford University Press, London.

Halliday, M (1985) *An Introduction To Functional Grammar*, London: Edward Arnold.

Hassall, T J (1997) *Requests by Australian Learners of Indonesian*, unpublished doctoral dissertation, Australian National University, Canberra.

Hasselgreen, A (2003) *Bergen ' Can Do' Project*, European Centre for Modern Languages.

Hawkins, J A and Filipović, L (2012) *Criterial features in L2 English: Specifying the Reference Levels of the Common European Framework*, English Profile Studies volume 1, Cambridge: UCLES/Cambridge University Press.

Heatley, A, Nation, I S P, and Coxhead, A (2002) *RANGE and FREQUENCY Programs*, available from http://www.vuw.ac.nz/lals/staff /Paul_Nation.

Herzog (n.d.) *An Overview of the History of the ILR Language Proficiency Skill Level Descriptions and Scale*, retrieved 22 February 2009 from http://www.govtilr.org/Skills/index.htm.

Hill, T (1997) The development of pragmatic competence in an EFL context (Doctoral dissertation, Temple University Japan), *Dissertation Abstracts International* 58, 3905.

Hornby, A (1954–56) *Oxford Progressive English for Adult Learners*, London: Oxford University Press.

Hornby, A (1959) *The Teaching of Structural Words and Sentence Patterns*, Oxford: Oxford University Press.

Houck, N and Gass, S M (1996) Non-native refusal: A methodological Perspective, in Gass, S M and Neu, J (Eds), *Speech Acts Across Cultures: Challenges to Communication In A Second Language*, Berlin: Mouton de Gruyter, 45-64.

Hudson, T (2005) Trends in assessment scales and criterion-referenced language assessment, *Annual Review of Applied Linguistics* 25, 205–227.

Hudson, T, Detmer, E, and Brown, J D (1995) *Developing prototypic measures of cross-cultural pragmatics*, Technical Report 7, Honolulu, HI: University of Hawai'i, Second Language Teaching and Curriculum Center.

Hulstijn, J H (2007) The shaky ground beneath the CEFR: Quantitative and qualitative dimensions of language proficiency, *Modern Language Journal* 91 (4), 663–667 (5).

Hulstijn, J H, Alderson, J C, & Schoonen, R (2010) Developmental stages in second language acquisition and levels of second-language proficiency: Are there links between them? in Bartning, I, Martin, M and Vedder, I (Eds), *Communicative proficiency and linguistic development: intersections between SLA and language testing research*, Eurosla Monographs Series 1, 11–20. Retrievable from http://eurosla.org/monographs/EM01/EM01home.html

Hymes, D (1964) Introduction: Towards ethnographies of communication, in Hymes, D and Gumperz, J (Eds) *The Ethnography of Communication*, American Anthropologist 66 (6), 1–34.

Hymes, D (1972) On communicative competence, in Pride, J and Holmes, J (Eds) *Sociolinguistics*, Harmondsworth: Penguin, 269-293.

Hymes, D (1974) *Foundations in sociolinguistics: an ethnographic approach*, Philadelphia, University of Pennsylvania Press.

Ingram, D E (1990) Australian second language proficiency rating, *AILA Review* 7, 46–61.

Ingram, D E (1996) *The ASLPR: Its origins and current developments*, paper presented at the NLLIA Language Expo '96 (Brisbane, Queensland, Australia, July 19–21, 1996). Eric Document ED402735. Retrieved from www.eric.ed.gov, 20 February 2009.

Interagency Language Roundtable (1985) *Interagency Language Roundtable Skill Level Descriptions*, Washington, DC: Government Printing office.

Jakobson, R (1960) Closing statement: linguistics: linguistics and poetics, in Sebeok T (Ed) *Style in Language*, Michigan: MIT Press, 350–377.

Jespersen, O (1933) *Essentials of English Grammar*, London: Allen and Unwin.

Johnson, K (1982) *Communicaive Syllabus Design and Methodology*, Oxford: Pergamon Press.

Johnson, K (2006) Revisiting Wilkins' notional syllabus, *International Journal of Applied Linguistics* 16 (3), 414–418.

Jones, N (2009) A comparative approach to constructing a multilingual proficiency framework: constraining the role of standard-setting, In Figueras, N and Noijons, J (Eds) *Linking to the CEFR levels: Research Perspectives*, Arnhem: Cito/EALTA, 37–44.

Kachru, B (1990) *The Alchemy of English: the Spread, Functions, and Models of Non-native Englishes*, Chicago: University of Illinois Press.

Kasper, G and Schmidt, R (1996) Developmental issues in interlanguage Pragmatics, *Studies of Second Language Acquisition* 18, 149–169.

Kasper, G and Rose, K (2003) *Pragmatics Development in a Second Language*, Oxford, UK: Blackwell.

Kaulfers, W V (1944) War time developments in modern language achievement Tests, *Modern Language Journal* 28, 136–150.

Keller, E (1981) Gambits: Conversational strategy signals, in Coulmas, F (Ed.), *Conversational Routine*, The Hague: Mouton, 93–113.

Khalifa, H and Weir, C (2009) *Examining Second Language Reading: Research and Practice in Assessing Second Language Reading*, Studies in Language Testing 29, Cambridge: UCLES/Cambridge University Press.

Kramsch, C (1986) From language proficiency to interactional competence, *Modern Language Journal* 70, 366–72.

Lantolf, J, and Frawley, W (1985) Oral proficiency testing: A critical analysis, *Modern Language Journal* 69 (4), 337–45.

Lazaraton, A (1991) *A conversation analysis of structure and interaction in the language interview*, unpublished doctoral dissertation, University of California, Los Angeles.

Leech, G (1980) *Explorations in Semantics and Pragmatics*, Amsterdam: John Benjamins.

Leech, G (1983) *Principles of Pragmatics,* London: Longman.

Leech, G N (1981) *Semantics* (2nd edition), Harmondsworth: Penguin.

Lenz, P and Schneider G (2004a) *A Bank of Descriptors for Self-assessment in European Language Portfolios*, Strasbourg: Council of Europe.

Lenz, P and Schneider, G (2004b) *Introduction to the bank of descriptors for self-assessment in European Language Portfolios*, retrieved 7 April 2010 from www.coe.int/T/DG4/Portfolio/documents/Introduction_descriptor.doc

Liskin-Gasparro, J E (1984) The ACTFL proficiency guidelines: Gateway to testing and curriculum, *Foreign Language Annals* 17 (5), 475–489.

Little, D (2007) The Common European Framework of Reference for Languages: Perspectives on the Making of Supranational Language Education Policy, *Modern Language Journal*, 91 (4), 645–655.

Liu, J (2006) *Measuring interlanguage pragmatic knowledge of EFL learners*, Frankfurt: Peter Lang.

Lonergan, J (2006) *Quality Assurance in FLT*, Paper presented to the ICC Annual Conference Riga, Latvia, 24 – 27 March 2006.

Lyons, J (Ed) *New Horizons in Linguistics*, Harmondsworth: Penguin.

Maeshiba, N, Yoshinaga, N, Kasper, G, and Ross, S (1996) Transfer and proficiency in interlanguage apologising, in Gass, S M and Neu, J (Eds), *Speech Acts Across Cultures: Challenges To Communication In A Second Language*, Berlin: Mouton de Gruyter, 155–187.

Mager, RF (1991) *Preparing Instructional Objectives* (2nd Edition), London: Kogan Page.

Malinowski, B (1922) *Argonauts of the Western Pacific: An Account of Native Enterprise and Adventure in the Archipelagoes of Melanesian New Guinea*, London: George Routledge & Sons.

Malinowski, B (1935) *Coral Gardens and Their Magic*, London: Allen and Unwin.

Martyniuk, W (2011) *Relating Language Examinations to the Common European Framework of Reference for Languages: Case Studies and Reflections on the use of the Council of Europe's Draft Manual*, Studies in Language Testing 33, Cambridge: Cambridge ESOL and Cambridge University Press.

Martyniuk, W and Noijons, J (2007) *Executive summary of results of a survey on the use of the CEFR at national level in the Council of Europe Member States*, Retrieved 2 September 2009, from http://www.coe.int.

McNamara, D S, Louwerse, M M, Cai, Z, and Graesser, A (2005) *Coh-Metrix*, Retrieved 5 December 2008, from http//:Coh-Metrix.memphis.edu.

McNamara, T F and Roever C (2006) *Language Testing: The Social Dimension*, Oxford: Blackwell.

Milanovic, M and Saville, N (Eds) (1996) *Performance Testing, Cognition and Assessment*, Cambridge: Cambridge University Press.

Milanovic, M and Weir, C J (forthcoming) *Measured Constructs: A History of the Constructs Underlying English Language Examinations 1913–2012*, Cambridge:UCLES/Cambridge University Press.

Mislevy, R (1992) *Linking Educational Assessments: Concepts, Issues, Methods and Prospects*, Princeton NJ: Educational Testing Service.

Mislevy, R (1995) Test theory and language-learning assessment, *Language Testing* 12 (5), 341–369.

Mitchell, R. and Myles, F (2004) *Second language Learning Theories* (2nd Edition), London: Arnold.

Morrow, K (Ed.) (2004) *Insights from the Common European Framework*, Oxford: Oxford University Press.

Mulligan, K (1987) Promisings and other social acts - their constituents and Structure, in Mulligan, K (Ed.), *Speech Act and Sachverhalt: Reinach and the Foundations of Realist Phenomenology*, Dordrecht: Nijhoff.

North, B (Ed.) (1992) *Transparency and Coherence in Language Learning in Europe: Objectives, Assessment and Certification, proceedings of the intergovernmental Symposium held at Rüschlikon, November 1991*, Strasbourg: Council for Cultural Cooperation.

North, B (1993) *The Development of descriptors on scales of proficiency: perspectives, problems, and a possible methodology*, NFLC Occasional Paper, National Foreign Language Center, Washington D.C., April 1993.

North, B (1994) *Scales of Language Proficiency: A Survey of Some Existing Systems*, Strasbourg: Council of Europe.

North, B (1996) *The development of a common framework scale of descriptors of language proficiency based on a theory of measurement*, unpublished PhD thesis, Thames Valley University.

North, B (2000) *The Development of a Common Framework Scale of Language Proficiency*, New York: Peter Lang.

North, B (2004) Relating assessments, examinations, and courses to the CEFR, in Morrow, K, *Insights from the Common European Framework*, Oxford: Oxford University Press, 77–90.

North, B (2007a) The CEFR illustrative descriptor scales, *The Modern Language Journal* 91 (4), 656–659.

North, B (2007b) *The CEFR levels: key points and key problems*, Paper presented at the 23rd ALTE Conference, Sevres, 18 April 2007.

North B and Schneider, G (1998) Scaling descriptors for language proficiency scales, *Language Testing* 15 (2), 217–262.

O'Neill, R, Kingsbury, R, Yeadon, T and Scott, R (1971) *Kernel Lessons Intermediate*, London: Longman.

Oscarsson, M (1980) *Approaches to Self-assessment in Foreign Language Learning*, Oxford: Pergamon.

O'Sullivan, B, Weir, C and Saville, N (2002) Using observation checklists to validate speaking test tasks. *Language Testing* 19 (1), 33–56.

Page, B (1992) Graded objectives schemes, in North, B (Ed.) *Transparency and Coherence in Language Learning in Europe; Objectives, Assessment and Certification, Symposium held in Ruschlikon, Switzerland, 10-16 November 1991*, Strasbourg: Council for Cultural Cooperation, 64–67.

Palmer, H E and Blanford, F G (1924) *Everyday Sentences in Spoken English (In Phonetic Transcription with Intonation Marks for the Use of Foreign Sudents* (2nd Edition), reprinted in IRLT (Eds) (1995–1999) *The Selected Writings of Harold E. Palmer, Vol.7*, Tokyo: Hon-no Tomosha.

Pawlikowska-Smith, G (2000) *Canadian Language Benchmarks 2000: English as a Second Language – for Adults*, Toronto: Centre for Canadian Language Benchmarks.

Pawlikowska-Smith, G (2002) *Canadian Language Benchmarks 2000: Additional Sample Task Ideas*, Toronto: Centre for Canadian Language Benchmarks.

Pike, K (1967) *Language in relation to a unified Theory of the Structure of Human Behaviour*, The Hague: Mouton.

Pollitt, A and Murray, N J (1996) What raters really pay attention to, in Milanovic, M and Saville, N (Eds) *Performance Testing, Cognition and Assessment*, Studies in Language Testing volume 3, Cambridge: Cambridge University Press, 74-91.

Richards and Rogers (2001) *Approaches and Methods in Language Teaching* (second edition), Cambridge: Cambridge University Press.

Richterich, R (1972) *A Model for the Definition of Adult Language Needs*, Council of Europe, Strasbourg: Pergamon Press.

Richterich, R (1983) (Ed.) *Case Studies in Identifying Language Needs*, Oxford: Pergamon Press.

Richterich, R and Schneider, G (1992) Transparency and coherence: why and for whom? In North, B (Ed.) *Transparency and Coherence in Language Learning in Europe; Objectives, Assessment and Certification, Symposium held in Ruschlikon, Switzerland, 10-16 November 1991*, Strasbourg: Council for Cultural Cooperation, 43–50.

Roberts, J (1983) Teaching with functional materials: the problem of stress and Intonation, *English Language Teaching Journal* 37 (3), 213–220.

Robins, R (1968) *General Linguistics; an Introductory Survey*, London: Longman.

Robinson, M (1992) Introspective methodology in interlanguage pragmatics Research, in Kasper, G (Ed.) *Pragmatics of Japanese as native and target language (Technical Report No. 3)*, Honolulu: University of Hawai'i at Manoa, Second Language Teaching and Curriculum Center, 27-82.

Roever, C (2005) *Testing ESL Pragmatics*, Bern: Peter Lang.

Rose, K R (2000) An exploratory cross-sectional study of interlanguage pragmatic development, *Studies in Second Language Acquisition* 22 (1), 27–67.

Rose, K R (2000) An exploratory cross-sectional study of interlanguage pragmatic development, *Studies in Second Language Acquisition* 22, 27–67.

Sacks, H, Schegloff A, Jeff erson G (1974) A simplest systematic for the organization of turn-taking for conversation, *Language* 50, 696–735.

Salamoura, A (2008) Aligning English Profile research data to the CEFR, *Research Notes* 33, 5–7.

Sammartino, P (1938) A language achievement scale, *Modern Language Journal* 22, 129–134.

Sarangi, S and Coulthard, M (Eds) (2000) *Discourse and Social Life*, London: Pearson.

Savignon, S (1985) Evaluation of Communicative Competence: The ACTFL Provisional Proficiency Guidelines, *Modern Language Journal* 69 (2), 129–34.

Savignon, S (1972), *Communicative Competence: An Experiment in Foreign Language Teaching*, Philadelphia: Center for Curriculum Development.

Saville, N and Hawkey, R (2010) The English Profile Programme – the first three Years, *English Profile Journal* 1(1), e7.

Scarcella, R (1979) On speaking politely in a second language, in Yorio, C A, Peters, K and Schachter, J (Eds) *On TESOL 1979: The Learner in Focus*, Washington, DC: Teachers of English to Speakers of Other Languages, 275-287.

Schank, R. C, and Abelson, R P (1977) *Scripts, Plans, Goals, and Understanding: An Inquiry into Human Knowledge Structures*, Hillsdale, N.J.: Laurence.

Schärer, R and North, B (1992) *Toward a common European framework for reporting language competency*, Washington, DC: National Foreign Language Center.

Schegloff, E A (1992) On talk and its institutional occasions, in Drew P and Heritage, J C (Eds) *Talk at Work*, Cambridge: Cambridge University Press, 101–134.

Schwartz, B (1969) *A Prospective View of Permanent Education. ERIC document ED-038-603*, Strasbourg: Council for Cultural Cooperation.

Schwartz, B (1974) *Permanent Education*, The Hague: Martinus Nijhoff.

Scott, M. (2006) *Oxford WordSmith Tools 4.0*, Retrieved 5 December 2008 from http://www. lexically.net/downloads/version4/html/index.html.

Searle, J (1969) *Speech Acts: An Essay In The Philosophy of Language*, Cambridge: Cambridge University Press.

Searle, J (1979) *Expression and Meaning: Studies in the Theory of Speech Acts*, Cambridge: Cambridge University Press.

Shaw, S and C.J. Weir (2007) *Examining Writing in a Second Language*, Studies in Language Testing volume 26, Cambridge: UCLES/Cambridge University Press.

Siegal, M (1996) The role of learner subjectivity in second language sociolinguistic competency: Western women learning Japanese, *Applied Linguistics* 17 (3), 356–382.

Sinclair, J and Coulthard, R (1975) *Towards An Analysis Of Discourse*, Oxford: Oxford University Press.

Skehan, P and Foster, P (1997) Task type and task processing conditions as influences on foreign language performance, *Language Teaching Research* 1 (3), 185–211.

Smith, P C and Kendall, J M (1963) Retranslation of expectations: an approach to the construction of unambiguous anchors for rating scales, *Journal of Applied Psychology* 47 (2), 149–154.

Spady, W (1994) *Outcomes Based Education: Critical Issues and Answers*, American Association of School Administration: Arlington, Virginia.

Sperber, D and Wilson, D (1995) *Relevance: Communication and Cognition* (2nd Edition), Oxford: Blackwell

Spolsky, B (1999) Standards, scales and guidelines in Spolsky, B (Ed.), *Concise Encyclopedia of Educational Linguistics*, Amsterdam: Elsevier.

Steffensen, M S, Joag-dev, C, and Anderson, R C (1979) A cross-cultural perspective on reading comprehension, *Reading Research Quarterly* 15 (1), 10–29.

Strevens, P (1980) *Teaching English as an International language*, Oxford: Pergamon Press.

Svanes, B (1992) Utviklingen av realisasjonsmonsteret for sprakhandlingen 'a be noen om a gjore noe' hos utenlandske studenter I lopet av 3 ar i Norge [Development of realization patterns of the speech act "asking someone to do something" by foreign students during three years in Norway], *Norsk Lingvistisk Tidsskift* 1, 1–50.

Swales, J (1990) *Genre Analysis: English in Academic and Research Settings*, Cambridge: Cambridge University Press.

Tan, S H (1990) The role of prior knowledge and language proficiency as predictors of reading comprehension among undergraduates, in de Jong, J H A L and Stevenson, D K (Eds), *Individualising the Assessment of Language Abilities*, Clevedon, PA: Multilingual Matters, 214-224.

Tannenbaum, R J and Wylie, E C (2005) *Mapping English Language Proficiency Scores Onto the Common European Framework*, TOEFL Research Report RR-88, Princeton: ETS.

Tarone, E (2005) English for Specific Purposes and interlanguage pragmatics, in Bardovi Harlig, K and Hartford, B (Eds) *Interlanguage Pragmatics: Exploring Institutional Talk*, Hillsdale, NJ: Lawrence Erlbaum Publishers, 157–176.

Thomas, J (1983) Cross-cultural pragmatic failure, *Applied Linguistics* 4 (2), 91–112.

Thorndike, E L (1921) *The Teachers Word Book*, New York: Teachers College.

Trim, J L M (1980) *Developing a Unit/Credit Scheme of Adult Language Learning*, Oxford, Pergamon.

Trim J L M (Ed.) (1981) *Modern Languages 1971–1981*, Report presented by CDCC Project Group 4, Strasbourg: Council of Europe.

Trim, J L M (2000) The Birth and early development of AILA, in AILA '99 Tokyo Organizing Committee (Eds) *Selected Papers from AILA '99 Tokyo.* Waseda, Waseda University Press.

Trim, J L M (Ed.) (2002) *Common European Framework of Reference for Languages: A Guide for Users*, Strasbourg: Council of Europe.

Trim, J L M (2005) *The role of the Common European Framework of Reference for Languages in teacher training*, Lecture delivered by J L M Trim, Graz, September 2005.

Trim, J L M (2009) *Breakthrough,* Cambridge: Cambridge University Press. (Available online from http://www.englishprofile.org)

Trim, J L M, Richterich, R, van Ek, J A and Wilkins, D A (1980) *Systems Development in Adult Language Learning*, Oxford, Pergamon.

Trim, J L M, Holec, H, Coste, D and Porcher, L (Eds) (1984) *Towards a More Comprehensive Framework For The Definition of Language Learning Objectives. Vol I: Analytical Summaries of the Preliminary Studies. Vol. II: Preliminary Studies*, Strasbourg, Council of Europe.

Trosborg, A (1987) Apology strategies in natives/nonnatives, *Journal of Pragmatics* 11, 147–167.

Trosborg, A (1995) *Interlanguage Pragmatics*, Berlin: Mouton de Gruyter.

van Ek, J A (1975) *The Threshold Level in a European Unit/Credit System for Modern Language Learning by Adults*, Strasbourg: Council of Europe.

van Ek, J A (1976) *The Threshold Level for Modern Language Learning in Schools*, London: Longman.

van Ek, J A (1981) Specification of communicative objectives, in Trim, J L M (Ed.), *Modern Languages (1971–1981)*, Strasbourg: Council for Cultural Cooperation.

van Ek, J A (1985) *Objectives for foreign language learning. Vol. I Scope*, Strasbourg, Council of Europe.

van Ek, J A (1986) *Objectives for foreign language learning. Vol. II Levels*, Strasbourg, Council of Europe.

van Ek, J A and Trim, J L M (1998a) *Waystage 1990* (Revised and corrected edition), Cambridge: Cambridge University Press.

van Ek, J A and Trim, J L M (1998b) *Threshold 1990* (Revised and corrected edition), Cambridge: Cambridge University Press.

van Ek, J A and Trim, J L M (2001) *Vantage*, Cambridge: Cambridge University Press.

van Els, T (1992) Revising the foreign languages examinations of upper secondary general education in the Netherlands, in North, B (Ed.) *Transparency and Coherence in Language Learning in Europe: Objectives, Assessment and Certification, proceedings of the intergovernmental Symposium held at Rüschlikon, November 1991*, 109–114.

van Lier, L (1989) Reeling, writhing, drawling, stretching, and fainting in coils: oral proficiency interviews as conversations, *TESOL Quarterly* 23 (3), 489–50.

Weir, C J (2005a) Limitations of the Council of Europe's Framework of reference (CEFR) in developing comparable examinations and tests, *Language Testing* 22 (3), 281–300.

Weir, C J (2005b) *Language Testing and Validation: An Evidence-Based Approach:* Basingstoke: Palgrave Macmillan.

West, M (1933) *Learn to Speak by Speaking*, London: Longmans, Green.

West, M (1953) *A General Service List of English Words, with Semantic Frequencies and a Supplementary Word-list for the Writing of Popular Science and Technology*, London: Longmans.

Widdowson, H G (1990) *Aspects of Language Teaching*, Oxford: Oxford University Press.

Wilds, C P (1975) The oral interview test, in Jones, R L and Spolsky, B (Eds), *Testing Language Proficiency*, Washington, DC: Center for Applied Linguistics, 29–44.

Wilkins, D (1972a) The linguistic and situational content of the common core in a unit/credit system, in Trim, J (Ed.) *Systems Development in Adult Language Learning*, Oxford: Pergamon.

Wilkins, D (1972b) *Linguistics and Language Teaching*, London: Edward Arnold.

Wilkins, D (1976) *Notional Syllabuses*, Oxford: Oxford University Press.

Wilkins, D (1978) Proposal for levels definition, in Trim, J L M, *Some Possible Lines of Development Of An Overall Structure for a European Unit / Credit*

Scheme For Foreign Language Learning By Adults, Strasbourg: Council of Europe, 71–78

Wittgenstein, L (1955) *Philosophical Investigations*, Oxford: Oxford University Press.

Wright, B D and Stone, M H (1979) *Best Test Design*, Chicago, Mesa Press.

Wu, J and Wu, R (2007) *The LTTC GEPT-CEFR calibration project*, The Language Training and Testing Center: Taipei, Taiwan, retrieved from http://www.lttc.ntu.edu.tw, 15 January 2010.

Wunderlich, D (Ed) (1972) *Linguistische Pragmatik*, Frankfurt: Athenäum.

Appendices

Appendix A: C1 level Can Do specifications for Profile Deutsch

(Trans. John Trim)

Global Can Do descriptors for oral interaction at Level C1

Can express him/herself spontaneously and fluently with almost no effort; pausing more often to search for the appropriate formulation only when dealing with abstract and more difficult themes.

Can in most cases understand idiomatic expressions and colloquialisms in conversation and use the most common ones as appropriate in the given situation.

Can express one's own thoughts and opinions with precision in a conversation and make one's own contribution skilfully, so that it fits in smoothly with that of others.

Can contribute flexibly and appropriately to conversations, expressing emotions, allusions and other speech intentions.

Can, with the help of appropriate phrases, take the floor in the course of a conversation, gain time for thought and indicate that one wishes to keep the floor (also C2).

Can steer conversation in a larger group, give others the floor or encourage them to take part (also C2).

Can face difficulties in expression flexibly, starting afresh, correcting oneself or reformulating an utterance.

Can use a variety of linguistic means to express one's thoughts and statements, so as to emphasise or clarify something.

Can deliver clear and well-structured spoken contributions to conversations, showing mastery of the means of organisation as well as of nexus in content and language.

Can set forth arguments in conversations and discussions clearly, linking together different themes, developing particular points in greater detail and rounding off the presentation with a suitable conclusion.

Can express oneself almost effortlessly in conversation, thanks to his/her extensive vocabulary and has no problem in compensating for gaps in vocabulary by paraphrasing with rarely any obvious hunting for words.

Can express him/herself with reasonable precision in conversation thanks to his/her extensive vocabulary and nuance assertions rather closely, clearly indicating the degree of certainty, doubt or probability.

Can express him/herself largely accurately and appropriately, thanks to his/her extensive vocabulary, so that mistakes in word usage rarely occur.

Can select from an extensive repertoire of grammatical structures and use complex structures to organise even lengthy contributions to conversation.

Can deliver even lengthy contributions to conversation so correctly that errors are rare and are scarcely noticed.

Can vary the intonation in conversation, and so place the stress as to express nuances of meaning.

Detailed Can Do descriptors for oral interaction at Level C1

Can exchange information on unusual themes or problems with officials or service personnel.
e.g. After being involved in an accident, can discuss with the representative of an insurance company who is to blame and what compromise solutions may be possible.

Can take part in a lively conversation among native speakers, referring to what other participants have said.
e.g. can discuss with German-speaking colleagues the pros and cons of various products at a trade fair and present the special features of his/her own firm's products.

Can express thoughts and opinions in informal discussions clearly and precisely, present arguments convincingly and react to the arguments put forward by others.
e.g. can discuss with your partner a crisis in the intimate relations of a pair who are your friends.

Can communicate information in a conversation, making allusions or differentiating according to emotional states, using for instance wit and irony (also C2).
e.g. can express commiseration and hope when discussing someone's serious illness, telling of similar cases which have had a positive outcome.

Can take part in formal discussions and negotiations, responding appropriately to the questions, assertions and objections raised by others.
e.g. can, as a teacher of German, present his/her own teaching methods to a seminar on teaching methodology and respond to critical comments and objections by other participants with objective arguments.

Can, when giving a talk at some event, reply appropriately to questions, assertions or objections raised by others.
e.g. can, acting as a travel guide for a German-speaking tourist group, respond to questions and special requests following a talk on excursion possibilities.

Can lead a debate or a discussion, opening the proceedings, acting as moderator and bringing the proceedings to a close (also C2).
e.g. can, as manager of a travel bureau, greet business partners to a meeting on price fixing, lead the negotiations and work out compromise solutions for any conflicts of interest.

Can, in an interview or similar discourse, answer questions fluently and without outside assistance, put forward his/her own thoughts, develop them and react to objections.
e.g. can answer questions raised by a colleague during an information session concerning the cultural, social and political situation of his/her country of origin and discuss in some detail expectations as to its future development.

Can conduct an interview or similar conversation, asking varied questions and reacting to the interviewee's responses.
e.g. can, as a music student, interview a musician and return, following the latter's rambling answers, to his/her prepared questions.

Can understand and exchange complex pieces of information and advice (also C2).
e.g. can, as a computer networking specialist, exchange information in a technical conversation with users concerning the network and discuss solutions for problems that may arise in the induction of a new user.

Can conduct telephone conversations with native German speakers effortlessly and respond to the partner's statements and allusions.
e.g. can console a friend, who is telling you her troubles on the telephone, with sympathy and give her concrete advice.

Global Can Do descriptors for written interaction at Level C1

Can conduct a clear, well-structured correspondence, bringing out the decisive points in the content and presenting his/her point of view in detail.

Can give written information on a variety of themes of a general or vocational character in a clear and readily legible form.

Can express him/herself clearly and precisely in writing, relating effectively to the addressee (also C2).

Can write clear and detailed reports on the most varied themes, relating to a range of addressees.

Can conduct a personal correspondence clearly and precisely, as well as expressing emotions and making jokes and allusions.

Can write texts which are largely correct and vary the vocabulary and style according to addressee, text type and theme.

Can in most cases understand idiomatic expressions and colloquialisms in correspondence and other written communications and use the most common ones him/herself as appropriate to the situation.

Can use the linguistic means for the organisation and coherence of textual components in a way corresponding to the communicative intention.

Can maintain a high level of grammatical correctness in his/her correspondence, with errors few and far between, so that they scarcely disturb the reader.

Can conform to the rules of orthography and punctuation consistently, apart from occasional slips of the pen.

Detailed Can Do descriptors for written interaction at Level C1

Can report events and describe experiences and feelings in detail in personal letters with flexible reference to the content of the partner's letters.
e.g. can write a letter to a female friend telling her about her own four-week-old baby, saying how much things have changed and how she feels about it all.

Can follow through a correspondence on the most varied subject matter with service providers, authorities or companies flexibly and independently.
e.g. can, as a tenant, conduct a correspondence with the property management concerning the laying of new flooring for his/her flat.

Can write formal letters raising or invoking contracts or agreed arrangements.
e.g. can write to his/her superior reminding him/her of the salary increase contractually due and requesting its implementation.

Can take note of and pass on pieces of information of the most varied character.
e.g. can summarise the proceedings and results of a meeting in an email to the participants, asking them to complement and if necessary amend the account.

Global Can Do descriptors for aural reception at Level C1

Can follow longer speeches and conversations, even when they are not clearly structured and when the interrelation of the parts is not explicit.

Can follow the contributions to group discussions and debates, even when the themes treated are abstract, complex and unfamiliar.

Can understand many everyday idiomatic expressions and colloquialisms and recognise a shift in style and register.

Can understand longer speeches and lectures on unfamiliar, abstract and complex themes, even despite occasional uncertainties, especially when the accent is unfamiliar.

Can recognise a broad spectrum of idiomatic expressions and colloquialisms and correctly recognise and evaluate a change of register, so that he/she has to confirm some details, especially when the speaker's accent is unfamiliar.

Detailed Can Do descriptors for aural reception at Level C1

Can understand conversation on abstract, complex themes from another discipline, even though sometimes particular items remain unclear.
e.g. can, as a student of sport, follow a discussion among students of German about Patrick Süskind's novel 'Das Parfum'.

Can understand many pieces of information, directions and guidelines (also C2).
e.g. can, when invited to join in a round of cards, understand the explanation of how the game 'Schafskopf' is played and what requires particularly careful attention.

Can identify particular pieces of information on public address systems even when the transmission quality is poor.
e.g. can understand an announcement at an open air concert that the next group has not arrived owing to its being stuck in a traffic jam and that as a result the programme has been rearranged.

Can understand detailed reports and commentaries, in which different opinions, connections and viewpoints are discussed.
e.g. can understand the report made by a visiting German colleague from a partner company on business developments over the past year and their probable causes.

Can understand literary short stories, even though occasional details remain unclear.
e.g. can, while driving, understand a story on an audio tape.

Can understand most lectures, discussions and debates relatively easily.
e.g. can, on the occasion of a 'Health Day', understand a platform discussion of the development and current situation of the National Health Service.

Can understand lectures, speeches and reports within the framework of his/ her study, training or profession, even when they are complex in content and in language.
e.g. can, within the framework of his/her training as a worker in the tourist industry, understand a complicated report on the new railway booking system.

Can understand a broad spectrum of radio broadcasts, even though the language spoken is not necessarily the standard variety.
e.g. can understand a longer radio crime drama featuring Commissioner Brenner in Vienna.

Can understand films, television series and theatre productions, even when they contain sloppy colloquial speech and idiomatic expressions.
e.g. can understand an exciting and entertaining film about the experiences of a Berlin family at the time of the fall of the Wall.

Can understand demanding television broadcasts such as news bulletins, current affairs programmes, interviews, discussion programmes and chat shows.
e.g. can understand a confrontation on television between the principal candidates of the two big parties contesting the German parliamentary elections shortly before polling day.

Global Can Do descriptors for written reception at Level C1

Can understand in detail long and complex texts even outside his/her field of specialisation, given that he/she is able to read difficult sections several times.

Can rapidly take in the content and significance of articles, written reports and news items dealing with a broad spectrum of vocationally relevant themes and decide whether a closer reading is worthwhile.

Can understand long, complex written texts encountered in the course of education or of social or professional life, grasping implicit attitudes and opinions.

Can understand both private and formal correspondence, even though on occasion unusual words and expressions remain unclear.

Detailed Can Do descriptors for written reception at Level C1

Can understand in detail long and complex directions for implements and processes even outside his/her field of specialisation, given that he/she is able to read difficult sections several times.

e.g. can, as a self-employed person, understand the guidance notes for completing the self-assessment income tax return.

Can understand longer, demanding texts and summarise their content
e.g. can understand the report of a conference of teachers of German and communicate the main points to a colleague by email.

Can understand detailed reports, analyses and commentaries, in which relationships, opinions and standpoints are discussed.
e.g. can, as a prospective student, recognise and understand the arguments for and against the introduction of centralised examinations in German contained in a report of the Commission for Foreign Students.

Can understand in a narrative text, over and above the action itself, the information it provides on the social, historical or political background.
e.g. can extract information on the social norms in Vienna around 1900 from a text of Arthur Schnitzler.

Can understand in detail long, complex and thematically very diverse texts, grasping delicate nuances of implicitly indicated attitudes and opinions (also C2).
e.g. can, reading between the lines, deduce the critical attitude of the author from an article on the history of female franchise in Switzerland.

Can understand everyday contracts in the private or vocational domain.
e.g. can understand the marital contract drawn up by a solicitor before the wedding.

Can understand all correspondence with the occasional recourse to a dictionary.
e.g. can, in a lawsuit with a former landlady, understand a complicated letter from the solicitor for the opposing party concerning the demands made in the current proceedings.

Can understand slang, idiomatic expressions and jokes in private correspondence.
e.g. can understand an email, from a friend who is at present on holiday, in which he makes fun in great detail of the accommodation and the food.

Can understand contemporary literary texts with no great exertion.
e.g. can understand the lyrical poetry of a contemporary author, taking as its theme everyday encounters.

Can extract information, ideas and opinions from specific texts in his/her own special field.
e.g. can, as an employee of a telecommunications company, understand a specialised article with detailed information on competing products.

Can rapidly scan long and complex texts of a general or specialised character to identify important items of information.
e.g. can rapidly scan the Diploma dissertation of a colleague to find out the most important results of a research project.

Global Can Do descriptors for oral production at Level C1

Can state the facts clearly, combining different themes, developing particular points more exactly and rounding off with a suitable conclusion.

Can express him/herself with reasonable precision thanks to his/her extensive vocabulary and nuance assertions rather closely, clearly indicating the degree of certainty, doubt or probability.

Can use a variety of common idiomatic expressions and colloquialisms appropriately in his/her discourse.

Can structure longer speeches and lectures appropriately with regard to the audience and the situation at the time.

Can formulate his/her statements and thoughts, using a variety of linguistic means to emphasise or clarify something.

Can, faced with difficulties in expression, start afresh, correct him/herself or reformulate an utterance.

Can express him/herself spontaneously and fluently with almost no effort; needing more often to search for the appropriate formulation only when dealing with abstract and more difficult themes.

Can speak clearly and in a well-structured way, showing mastery of the means of organisation as well as of nexus in content and language.

Can express oneself almost effortlessly in conversation, thanks to his/her extensive vocabulary and has no problem in compensating for gaps in vocabulary by paraphrasing with rarely any obvious hunting for words.

Can express him/herself largely accurately and appropriately, thanks to his/her extensive vocabulary, so that errors in word usage rarely occur.

Can deliver even lengthy contributions to conversation so correctly that errors are rare and are scarcely noticed.

Can select from an extensive repertoire of grammatical structures and use complex structures to organise even lengthy contributions to conversation.

Can vary the intonation in conversation, and so place the stress as to express nuances of meaning.

Detailed Can Do descriptors for oral production at Level C1

Can state complex facts clearly and in detail.
e.g. can report on the state of development of Blended Learning in his/her own country and present the results of experience (advantages and disadvantages) in a well-structured way.

Can describe facts in detail, incorporating subordinate themes, dealing more closely with certain points and rounding off the presentation with a suitable conclusion.
e.g. can, as an applicant for a position, give an account of which experiences and previous activities qualify him/her for this appointment.

Can express thoughts and attitudes clearly and support them with sound argument.
e.g. can, at the beginning of an in-service teacher training course, formulate his/her expectations and wishes, as well as giving reasons for taking part.

Can tell stories, introducing digressions and dealing with certain points in greater detail, then rounding everything off with a suitable conclusion.
e.g. can, as an au pair girl, tell a child a folk-tale from her own country, giving many details.

Can deliver a clear and well-structured lecture on a complex topic, presenting his/her own point of view in some detail, underpinning it with subsidiary points, suitable examples or sound reasoning.
e.g. can, as a lecturer in General Linguistics, present his/her own practice in testing to an in-service course on 'testing and examining' indicating the specific conditions and making clear the weaknesses as well as the strengths of the testing methods selected with suitable examples.

Can make an oral summary of a long and demanding text.
e.g. can retain in memory, with the aid of his/her own notes, the important contributions made during a discussion and formulate orally a provisional interim result.

Can read a clearly articulated paper in his/her own specialised field of interest, deviating when necessary from a prepared text and responding to questions from the audience.
e.g. can, when it is indicated that some aspect of the paper, for instance 'action orientation', is still less than clear, depart from the prepared paper and go more deeply into this aspect giving concrete examples.

Can make public announcements, giving emphasis to what is important by means of stress and intonation.
e.g. can announce a guest speaker at a meeting of the society 'Friends of the Cinema' with an appreciation of his/her experience as a director.

Global Can Do descriptors for written production at Level C1

Can express him/herself in writing on a variety of themes of a general or vocational character in a clear and readily legible form.

Can compose clear, well-structured texts on complex themes, emphasising the main points, presenting his/her own standpoint in detail and supporting it with subsidiary points, appropriate examples and/or reasoning, and round the text off with a suitable conclusion.

Can write texts which are largely correct and vary the vocabulary and style according to addressee, text type and theme.

Can formulate his/her statements and thoughts using various linguistic means, emphasising or clarifying particular statements according to the purpose.

Can use the proper technical and idiomatic expressions corresponding to his/her field of specialisation with no great problems.

Can maintain a high level of grammatical correctness in his/her correspondence, with errors few and far between, so that they scarcely disturb the reader.

Can conform to the rules of orthography and punctuation consistently, apart from occasional slips of the pen.

Detailed Can Do descriptors for written production at Level C1

Can write texts on complex themes which are reader-friendly, clear and well-structured, giving prominence to the most important points.
e.g. can summarise his/her own research in a well-structured, detailed paper to a seminar on Indo-European languages.

Can present his/her opinion on a theme or event, giving prominence to the main ideas and illustrating his/her argument with detailed examples.
e.g. can submit a working paper for a publisher's conference to consider the planned merger of the editorial divisions for English and German giving reasons for believing the scheme to be practicable.

Can present his/her own standpoint in a commentary, giving prominence to the main points and supporting his/her views with detailed arguments.
e.g. can, as a computer expert, write a critical review of a new software package, giving examples to illustrate its disadvantages.

Can compose clear, well-structured, detailed fictional texts in a style at once personal and appropriate to the texts.
e.g. can, as a participant in a language course, write dialogues to a silent film sequence, the language of which is appropriate both to the characters and to the situation.

Can take up arguments from various sources in a text and weigh them against each other.
e.g. can, as an insurance consultant, put together a summary from reports in various media, from which the advantages and disadvantages of a planned measure in the field of health can be seen to follow.

Can summarise long and demanding texts, both factual and literary, not only for his/her own personal use.
e.g. can, as a biology student, produce a short, concise document summarising a lengthy textbook article on 'the conditions for the viability of fish in alpine lakes', to help his/her fellow students prepare for their examinations.

Can make notes during a lecture on a subject in his/her special field, which are sufficiently detailed to be of use to others.
e.g. can, as a student of the teaching of German as a foreign language, take down the most important content of a lecture on language teaching methodology for a sick fellow student.

Can compose advertisements and public announcements (also C2).
e.g. can, as a member of staff in the personnel department, draft an advertisement for a post which has been vacated.

Global Can Do descriptors for oral mediation from German at Level C1

Can rapidly grasp the important content of complex German texts on both concrete and abstract themes from his/her own or some other special fields of interest, and pass it on to others in a common language with the help of notes.

Can make independent notes to set down in writing the important content of a many-layered written German text on themes of general or personal interest and then pass it on orally, perhaps at a later time, to other persons in a common language.

Can pass on the important content of longer and complex speeches in German on familiar or sometimes less familiar topics to other persons in a common language, if necessary inserting enquiries concerning particular formulations or technical concepts.

Can pass on single statements of fact and opinion in German texts on various topics in the public and private domains, which are spoken quickly or which deviate slightly from the standard language, to other persons in a common language in a structured way.

Detailed Can Do descriptors for oral mediation from German at Level C1

Can pass on the important content of longer and complex speeches in German on familiar or sometimes less familiar topics to other persons in a common language, if necessary inserting enquiries concerning particular formulations or technical concepts.

e.g. can pass on the presentation in German of a newly developed medical product to a non-German-speaking doctor or patient in a common language.

Can pass on single statements of fact and opinion in German texts on various topics in the public and private domains, which are spoken quickly or which deviate slightly from the standard language, to other persons in a common language in a structured way.

e.g. can pass on, from a talk explaining the structure of the Luxemburg national health service, delivered in German with a Luxemburg accent, some central features of the system to speakers of other languages in a common language.

Can rapidly grasp the important content of complex German texts on both concrete and abstract themes from his/her own or some other special fields of interest, and pass it on to others in a common language with the help of notes.

e.g. can pass on information concerning the special characteristics of a piece of software contained in a German language software description to a colleague in a common language.

Can make independent notes to set down in writing the important content of a many-layered written German text on themes of general or personal interest and then pass it on orally, perhaps at a later time, to other persons in a common language.

e.g. can pass on the content of the German language instructions for the construction of a flat-pack item of furniture to a non-German-speaking customer in a common language.

Global Can Do descriptors for oral mediation from another language into German at Level C1

Can pass on in German, clearly and for the most part correctly, the central contents of a longer and complex oral presentation in another language dealing with general topics or ones from his/her own field.

Can pass on orally in German the greater part of the contents of longer, even unstructured, oral texts in another language dealing with themes in the private and public domains in a clear and explanatory way.

Can pass on orally in German important contents and standpoints in longer, many-layered texts written in another language dealing with concrete and abstract themes in his/her own field or in other particular fields of special interest clearly and completely.

Detailed Can Do descriptors for oral mediation from another language into German at Level C1

Can pass on in German, clearly and for the most part correctly, the central contents of a longer and complex oral presentation in another language dealing with general topics or ones from his/her own field.
e.g. can pass on in German to his/her circle of friends information from a speech delivered in another language by a politician dealing with the current situation in a crisis area.

Can pass on orally in German the greater part of the contents of longer, even unstructured, oral texts in another language dealing with themes in the private and public domains in a clear and explanatory way.
e.g. can pass on in German what is said by parents speaking another language at a parent–teacher evening to the German-speaking teacher.

Can pass on orally in German important contents and standpoints in longer, many-layered texts written in another language dealing with concrete and abstract themes in his/her own field or in other particular fields of special interest clearly and completely.
e.g. can convey to German-speaking participants at a trade fair the differences between the various regulations specific to each country contained in technical literature written in another language.

Global Can Do descriptors for oral mediation from German into German at Level C1

Can simplify and pass on in German, clearly and intelligibly, complex statements made in German on particular themes in the public and private domains.

Can deal with problems of understanding information and points of view in his/her own special field of interest expressed in German by passing them on orally in German in a clear, fluent and explanatory fashion.

Can pass on in oral communication, in a simplified and well-structured form, the central statements and arguments contained in complex written German texts dealing with different themes of current or personal interest, occasionally querying particular formulations or technical concepts.

Detailed Can Do descriptors for oral mediation from German into German at Level C1

Can simplify and pass on in German, clearly and intelligibly, complex statements made in German on particular themes in the public and private domains.
e.g. can explain to a child's parents, who have not been living in a German-speaking country very long, the diagnosis and treatment plan of the German-speaking dentist.

Can deal with problems of understanding information and points of view in his/her own special field of interest expressed in German by passing them on orally in German in a clear, fluent and explanatory fashion.
e.g. can make clear to a friend in German what exactly are the special regulations for a golf tournament announced in German by the organiser.

Can pass on in oral communication, in a simplified and well-structured form, the central statements and arguments contained in complex written German texts dealing with different themes of current or personal interest, occasionally querying particular formulations or technical concepts.
e.g. can pass on to a friend in simplified form the latest findings regarding a range of diets reported in a German specialised journal.

Global Can Do descriptors for oral mediation between German and another language at Level C1

Can convey reciprocally the significant contents of the various contributions to a conversation on unfamiliar as well as familiar topics in a clear and complementary fashion by making use of particular items of information available to him/her and occasionally asking questions.

Can reproduce clearly and reciprocally almost all items of information and content of central importance in an everyday conversation between speakers of German and those of other languages.

Can reproduce clearly and reciprocally most of the content of the contributions to a discussion between speakers of German and those of other languages on themes from his/her own field of interest, occasionally asking questions.

Detailed Can Do descriptors for oral mediation between German and another language at Level C1

Can convey reciprocally the significant contents of the various contributions to a conversation on unfamiliar as well as familiar topics in a clear and complementary fashion by making use of particular items of information available to him/her and occasionally asking questions.

e.g. can pass on reciprocally the individual contributions to a conversation between a German-speaking divorce lawyer and his/her client, who is a speaker of another language.

Can reproduce clearly and reciprocally almost all items of information and content of central importance in an everyday conversation between speakers of German and those of other languages.

e.g. can assist the negotiations at an employment interview between a speaker of another language and a German-speaking domestic help by passing on reciprocally the content of all that is said and drawing the attention of both sides to supplementary information.

Global Can Do descriptors for written mediation from German at Level C1

Can pass on independently in writing the central contents of longer written texts on many-layered themes of general and personal interest to speakers of other languages in a common language.

Can record in writing in a prescribed form in a common language the important contents of longer, complex oral texts in German, on concrete and abstract themes of current interest and in his/her own field of special interest, for speakers of other languages.

Detailed Can Do descriptors for written mediation from German at Level C1

Can pass on independently in writing the central contents of longer written texts on many-layered themes of general and personal interest to speakers of other languages in a common language.

e.g. can pass on in writing in a common language to an interested friend relevant information about a Rhine cruise contained in German-language travel agents' brochures.

Can record in writing in a prescribed form in a common language the important contents of longer, complex oral texts in German, on concrete and abstract themes of current interest and in his/her own field of special interest, for speakers of other languages.

e.g. can record important details with notes at an information session concerning the forthcoming final examinations for the benefit of a sick fellow student so that he can complete the application form.

Global Can Do descriptors for written mediation from another language into German at Level C1

Can record lucidly in writing for German speakers the central contents of longer, complex oral texts in another language from a variety of areas of private and public life together with particular complementary observations.

Can record in writing for German speakers the central contents of longer, complex written texts on concrete and abstract themes of current, personal or specialised themes clearly and free from errors of an orthographic or grammatical nature such as to distort the meaning.

Detailed Can Do descriptors for written mediation from another language into German at Level C1

Can record in writing for German speakers the central contents of longer, complex written texts on concrete and abstract themes of current, personal or specialised themes clearly and free from errors of an orthographic or grammatical nature such as to distort the meaning.

e.g. can pass on in writing in German a report written in another language concerning damage sustained in a car accident to a German-speaking colleague dealing with the case.

Can record lucidly in writing for German speakers the central contents of longer, complex oral texts in another language from a variety of areas of private and public life together with particular complementary observations.

e.g. can record in writing in German for an interested colleague the most important recommendations on favourable investment opportunities contained in a television programme in another language.

Appendix B: Functional progression in the T-series

Vantage (B2 and above)	Threshold (B1)	Waystage (A2)	Breakthrough (A1)
1 imparting and seeking information	1. imparting and seeking factual information	1 imparting and seeking factual information	1 the learner CAN impart and elicit factual information
1.1 identifying and specifying	1.1 identifying (defining)	1.1 identifying (defining)	1.1 identifying
1.2 stating and reporting (describing, narrating)	1.2 reporting (describing and narrating)	1.2 reporting (describing and narrating)	1.2 reporting (describing and narrating)
1.3 correcting	1.3 correcting	1.3 correcting	1.3 correcting
1.3.1 correcting a positive statement	1.3.1 correcting a positive statement		
1.3.2 correcting a negative statement	1.3.2 correcting a negative statement		
1.4 asking	1.4 asking	1.4 asking	1.4 asking
1.4.1 for a confirmation or denial	1.4.1 for confirmation	1.4.1 for confirmation	1.4.1 for confirmation
1.4.2 demanding confirmation or denial			
1.4.3 expecting confirmation			
1.4.4 demanding confirmation			
1.4.5 querying a statement			
1.4.6 asking for a piece of information	1.4.2 for information	1.4.2 for information	1.4.2 for information

Vantage (B2 and above)	Threshold (B1)	Waystage (A2)	Breakthrough (A1)
1.4.7 seeking identification	1.4.3 seeking identification	1.4.3 seeking identification	1.4.3 seeking identification
1.4.8 asking for specification			
1.4.9 expressing curiosity			
1.5 answering questions	1.5 answering questions	1.5 answering questions	1.5 answering questions
1.5.1 confirming or disconfirming	1.5.1 for confirmation	1.5.1 for confirmation	1.5.1 for confirmation
1.5.2 giving information	1.5.2 for information	1.5.2 for information	1.5.2 for information
1.5.2.1 time	1.5.2.1 time		
1.5.2.2 place	1.5.2.2 place		
1.5.2.3 manner	1.5.2.3 degree		
1.5.2.4 degree	1.5.2.4 manner		
1.5.2.5 reason	1.5.2.5 reason		
1.5.3 identifying	1.5.3 seeking identification	1.5.3 seeking identification	1.5.3 for identification
1.5.3.1 identifying a person			
1.5.3.2 identifying a person's occupation, role etc.			
1.5.3.3 identifying the possessor			
1.5.3.4 identifying a thing			

1.5.4 specifying

1.5.5 questions asking for confirmations information, identification or specifications can be answered by expressions of ignorance			2 the learner CAN express and find out attitudes.
2 expressing and finding out attitudes	2 expressing and finding out attitudes	2 expressing and finding out attitudes	2.1 factual: agreement, etc.
2.1 attitudes to matters of fact	2.1 factual: agreement, etc.	2.1 factual: agreement	2.1.1 expressing agreement with a statement
2.1.1 expressing agreement with a statement	2.1.1 expressing agreement with a statement	2.1.1 expressing agreement with a statement	
2.1.1.1 expressing strong agreement		2.1.1.1 expressing agreement with a positive statement	
2.1.1.2 expressing agreement with a positive statement	2.1.2 expressing agreement with a positive statement	2.1.1.2 expressing agreement with a negative statement	
2.1.1.3 expressing agreement with a negative statement	2.1.3 expressing agreement with a negative statement		
2.1.1.4 expressing reluctant agreement			
2.1.1.5 conceding a point			
2.1.1.6 expressing agreement with reservations			

Vantage (B2 and above)	Threshold (B1)	Waystage (A2)	Breakthrough (A1)
2.1.1.7 demurring			
2.1.2 expressing disagreement with a statement	2.1.2 expressing disagreement with a statement	2.1.2 expressing disagreement with a statement	2.1.2 expressing disagreement with a statement
2.1.2.1 expressing strong disagreement			
2.1.2.2 expressing disagreement with a positive statement	2.1.2.1 expressing disagreement with a positive statement	2.1.2.1 expressing disagreement with a positive statement	
2.1.2.3 expressing disagreement with a negative statement	2.1.2.2 expressing disagreement with a negative statement	2.1.2.2 expressing disagreement with a negative statement	
2.1.2.4 expressing weak disagreement			
2.1.3 enquiring about agreement or disagreement	2.1.3 enquiring about agreement or disagreement	2.1.3 enquiring about agreement and disagreement	2.1.3 enquiring about agreement and disagreement
2.1.4 inviting agreement			
2.1.5 inviting disagreement with a statement			
2.1.6 denying statements	2.1.4 denying statements	2.1.4 denying statements	2.1.4 denying something
2.2 expressing knowledge, memory, belief	2.2 factual: knowledge	2.2 factual: knowledge	2.2 factual: knowledge

2.2.1 expressing knowledge (or not) of a person, thing or fact	2.2.1 stating whether one knows or does not know a person, thing or fact	2.2.1 stating whether one knows or does not know something or someone	2.2.1 stating whether one knows or does not know something, someone, or a fact
2.2.2 asking about knowledge	2.2.2 enquiring whether someone knows or does not know a person, thing or fact	2.2.2 enquiring whether one knows or does not know something or someone	2.2.2 enquiring whether someone knows or does not know something, someone, or a fact
2.2.3 asserting ignorance			
2.2.4 expressing remembering or forgetting persons, things, facts, actions	2.2.3 stating whether one remembers or has forgotten a person, thing, fact or action		
2.2.5 enquiring about remembering or forgetting	2.2.4 enquiring whether one remembers or has forgotten a person, thing, fact or action		
2.2.6 reminding			
2.2.7 expressing degrees of certainty			
2.2.7.1 confident assertion			
2.2.7.2 tentative assertion			
2.2.7.3 expressing uncertainty			
2.2.7.4 expressing doubt, incredulity			
2.2.7.5 expressing bewilderment			

Vantage (B2 and above)	Threshold (B1)	Waystage (A2)	Breakthrough (A1)
2.3 expressing modality	2.3 factual: modality	2.3 factual: modality	2.3 factual: certainty
2.3.1 expressing degrees of probability	2.3.1 expressing degrees of probability	2.3.3 expressing how (un)certain one is of something	2.4.1 expressing how certain one is of something
	2.3.5 expressing degrees of certainty	2.3.3.1 strong positive	
		2.3.3.2 positive	
		2.3.3.3 intermediate	
		2.3.3.4 weak	
		2.3.3.5 negative	
	2.3.6 enquiring about degrees of certainty	2.3.4 enquiring how (un)certain others are of something	2.4.2 enquiring how certain someone is of something
2.3.2 enquiring about probability/ possibility	2.3.2 enquiring as to degrees of probability		
2.3.3 expressing necessity (including logical deduction)	2.3.3 expressing or denying necessity (including logical deduction)		
2.3.4 denying necessity			
2.3.5 enquiring as to necessity (including logical deduction)	2.3.4 enquiring as to necessity (including logical deduction)		

2.5 obligation	2.3.5 expressing one is (not) obliged to do something	2.3.7 expressing obligation	2.3.6 expressing obligation
2.5.1 expressing obligation to do something			2.3.7 denying obligation
2.5.2 enquiring whether one is obliged to do something	2.3.6 enquiring whether one is obliged to do something	2.3.8 enquiring about obligation	2.3.8 enquiring about obligation
2.3.1 expressing ability and inability	2.3.1 expressing ability and inability	2.3.9 expressing ability/inability to do something	2.3.9 expressing ability to do something
			2.3.10 denying ability to do something
2.3.2 enquiring about ability and inability	2.3.2 enquiring about ability and inability	2.3.10 enquiring about ability or inability to do something	2.3.11 enquiring about ability to do something
2.6 permission		2.3.11 expressing that something is or is not permitted, or permissible	2.3.12 expressing permissibility
		2.3.12 enquiring whether something is or is not permitted or permissible (including seeking permission)	
2.6.2 seeking permission	2.3.8 seeking permission		2.3.14 enquiring about permissibility
2.6.1 giving permission	2.3.7 giving permission	2.3.13 granting permission	2.3.13 granting permission
2.6.3 stating that permission is not given	2.3.9 stating that permission is withheld	2.3.14 withholding permission	2.3.13 denying permissibility

Vantage (B2 and above)	Threshold (B1)	Waystage (A2)	Breakthrough (A1)
2.4 expressing and enquiring about volition	2.4 volitional	2.4 volitional	2.7 volitional
2.4.1 expressing wishes/wants/desires	2.4.1 expressing wants/desires	2.4.1 expressing want, desire	2.7.1 expressing wants, desires
2.4.2 expressing negative wishes/wants/desires			
2.4.3 enquiring about wishes/wants/desires	2.4.2 enquiring about wants/desires	2.4.2 enquiring about want, desire	2.7.2 enquiring about wants, desires
2.4.4 enquiring about intentions	2.4.3 expressing intentions	2.4.3 expressing intention	2.7.3 expressing intention
2.4.5 expressing negative intentions			
2.4.6 enquiring about intentions	2.4.4 enquiring about intentions	2.4.4 enquiring about intention	2.7.4 enquiring about intention
2.5 expressing and enquiring about emotions	2.5 emotional	2.5 emotional	2.8 emotional
			2.8.1 expressing and reporting emotional states
			2.8.2 enquiring about emotional states
2.5.1 expressing pleasure, happiness	2.5.1 expressing pleasure, liking	2.5.1 expressing pleasure, liking	2.8.3 expressing pleasure, liking

2.5.2 expressing unhappiness, sadness	2.5.2 expressing displeasure, unhappiness	2.5.2 expressing displeasure, dislike	2.8.4 expressing displeasure, dislike
2.5.3 enquiring about happiness/ unhappiness	2.5.3 enquiring about pleasure/ displeasure, happiness/ unhappiness	2.5.3 enquiring about pleasure, liking, displeasure, dislike	2.8.5 enquiring about (dis)pleasure, (dis)like
2.5.4 enquiring about the cause of unhappiness/dissatisfaction/ disappointment			
2.5.5 exhorting someone not to be dejected			
2.5.6 expressing regret/sympathy/ condolence	2.6.7 expressing regret, sympathy	2.6.5 expressing regret	2.9.5 expressing regret
2.5.7 expressing fellow-feeling, empathy			-
2.5.8 expressing hope, expectation	2.5.15 expressing hope	2.5.4 expressing hope	2.8.6 expressing hope
2.5.9 expressing disappointment	2.5.16 expressing disappointment	2.5.8 expressing disappointment	2.8.8 expressing disappointment
2.5.10 expressing fear/anxiety	2.5.17 expressing fear		
2.5.11 enquiring about fear/ anxiety/worry	2.5.19 enquiring about fear/worry		
2.5.12 expressing pain, anguish, suffering			
2.5.13 enquiring about pain, anguish, suffering			

Vantage (B2 and above)	Threshold (B1)	Waystage (A2)	Breakthrough (A1)
2.5.14 reassuring a worried, frightened person, comforting a sufferer	2.5.18 giving reassurance		2.8.10 giving reassurance
2.5.15 expressing relief			
2.5.16 expressing liking, affection	2.5.4 expressing liking	2.5.1 expressing pleasure, liking	2.8.3 expressing pleasure, liking
2.5.17 expressing dislike	2.5.5 expressing dislike	2.5.2 expressing displeasure, dislike	2.8.4 expressing displeasure, dislike
2.5.18 enquiring about like and dislike	2.5.6 enquiring about likes and dislikes	2.5.3 enquiring about pleasure, liking, displeasure, dislike	2.8.5 enquiring about (dis)pleasure, (dis)like
2.5.19 expressing preference	2.4.5 expressing preference	2.4.5 expressing preference	2.7.5 expressing preference
2.5.20 enquiring about preferences	2.4.6 enquiring about preference		
2.5.21 expressing satisfaction		2.5.5 expressing satisfaction	2.8.7 expressing satisfaction
2.5.22 expressing dissatisfaction	2.5.7 expressing dissatisfaction	2.5.6 expressing dissatisfaction	2.8.8 expressing dissatisfaction
2.5.23 enquiring about satisfaction/dissatisfaction	2.5.8 enquiring about satisfaction/ dissatisfaction	2.5.7 enquiring about satisfaction	2.8.9 enquiring about satisfaction
2.5.24 complaining			
2.5.25 expressing bad temper			
2.5.26 reacting to bad temper			
2.5.27 apologising for bad temper			
2.5.28 expressing interest	2.5.9 expressing interest		

2.5.29 expressing lack of interest	2.5.10 expressing lack of interest		
	2.5.11 enquiring about interest or lack of interest		
2.5.30 expressing surprise	2.5.12 expressing surprise		
2.5.31 enquiring about surprise	2.5.13 expressing lack of surprise		
2.5.32 expressing lack of surprise	2.5.14 enquiring about surprise		
2.5.33 expressing indifference		2.6.6 expressing indifference	2.9.6 expressing indifference
2.5.34 enquiring about indifference			
2.5.35 expressing fatigue, resignation			
2.5.36 expressing gratitude	2.5.20 expressing gratitude	2.5.9 expressing gratitude	2.8.9 expressing gratitude
2.5.37 reacting to an expression of gratitude	2.5.21 reacting to an expression of gratitude		
2.6 expressing moral attitudes	2.6 moral	2.6 moral	2.9 moral
2.6.1 expressing moral obligation	2.6.3 expressing moral obligation		
2.6.2 expressing approval	2.6.4 expressing approval	2.6.3 expressing approval	2.9.3 expressing approval
2.6.3 expressing disapproval, protest	2.6.5 expressing disapproval		
2.6.4 enquiring about approval/disapproval	2.6.6 enquiring about approval/disapproval		

Vantage (B2 and above)	Threshold (B1)	Waystage (A2)	Breakthrough (A1)
2.6.5 attaching/accepting blame			
2.6.6 denying blame			
2.6.7 apologising/asking forgiveness	2.6.1 offering an apology	2.6.1 apologising	2.9.1 apologising
2.6.8 apologising for disturbing someone			
2.6.9 accepting an apology, granting forgiveness	2.6.2 accepting an apology	2.6.2 granting forgiveness	2.9.2 granting forgiveness
		2.6.4 expressing appreciation	2.9.4 expressing appreciation
3 deciding and managing courses of action: suasion	3 deciding on courses of action (suasion)	3 getting things done (suasion)	3 the learner CAN get things done (suasion)
3.1 suggesting a joint course of action (involving both speaker and addressee)	3.1 suggesting a course of action (involving both speaker and addressee)	3.1 suggesting a course of action (including the speaker)	3.1 suggesting a course of action
3.2 agreeing to a suggestion	3.2 agreeing to suggestion		
3.3 requesting someone to do something	3.3 requesting someone to do something	3.2 requesting others to do something	3.2 requesting others to do something
3.3.1 urgent requests			
3.3.2 giving instructions and orders			

3.3.3 ordering goods/a meal/ drinks/etc.			
3.3.4 asking someone for something	3.14 asking someone for something		
3.3.5 making polite requests			
3.3.6 dropping hints for someone to act on			
3.3.7 pleading			
3.3.8 asking for assistance	3.8 requesting assistance	3.10 requesting assistance	3.10 requesting assistance
3.4 responding to a request	3.9 offering assistance	3.9 offering assistance	3.9 offering assistance
3.4.1 agreeing to a request willingly			
3.4.2 agreeing with reservations			
3.4.3 agreeing with reluctance			
3.4.4 demurring			
3.4.5 refusing			
3.4.6 expressing defiance			
3.4.6.1 defiance of an order			
3.4.6.2 defiance of a prohibition			

Vantage (B2 and above)	Threshold (B1)	Waystage (A2)	Breakthrough (A1)
3.4.6.3 defiance of a sated intention			
3.5 offering assistance			
3.6 giving advice	3.4 advising someone to do something	3.7 advising others to do something	3.7 advising others to do something
3.7 giving warnings	3.5 warning others to do something or to refrain from doing something	3.8 warning others to take care or to refrain from doing something	3.8 warning
3.8 giving encouragement	3.6 encouraging others to do something		
	3.7 instructing or directing someone to do something		
3.9 asking permission	3.10 seeking permission		
3.10 granting permission	3.11 giving permission		
3.10.1 granting permission willingly			
3.10.2 granting permission with reservations			
3.10.3 granting permission with reluctance			
3.10.4 demurring			

3.11 refusing or withholding permission		3.12 stating that permission is withheld
3.12 prohibiting someone from doing something		
3.13 offering to do something for someone		
3.14 offering somebody something		
3.15 inviting someone to do something	3.10 inviting someone to do something	3.3 inviting others to do something
3.15.1 pressing invitations		
	3.11 accepting an offer or invitation	3.4 accepting an offer or invitation
3.15.2 tentative invitations		
3.16 declining an offer or invitation	3.12 declining an offer or invitation	3.5 declining an offer or invitation
	3.13 enquiring whether an invitation or offer is accepted or declined	3.6 enquiring whether an invitation or offer is accepted or declined
3.16.1 firm refusal		
3.16.2 demurring or weak refusal (inviting renewal of offer/ invitation)		

Vantage (B2 and above)	Threshold (B1)	Waystage (A2)	Breakthrough (A1)
3.17 enquiring whether offer/invitation is accepted			
4 socialising	4 socialising	4 socialising	4 the learner CAN socialise
4.1 attracting attention	4.1 attracting attention	4.1 attracting attention	4.1 attracting attention
4.2 greeting people	4.2 greeting people	4.2 greeting people	4.2 greeting people
4.2.1 greeting strangers or acquaintances	4.2.1 when meeting a friend or acquaintance	4.3 when meeting people	
4.2.2 greeting friends of close acquaintances			
4.3 replying to a greeting	4.3 replying to a greeting from a friend or acquaintance		4.3 responding
4.3.1 if in normal health			
4.3.2 if recovering from an illness etc.			
4.4 addressing	4.4 addressing	4.4 addressing somebody	4.4 addressing people
4.4.1 addressing a friend or a relative	4.4.1 addressing a friend or acquaintance		
4.4.2 addressing an acquaintance			
4.4.3 addressing a stranger (official, customer, member of public, etc.)	4.4.2 addressing a stranger		

4.4.3 addressing a customer or a member of the general public

- 4.4.3.1 formal address
  - 4.4.3.1 formal
  - 4.4.3.2 popular, familiar
- 4.4.3.2 informal address (N.B. no address form)
  - 4.4.3.3 informal
- 4.4.4 terms of endearment
- 4.5 making introductions
  - 4.5 introducing someone to someone else
    - 4.5 introducing somebody
      - 4.5 introducing someone
  - 4.5.1 formal
    - 4.5.1 formal
  - 4.5.2 informal introductions
    - 4.5.2 informal
  - 4.5.3 introducing oneself
    - 4.6 when being introduced to someone or when someone is introduced to you
      - 4.6 reacting to being introduced
        - 4.6 reacting to being introduced
  - 4.5.3.1 more formal
    - 4.6.1.1.1 formal
  - 4.5.3.2 informal
    - 4.6.1.1.2 informal
  - 4.5.4 when being introduced or when someone is introduced to you
  - 4.5.5 enquiring whether an introduction is needed
- 4.6 making someone welcome

Vantage (B2 and above)	Threshold (B1)	Waystage (A2)	Breakthrough (A1)
4.7 at a meal			
4.7.1 at a meal before eating			
4.7.2 at a meal inviting guests to serve themselves			
4.8 proposing a toast	4.8 proposing a toast	4.8 proposing a toast	4.8 proposing a toast
4.9 congratulating someone	4.7 congratulating someone	4.7 congratulating	4.7 congratulating someone
4.10 good wishes			
4.10.1 someone's birthday			
4.10.2 at festival times			
4.10.3 wishing someone success			
4.10.4 when someone is going out, or on holiday			
4.10.5 when parting from someone			
4.11 taking leave	4.9 taking leave	4.9 taking leave	4.9 taking leave
4.11.1 formal	4.9.1 formal		
4.11.2 informal	4.9.2 informal		
4.11.3 colloquial			

4.11.4 if you are not expected to meet again	4.9.3 if you are not expected to meet again		5 the learner CAN structure discourse.
5. structuring discourse	5. structuring discourse	5. structuring discourse	
5.1 opening	5.1 opening	5.1 opening	5.1 opening a conversation
5.1.1 on formal occasions	5.1.1 on formal occasions		
5.1.2 as participant in a meeting	5.1.2 as participant in a meeting		
5.1.3 informally			
5.2 introducing a theme	5.4 introducing a theme		
5.2.1 at the start of a discourse			
5.2.2 introducing a topic			
5.2.3 introducing a report/ narrative or description			
5.2.4 introducing an anecdote			
5.3 expressing an opinion	5.5 expressing an opinion		
5.4 enumerating	5.6 enumerating	5.4 enumerating	5.4 enumerating
5.5 exemplifying	5.7 exemplifying		
5.6 emphasising	5.8 emphasising		
5.6.1 in speech	5.8.1 in speech		

Vantage (B2 and above)	Threshold (B1)	Waystage (A2)	Breakthrough (A1)
5.6.2 in writing	5.8.2 in writing		
5.6.2.1 emphasis in hand- or type-written texts	5.8.2.1 in hand- or type-written texts		
5.6.2.2 emphasis on printed or word-processed texts	5.8.2.2 in printed texts		
5.7 defining			
5.8 summarising	5.9 summarising	5.5 summing up	5.5 summing up
5.9 changing the theme	5.10 changing the theme		
5.10 asking someone to pass to a new theme	5.11 asking someone to change the theme		
5.11 asking someone's opinion	5.12 asking someone's opinion		
5.12 showing that one is following a person's discourse	5.13 showing that one is following a person's discourse		
5.13 interrupting, asking for the floor	5.14 interrupting		
5.14 objecting/protesting			
5.15 asking someone to be silent	5.15 asking someone to be silent		
	5.16 giving over the floor		
5.16 indicating a wish to continue	5.17 indicating a wish to continue		

5.17 encouraging someone to continue	5.18 encouraging someone to continue		
5.18 indicating that one is coming to an end	5.19 indicating that one is coming to an end		
5.19 closing	5.20 closing	5.6 closing	5.6 closing
5.19.1 at the end of a speech	5.20.1 at the end of a speech		
5.19.2 at the end of a conversation	5.20.2 at the end of a conversation		
5.20 using a telephone	5.21 telephone	5.7 telephone	5.7 using the telephone.
5.20.1 opening the conversation by answering the call	5.21.1 on answering a call	5.7.1 opening (on lifting the handset)	5.7.1 opening
5.20.2 response by initiator of call	5.21 response by initiator of call		
5.20.3.1 asking for a person	5.21.3.1 asking for a person		
5.20.3.2 asking for an extension	5.21.3.2 asking for an extension	5.7.2 asking for extension	5.7.2 asking for an extension
5.20.4 verifying caller			
5.20.5 asking someone to wait	5.21.4 asking someone to wait		
5.20.6 asking whether one is heard and heard/understood	5.21.5 asking whether you're heard and understood		
	5.21.5 giving signals that you are hearing and understanding		
5.20.7 announcing new call	5.21.7 announcing new call	5.7.3 giving notice of a new call	5.7.3 requesting or giving notice of a new call

Vantage (B2 and above)	Threshold (B1)	Waystage (A2)	Breakthrough (A1)
5.20.8 signing off signals			
5.21 letters (in addition to 5.1 –19)	5.21 letters	5.8 letter	5.8 opening and closing a letter
5.21.1 opening formulae	5.21.1 opening	5.8.1 opening	5.8.1 opening
5.21.1.1 to strangers whose name is not known, companies	5.21.1.1 if name is not known		
5.21.1.2 to acquaintances and named strangers	5.21.1.2 if name is known		
5.21.1.3 to family friends and closer acquaintances			
5.21.2 closing formulae	5.21.2 closing	5.8.2 closing	5.8.2 closing
5.21.2.1 to strangers whose name is not known			
5.21.2.2 to acquaintances and named strangers			
5.21.2.3 to family friends and closer acquaintances			
5.21.2.4 on terms of endearment only			
6 assuring and repairing communication	6. communication repair	6 communication repair	6 the learner CAN repair snags in communication

6.1 signalling non-understanding	6.1 signalling non-understanding	6.1 signalling non-understanding	6.1 signalling non-understanding
6.2 asking for repetition	6.2 asking for repetition of sentence	6.2 asking for overall repetition	6.2 asking for overall repetition
6.2 1 of the whole utterance			
6.2 2 of a particular word or phrase	6.3 asking for repetition of word or phrase	6.3 asking for partial repetition	6.3 asking for partial repetition
6.3 asking for confirmation	6.4 asking for confirmation	6.5 asking for confirmation of understanding	6.5 asking for confirmation of understanding
6.3.1 asking for confirmation of text	6.4.1 asking for confirmation of text		
6.3.2 asking for confirmation of understanding	6.4.2 asking for confirmation of understanding		
6.4 asking for definition or clarification	6.5 asking for clarification	6.4 asking for clarification	6.4 asking for clarification
6.5 asking someone to spell something	6.6 asking someone to spell something	6.6 asking to spell something	6.6 asking for a word to be spelled out
6.6 asking for something to be written down	6.7 asking for something to be written down	6.7 asking to write something down	6.7 asking for something to be written down
6.7 expressing ignorance	6.8 expressing ignorance of an expression	6.8 expressing ignorance	6.8 expressing ignorance of an expression
6.8 appealing for assistance	6.9 appealing for assistance	6.9 appealing for assistance	6.9 appealing for assistance
6.8 appealing for assistance in finding an expression			

Vantage (B2 and above)	Threshold (B1)	Waystage (A2)	Breakthrough (A1)
6.9 filling hesitation pauses while looking for a forgotten word or phrase	5.2.1 hesitating, looking for words	5.2 hesitating, looking for words	5.2 expressing hesitation, looking for words
6.10 substituting for a forgotten noun or name	5.2.2 hesitating for forgotten name		
6.10.1 using a meaningless noun or name			
6.10.2 paraphrasing	6.11 paraphrasing		
6.11 asking someone to speak more slowly	6.10 asking someone to speak more slowly	6.10 asking to slow down	6.10 asking a speaker to slow down
6.12 what to do if the interlocutor does not understand			
6.12.1 repeating what one has said	6.12 repeating what one has said		
6.12.2 spelling out a word or expression	6.14 spelling out a word or expression		
6.12.3 correcting oneself	5.3 correcting oneself	5.3 correcting oneself	5.3 correcting oneself
6.13 asking if you have been understood	6.13 asking if you have been understood		
6.14 supplying a word or expression	6.15 supplying a word or expression		

Appendix C: Draft illustrative generative Can Do statements for the C levels

1. Spoken Interaction

Code	Activity Can . . .	Topic/Setting Concerned with . . .	Input Based on . . .	Text Producing . . .	Qualities – how well? Linguistic/Pragmatic/Sociolinguistic/ Strategic	Restrictions Provided that . . .
SI-B	discuss the nature and relative merits of particular choices	goods or services, procedures, courses of action		[spoken interaction]	— is readily comprehensible — intonation is used to support meaning — uses a range of grammatical forms and vocabulary appropriate to the audience, topic and social context — adjusts level of formality and style of speech to suit social context: formal, informal, colloquial — contributions are relevant and are integrated into the flow of the discourse	•

Code	Activity Can...	Topic/Setting Concerned with...	Input Based on...	Text Producing...	Qualities – how well? Linguistic/Pragmatic/Sociolinguistic/ Strategic	Restrictions Provided that...
					using linking words, repetition of words used by other participants — repairs interaction as necessary	
SI-C	follow and contribute to complex interactions between third parties	abstract, complex unfamiliar topics		[spoken interaction] group discussion	— turn taking is natural — contributions are relevant and are integrated into the flow of the discourse — using linking words, repetition of words used by other participants — conveys ideas with some precision, does not resort to simplification — is readily comprehensible — intonation is used to support meaning — uses a range of grammatical forms and vocabulary appropriate to the audience, topic and social context — adjusts level of formality and style of speech to suit social context: formal, informal, colloquial — repairs interaction as necessary	•
SI-D	evaluate, restate and challenge	matters within their academic or professional competence	contributions from other participant	[spoken interaction]	— contributions are relevant and are integrated into the flow of the discourse — using linking words, repetition of words used by other participants — is readily comprehensible — intonation is used to support meaning — uses a range of grammatical forms and vocabulary appropriate to the audience, topic and social context	•

SI-E	frame critical remarks or express strong disagreement in such a way as to minimise any offence	familiar topics/matters within their academic or professional competence	[spoken interaction]	<ul><li>adjusts level of formality and style of speech to suit social context: formal, informal, colloquial</li></ul><ul><li>remarks are relevant</li><li>contributions are relevant and are integrated into the flow of the discourse using linking words, repetition of words used by other participants</li><li>adjusts level of formality and style of speech to suit social context: formal, informal, colloquial</li><li>is readily comprehensible; intonation is used to support meaning</li><li>uses a range of grammatical forms and vocabulary appropriate to the audience, topic and social context</li><li>repairs interaction as necessary</li></ul>
SI-F	express sympathy or condolence, enquire into the causes of unhappiness or sadness and offer comfort	personal relationships/ counselling roles	[spoken interaction] conversation	<ul><li>is readily comprehensible</li><li>uses intonation and word choice to express mood, distinguishing between shades of feeling</li><li>uses a range of grammatical forms and vocabulary appropriate to the audience, topic and social context</li><li>adjusts level of formality and style of speech to suit social context: formal, informal, colloquial</li></ul>
SI-G	discuss work with colleagues	matters within their academic or professional competence	[spoken interaction]	<ul><li>using appropriate technical terminology</li><li>is readily comprehensible</li><li>intonation is used to support meaning</li><li>conveys ideas with some precision, does not resort to simplification</li></ul>

Code	Activity Can . . .	Topic/Setting Concerned with . . .	Input Based on . . .	Text Producing . . .	Qualities – how well? Linguistic/Pragmatic/Sociolinguistic/Strategic	Restrictions Provided that . . .
					— uses a range of grammatical forms and vocabulary appropriate to the audience, topic and social context — adjusts level of formality and style of speech to suit social context: formal, informal, colloquial — contributions are relevant and are integrated into the flow of the discourse using linking words, repetition of words used by other participants — repairs interaction as necessary	•
SI-H	indicate levels of willingness or reluctance and state conditions when agreeing to requests or granting permission		requests	[spoken interaction]	— is readily comprehensible — intonation is used to support meaning — uses a range of grammatical forms and vocabulary appropriate to the audience, topic and social context — adjusts level of formality and style of speech to suit social context: formal, informal, colloquial	•
SI-I	invite participation, introduces issues, manages contributions	meetings on matters within their academic or professional competence		[spoken interaction]	— plays a leading part in discussion or negotiation — is readily comprehensible — intonation is used to support meaning — uses a range of grammatical forms and vocabulary appropriate to the audience, topic and social context	•

				— adjusts level of formality and style of speech to suit social context: formal, informal, colloquial — repairs interaction as necessary
SI-J	summarise and evaluate main points in discussion	meetings on matters within their academic or professional competence	[spoken interaction] extended discussion or negotiation	— able to gain and hold floor — summary is accurate — is readily comprehensible — intonation is used to support meaning — uses a range of grammatical forms and vocabulary appropriate to the audience, topic and social context — adjusts level of formality and style of speech to suit social context: formal, informal, colloquial
SI-K	enquire about and negotiate special treatment	prices and conditions of sale – rates, terms and conditions	[spoken interaction] extended negotiation	— using appropriate technical terminology — is readily comprehensible — intonation is used to support meaning — conveys ideas with some precision, does not resort to simplification — uses a range of grammatical forms and vocabulary appropriate to the audience, topic and social context — adjusts level of formality and style of speech to suit social context: formal, informal, colloquial — repairs interaction as necessary
SI-L	complain and negotiate redress	poor service e.g. returning faulty, inappropriate or unwanted service agreements	[spoken interaction] extended negotiation	— using appropriate technical terminology — is readily comprehensible — intonation is used to support meaning — conveys ideas with some precision, does not resort to simplification

Code	Activity Can...	Topic/Setting Concerned with...	Input Based on...	Text Producing...	Qualities – how well? Linguistic/Pragmatic/Sociolinguistic/Strategic	Restrictions Provided that...
		goods and negotiating for a replacement or refund			— uses a range of grammatical forms and vocabulary appropriate to the audience, topic and social context — adjusts level of formality and style of speech to suit social context: formal, informal, colloquial — repairs interaction as necessary	•
SI-M	apologise and ask for understanding of their position	legal, regulatory matters: in case of infringements of regulations		[spoken interaction] exchanges with officials	— is readily comprehensible — intonation is used to support meaning — uses a range of grammatical forms and vocabulary appropriate to the audience, topic and social context — adjusts level of formality and style of speech to suit social context: formal, informal, colloquial — repairs interaction as necessary	• infringements are minor
SI-N	express regrets and negative wishes or intentions			[spoken interaction]	— is readily comprehensible — intonation is used to support meaning — uses a range of grammatical forms and vocabulary appropriate to the audience, topic and social context — adjusts level of formality and style of speech to suit social context: formal, informal, colloquial — repairs interaction as necessary	•
SI-O	establish solidarity with		complaints about third	[spoken interaction]	— contributions are integrated into the flow of the discourse using linking words, repetition	•

		parties/ conditions		
	interlocutors through sympathetic questioning and expressions of agreement		informal conversation (with friends)	— of words used by other participants — adjusts level of formality and style of speech to suit social context: formal, informal, colloquial — is readily comprehensible — uses intonation and word choice to express mood, distinguishing between shades of feeling — uses a range of grammatical forms and vocabulary appropriate to the audience, topic and social context — repairs interaction as necessary •
SI-P	complex, abstract ideas academic/ professional matters	ask for explanation or clarification and negotiate understanding	[spoken interaction] discussion	— is readily comprehensible — intonation is used to support meaning — uses a range of grammatical forms and vocabulary appropriate to the audience, topic and social context — adjusts level of formality and style of speech to suit social context: formal, informal, colloquial — repairs interaction as necessary
SI-Q		negotiate a course of action with a partner or group, reporting on what others have said, summarising, elaborating and weighing up multiple points of view	[spoken interaction] discussion	• contributions are integrated into the flow of the discourse using linking words, repetition of words used by other participants — is readily comprehensible — intonation is used to support meaning — uses a range of grammatical forms and vocabulary appropriate to the audience, topic and social context — adjusts level of formality and style of speech to suit social context: formal, informal, colloquial — repairs interaction as necessary

2. Spoken Production

Code	Activity Can...	Topic/Setting Concerned with...	Input Based on...	Text Producing...	Qualities – how well? Linguistic/Pragmatic/Sociolinguistic/Strategic	Restrictions Provided that...
SP-A	interpret specialist topics to the layperson	complex technical topics		[spoken production] addressing audiences	— able to speak at length as required — is readily comprehensible — intonation is used to support meaning — good command of non-technical circumlocution, idiomatic expressions and colloquialisms — uses a range of grammatical forms and vocabulary appropriate to the audience, topic and social context — manipulates the order of elements to control information focus — makes topic accessible to the layperson — adjusts level of formality and style of speech to suit social context: formal, informal, colloquial — consistent register — checks comprehension	topics relate to his/her field of interest, presentation prepared independently
SP-B	qualify assertions	complex technical/ abstract topics		[spoken production] addressing audiences	— able to speak at length as required — is readily comprehensible — intonation is used to support meaning — uses a range of grammatical forms and vocabulary appropriate to the audience, topic and social context — indicating levels of confidence or uncertainty — clear — demonstrates flexibility and control of nuances — well-structured and developed	
SP-C	define or specify	complex technical/		[spoken production]	— is readily comprehensible — intonation is used to support meaning	topics relate to his/her field of

	addressing audiences	abstract topics	— uses a range of grammatical forms and vocabulary appropriate to the audience, topic and social context — clear — demonstrates flexibility and control of nuances in detail, distinguishing between objects or concepts that closely resemble each other — at length — well-structured and developed	interest
SP-D	give instruction	series of complex professional/ academic procedures	[spoken production] [sustained monologue] — is readily comprehensible — intonation is used to support meaning — uses a range of grammatical forms and vocabulary appropriate to the interlocutor(s), topic and social context — using appropriate technical terminology — clear — at length — detailed — well-structured and developed — conveys ideas with some precision, does not resort to simplification — checks comprehension as necessary	instructions to a work colleague or student with some technical knowledge
SP-E	speculate or hypothesise, comparing and evaluating a number of possible developments		[spoken production] [sustained monologue] — clear — detailed — at length — well-structured and developed — is readily comprehensible — intonation is used to support meaning — conveys ideas with some precision, does not resort to simplification — uses a range of grammatical forms and vocabulary appropriate to the interlocutor(s), topic and social context	

3. Spoken Reception

Code	Activity Can . . .	Text when listening to . . .	Text characteristics characterised by . . .	Topic/Setting concerned with . . .	Qualities – how well?	Restrictions Provided that . . .
SR-A	make notes to extract and reconstruct the main points and key supporting details	presentations, lectures or documentary broadcasts	extended monologue	complex public, academic or professional topics involving detailed propositional information that is new to the listener and includes abstract concepts	produces accurate and detailed summary or text level representation of factual content summarises the main points accurately responds to questions of detail	standard accents, familiar to the listener rate of speech is natural
SR-B	extract the gist and distinguish between opinions	informal meetings and discussions	multi-participant discussion with non-linear organisation, frequent colloquialisms and overlapping turns	personal or public topics of general interest	identifies the main points being made by participants identifies all areas of agreement and disagreement between participants	conversation is animated – at a fast natural rate voices are easily differentiated or audio is supported by images language is standard, but a range of accents are used
SR-C	identify the emotions or attitudes of speakers	informal meetings and discussions	multi-participant discussion marked by non-linear organisation, colloquialisms and overlapping turns	personal, public, academic, professional topics	accurately identifies the attitudes or emotions conveyed implicitly by stress, pitch and intonation, lexical choices	conversation is animated – at a fast natural rate voices are easily differentiated or audio is supported by images language is standard, but a range of accents are used
SR-D	extract gist, detail, purposes and main points	formal discussions on academic, public or professional topics	dialogues, multi-participant discussion with formal turn taking and organisation – may be mediated by a chairperson	complex public, academic or professional topics involving detailed propositional information that is new to the listener: facts, definitions	produces accurate and detailed summary or text level representation of factual content, showing relationships between ideas accurately responds to questions of detail	contributions are clearly presented – intended for an audience as well as fellow participants standard accent, familiar to the listener

SR-E	extract, select and integrate detailed information required to carry out related tasks	multiple sources	variety of spoken text types: extended monologues, multi-participant discussions	complex, abstract personal, public, academic, professional topics	extracts and evaluates information and opinions from different sources integrates these in preparation for a report, essay or position paper etc.	standard accent, familiar to the listener discussions are formal and structured
SR-F	identify, analyse and evaluate the use of interactive spoken language for persuasion	formal debates, interviews, business interactions, situations of personal or public conflict	dialogues, multi-participant discussions	personal, public, academic, professional topics	identifies how linguistic resources (stress, pitch and intonation, lexical choices) are used by participants to resolve conflict, build consensus, promote views etc. and evaluates the success of these strategies in an interaction	in dialogues/discussions, voices are easily differentiated or audio is supported by images language is standard, but a range of accents are used
SR-G	evaluate presentations in relation to their purpose and audience	presentations, speeches	extended monologue	personal, public, academic, professional topics	identifies speaker purpose and intended audience evaluates the use of language in relation to these: suggests improvements	language is standard, but a range of accents may be used rate of speech is natural
SR-H	integrate information and detailed instructions to carry out complex tasks involving multiple elements	multiple sources	extended monologues, dialogues	personal, public, academic, professional topics	brings together information from different sources to describe a task to be carried out and steps to complete the task	language is standard, but a range of accents may be used rate of speech is natural unfamiliar process or procedure the context is familiar – personal to the listener or within the listener's academic/ professional field

4. Written Interaction

Code	Activity Can . . .	Topic/Setting Concerned with . . .	Input Based on . . .	Text Producing . . .	Qualities – how well? Linguistic/Pragmatic/Sociolinguistic	Restrictions Provided that . . .
WI-A	Write in support of a candidate for a job or award	personal or professional	resume	[written interaction] letter/email of reference	maintains high levels of linguistic accuracy over extended text makes effective use of linguistic modality to signal the strength of claim, argument, or position complex clear appropriate and effective logical structure which helps the reader to find significant points reaches a position or conclusion well-structured and developed logical uses conventional elements of genre structure style appropriate to the genre adopted and to the reader in mind	
WI-B	Write a persuasive application	academic or professional employment	personal information	[written production] job/study application letter/email	maintains high levels of linguistic accuracy over extended text makes effective use of linguistic modality to signal the strength of claim, argument, or position complex clear appropriate and effective logical structure which helps the reader to find significant points reaches a position or conclusion well-structured and developed logical	employment/ study within his/her field of interest

					uses conventional elements of genre structure style appropriate to the genre adopted and to the reader in mind
WI-C	Evaluate, restate and challenge an argument	professional or academic	online discussion	[written interaction] online discussion	maintains high levels of linguistic accuracy over [in real time] extended sequence of turns clear uses conventional elements of genre structure style appropriate to the genre adopted and to the reader in mind repairs interaction as necessary
WI-D	Ask for explanation or clarification and negotiate understanding	complex, abstract ideas academic/ professional matters		[written interaction] online discussion	maintains high levels of linguistic accuracy over [in real time] extended sequence of turns clear uses conventional elements of genre structure style appropriate to the genre adopted and to the reader in mind repairs interaction as necessary
WI-E	express sympathy or condolence and offer comfort	sensitive personal matters	news of bereavement/ divorce	[written interaction] letter of sympathy, condolence	maintains high levels of linguistic accuracy over extended text makes effective use of linguistic modality to signal the strength of claim, argument, or position complex clear well-structured and developed logical uses conventional elements of genre structure style appropriate to the genre adopted and to the reader in mind

5. Written Production

Code	Activity Can...	Topic/Setting Concerned with...	Input Based on...	Text Producing...	Qualities – how well? Linguistic/Pragmatic/Sociolinguistic	Restrictions Provided that...
WP-A	incorporate information drawn from the work of others into his/her own text	complex academic or professional topics	professional or academic texts	[written production] reports, articles or essays	clear appropriate and effective logical structure which helps the reader to find significant points without infringing conventionally-accepted academic/professional standards of the use of others work	
WP-B	set out multiple perspectives on an intellectual issue	complex academic or professional topics	professional or academic texts	[written production] reports, articles or essays	maintains high levels of linguistic accuracy over extended text makes effective use of linguistic modality to signal the strength of claim, argument, or position makes clear author's own stance on the issue clearly distinguishes own ideas and opinions from those of (multiple) sources style appropriate to the genre adopted	topic within his/her field of interest
WP-C	describe and interpret	complex academic or professional topics	empirical data from research	[written production] reports, articles or essays	maintains high levels of linguistic accuracy over extended text at length (500 words plus) clear reaches a position or conclusion well-structured and developed style appropriate to the genre adopted	
WP-D	present specialist material	complex academic or professional topics	research or professional/academic texts	[written production] reports, articles or essays for a general audience	maintains high levels of linguistic accuracy over extended text at length (500 words plus) uses suitably non-technical words and phrases clear	topic within his/her field of interest opportunities for redrafting and revision

					well-structured and developed style appropriate to the genre adopted and to the reader in mind accessible to an audience that is not familiar with the topic	
WP-E	define or specify	complex academic or professional topics	personal experiences/ texts	[written production] reports, articles or essays	at length (500 words plus) in detail, distinguishing between objects or concepts that closely resemble each other maintains high levels of linguistic accuracy over extended text clear complex logical well-structured and developed	
WP-F	write an introduction	complex academic or professional topics	co-text	[written production] longer reports, articles or dissertations	maintains high levels of linguistic accuracy over extended text at length (500 words plus) complex clear well-structured and developed logical uses conventional elements of genre structure presenting key elements to be developed in succeeding text	topic within his/her field of interest opportunities for redrafting and revision
WP-G	write a conclusion	complex academic or professional topics	co-text	[written production] longer reports, articles or dissertations	maintains high levels of linguistic accuracy over extended text at length (500 words plus) complex clear well-structured and developed logical uses conventional elements of genre structure reviews and summarises an extended exposition or argument	topic within his/her field of interest opportunities for redrafting and revision

6. Written Reception

Code	Activity Can . . .	Text when reading . . .	Text characteristics characterised by . . .	Topic/Setting concerned with . . .	Qualities – how well?	Restrictions Provided that . . .
WR-A	demonstrate comprehensive understanding	articles in serious newspapers or magazines; reference books; specialised academic/ professional publications	lengthy, complex sentences infrequent, sometimes technical vocabulary formal register	complex public, academic or professional topics conveying detailed propositional information that is new to the reader: facts, definitions	produces accurate and detailed summary or text level representation of factual content, showing relationships between ideas accurately responds to questions of detail	access to reference tools opportunities for re-reading texts addressed to general educated readership OR texts addressed to professional/ academic community to which learner belongs
WR-B	integrate ideas across texts: compare, contrast, synthesise	articles in serious newspapers or magazines; reference books; specialised academic/ professional publications	lengthy, complex sentences infrequent, sometimes technical vocabulary formal register	complex, public, academic or professional topics including abstract ideas	identifies all main areas of agreement and disagreement across texts selects elements from two or more texts to construct a balanced response to a question	access to reference tools opportunities for re-reading texts addressed to general educated readership OR texts addressed to professional/academic community to which learner belongs
WR-C	demonstrate understanding of implicit attitudes and opinions	articles in serious newspapers or magazines; reference books; specialised academic/	linguistic means for conveying attitude include use of metaphor/ marked syntax/ lexical connotation	complex public, academic or professional topics; conveying attitudes and opinions	accurately summarises the views of the writer	access to reference tools opportunities for re-reading texts addressed to general educated readership OR

	Text types	Text characteristics	Topics	Expected response	Conditions
WR-D demonstrate comprehensive understanding	professional publications personal messages in informal letters, emails etc. informal articles, weblogs etc.	texts characterised by: lengthy, complex sentences infrequent, sometimes technical vocabulary formal register informal register colloquial expressions elliptical cohesion cultural references	complex public, academic or professional topics conveying detailed propositional information that is new to the reader: facts, definitions	produces accurate and detailed summary or text level representation of factual content, showing relationships between ideas accurately responds to questions of detail	texts addressed to professional/academic community to which learner belongs access to reference tools opportunities for re-reading texts addressed to general educated readership OR texts addressed to professional/academic community to which learner belongs
WR-E demonstrate understanding of implicit attitudes and opinions	personal messages in informal letters, emails etc. informal articles, weblogs etc.	linguistic means for conveying attitude include use of metaphor/ marked syntax/ lexical connotation informal register colloquial expressions elliptical cohesion cultural references	personal topics; conveying emotions, attitudes and opinions	accurately summarises the views of the writer	access to reference tools opportunities for re-reading
WR-F critically interpret	literary writings articles in serious newspapers or magazines; specialised	formal register lengthy, complex sentences infrequent, sometimes technical vocabulary	personal, public, educational or professional topics	accurately represents the views of the writer and engages critically with them to reach a conclusion	access to reference tools opportunities for re-reading

Code	Activity Can...	Text when reading...	Text characteristics characterised by...	Topic/Setting concerned with...	Qualities – how well?	Restrictions Provided that...
		academic/ professional publications personal messages in informal letters, emails etc.	OR informal register colloquial expressions elliptical cohesion cultural references			
WR-G	can demonstrate awareness of the impact on the reader of features of style: lexical and grammatical choices, discourse organisation	literary writings articles in serious newspapers or magazines; specialised academic/ professional publications personal messages in informal letters, emails etc.	formal register lengthy, complex sentences infrequent, sometimes technical vocabulary OR informal register colloquial expressions elliptical cohesion cultural references	personal, public, educational or professional topics	successfully identifies genre, tone, purpose, stylistic features and likely impact	access to reference tools opportunities for re-reading
WR-H	demonstrate broad understanding	articles in serious newspapers or magazines; reference books; specialised academic/ professional publications	lengthy, complex sentences infrequent, sometimes technical vocabulary formal register	complex public, academic or professional topics conveying detailed propositional information that is new to the reader: facts, definitions	produces accurate general overview of content reproduces all main ideas accurately responds to questions of gist	under time pressure texts addressed to general educated readership OR texts addressed to professional/academic community to which learner belongs

Author index

Abelson, R P 27
Alderson, J C 48, 49, 56, 70, 71, 115, 120, 124, 148, 151, 152–154, 156
Alexander, L G xxx, 9,
Anderson, R C 136
Austin, J xxviii, 11–13

Bachman, L F 19, 20, 54, 58, 87, 120
Baldegger, M xxx
Bardovi-Harlig, K 34, 35, 36
Bausch, K 48
Blanford, F G xxviii
Block, J H 41
Bloom, B S 41
Bloomfield, L 11, 15
Blum-Kulka, S 34–35
Bonnet, G 60
Bormuth, J R 132
Breen, M P 51
Brennan, R L 45
Brindley, G 69
Brown, H D 10
Brown, J D 36, 132
Brown, P 15
Brumfit, C J 51
Bühler, K 15
Bunch, M 62, 148
Bung, K xxviii

Cai, Z 123
Canale, M 19–20, 54
Candlin, C 51
Capel, A xxvii, 2, 10, 77–78, 115–116, 125, 147, 164
Carroll, B J 60
Carroll, J B 41, 46
Celce-Murcia, M 11, 19, 173
Chalhoub-Deville, M 43
Chiba, M 35
Chihara, T 136
Cizek, G J 62, 148
Clapham, C 135
Clark, J 43
Clifford, R 43, 87
Cobb, T 94
Coltheart, M 134
Cook, G 28
Coriat, R 119–120

Coste, D xxi, xxix, xxxiv
Coulthard, M 13
Coulthard, R 12
Council of Europe xx, xxiii–xxv, xxviii, xxix, xxxii–xxxiv, xxxvii–xxxviii, xli, 1–3, 7–9, 11, 12, 14, 17, 19, 20, 24, 29–31, 33, 34, 37–39, 41, 42, 45–63, 67, 71, 75, 78–81, 88, 90, 115–116, 129, 143, 148–150, 157, 159–164, 170–173
Courtillon, J xxix
Coxhead, A 123
Crossey, M 61
Crossley, S 119, 132
Crystal, D 36
Cummins, J 113

Davidson, F 70
de Jong, J H A L 58, 86
Detmer, E 36
Dornyei, Z 11, 19, 173
Dunlea, J 70

Eckersley, C 9
Ehrlich, M F 132
Ellis, R 35
Enright, M 120

Faucett, L 9
Feldt, L S 45
Fellbaum, C 134
Ferenczi, V xxix
Filipović, L 2, 10, 34, 77–78, 115–116, 143, 147, 161, 167–168, 171, 173
Figueras, N 71
Firth, J xxviii, 11, 12, 16
Flowerdew, J 14, 24–25
Fortus, R 119–120
Foster, P 61, 169
Frawley, W 44, 48, 70
Freedle, R 119–120, 132
Fulcher, G 70
Fund, S 119–120

Garfinkel, H 12
Gass, S M 35
Glaboniat, M 70, 78
Goffman, E 27

Golato, A 36
Goldman, S R 132
Grabe, W 120
Graesser, A 123
Greenfield, J 118–119, 132
Grice, H 14–15

Halliday, M 16–19
Hartford, B S 35–36
Hassall, T J 35
Hasselgreen, A 77
Hawkey, R 1
Hawkins, J A 2, 10, 34, 77–78, 115–116,
    143, 147, 161, 167–168, 171, 173
Heatley, A 123,125
Herzog (nd) 43
Hill, T 35
Holec, H xxxi
Hornby, A 9
Houck, N 35
House, J 34
Hudson, T 36, 49
Hulstijn, J H 1, 7, 40, 48–49, 58
Hymes, D xxviii, 11, 14, 15, 17, 19, 53

Ingram, D E 44, 46

Jakobson, R 14–17
Jefferson G 12, 27
Jespersen, O 18
Joag-Dev, C 136
Johnson, K 10
Jones, N 148

Kachru, B 82
Kasper, G 34–35
Kaulfers, W V xxiii
Keller, E 27
Kendall, J M 47
Khalifa, H 71, 116–120, 124–125, 162
Kingsbury, R 9
Koda, K 132
Kostin, I 119–120
Kramsch, C 43–44, 48
Krumm, H 48

Lantolf, J 44, 48, 70
Lazaraton, A 44
Leech, G N 15, 25, 34
Lenz, P 77, 80–81
Levinson, S 15
Liskin-Gasparro, J E 43–44
Little, D 60
Liu, J 36
Lonergan, J 87
Louwerse, M M 123
Lyons, J 18

Maeshiba, N 35
Mager, R F 42, 47, 60, 150
Malinowski, B 11–12
Martins-Baltar, M xxix
Martyniuk, W 61, 71
Matsudaira, T 70
McNamara, D S 67, 70, 119, 123, 132
Milanovic, M 7
Mislevy, R 45, 49
Mitchell, R 34
Morrow, K 70
Mosenthal, P 120
Mulcahy-Ernt, P 120
Müller, M 70, 78
Mulligan, K 11
Murray, N J 47
Myles, F 34

Nation, I S P 123
Neff, A xxx
Noijons, J 61, 71
North, B xxi, xxxiv, xxxvii, 41, 43, 44,
    46–49, 51, 54–55, 58, 60, 62, 113,
    172

O'Neill, R 9, 10
Oller, J 136
Olshtain, E 20, 35
Oscarsson, M xxxiii
O'Sullivan, B 37

Page, B 44, 46, 49
Palmer, H E xxviii, 19–20, 54, 87
Pape, E xxx
Pawlikowska-Smith, G 67–69, 85, 101,
    107–108
Pike, K 12
Pollitt, A 47
Porcher, L xxxi

Rakestraw, J A 132
Richards and Rogers 10
Richterich, R xxviii–xxix, 24, 49
Roberts, J 25
Robins, R 12
Robinson, M 35
Roever C 36, 67, 70
Rose, K R 34–35
Ross, S 35
Rusch, P 70, 78

Sacks, H 12, 27
Sakurai, T 136
Salamoura, A 169
Sammartino, P xxiii
Sarangi, S 13
Savignon, S 19, 44, 48, 58

Saville, N 1, 37
Scarcella, R 35
Schank, R C 27
Schärer, R 41, 43
Schedl, M 120
Schegloff, E A 12, 27, 55
Schmidt, R 34
Schmitz, H 70, 78
Schneider, G xxxvii, 46, 49, 77, 80–81
Schoonen, R 1, 7, 40
Schwartz, B 8
Scott, M 123
Scott, R 9, 10
Searle, J 12–15, 17
Shaw, S 71, 162
Siegal, M 36
Sinclair, J 12
Skehan, P 169
Smith, P C 47, 67–69
Spady, W 42, 69
Sperber, D 15
Spolsky, B xxii–xxiii
Steffensen, M S 136
Stone, M H 47
Strevens, P 10
Svanes, B 35
Swain, M 19–20, 54
Swales, J 27, 51

Tan, S H 135
Tannenbaum, R J 70
Tarone, E 35
Thomas, J 11, 36

Thorndike118
Thurrell, S 11, 19, 173
Trim, J L M xxi–xli, 2, 7–9, 12, 18, 20, 22,
    24–28, 31–32, 39–40, 44, 51, 53, 82,
    100, 148–150, 165, 167–168, 171
Trosborg, A 35,

van Ek, J A xxi, xxviii–xxxii, 1, 2, 14, 18,
    20–22, 24–28, 31, 32, 40, 42, 44, 48, 50,
    54, 96, 100, 165, 167, 168, 171,
van Els, T 44
van Lier, L 44

Weir, C J 7, 37, 48, 60, 68, 71, 116, 117,
    119–120, 124–125, 135, 161–162
Wertenschlag, L 70, 78
West, M 9
West, R 60
Widdowson, H G 10
Wilds, C P 46
Wilkins, D xxiv, xxviii, xxx, 1, 9–10, 17–18,
    22, 31, 41, 80, 88, 90–91, 93, 108, 149,
    172
Wilson, D 15
Wittgenstein, L 11
Wright, B D 47
Wu, J 70
Wu, R 70
Wunderlich, D 27
Wylie, E C 70

Yeadon, T 9
Yoshinaga, N 135

Subject index

abstract (information in text) xxxviii, 21, 63, 64, 98–103, 107, 111–112, 115–116, 119–120, 129, 134–135, 156, 197–202
academic domain of language use 68
accuracy xxxii, xxxix, 30–31, 50–51, 60, 104, 113, 139–141, 172, 238–241
achievement xxxvi–xxxvii, 41, 45, 48, 69
(communicative) activities 48, 50, 55, 75, 88, 103, 108–109, 113, 117, 159, 172
(language) activities xxviii, xxxv–xxxvi, xxxix–xl, 11, 21, 27, 40, 50–58, 60, 77, 79–83, 86–87, 89–90, 115–116, 150–151, 155–157, 160–161, 173
(language) acquisition 34–38, 48
analysis of variance (anova) 127–130, 133–135
appropriateness 29, 51
aptitude 22, 41
assessment xxii, xxv, xxix, xxxiii–xxxix, 1, 3, 19, 22, 36, 43, 45–50, 61–62, 67–71, 77–80, 83–85, 87, 110, 113, 154, 171
assignments 68
attainment xxiv–xxv, xxxiii, 82–83, 87
audience xxix, 34, 49–52, 56–57, 77, 96, 99, 103–108, 110–112, 148, 157, 159, 170, 194, 195, 227–241
(textual) authenticity 67, 101, 120

band scales xxxvii–xxxix, 54, 59, 84, 86, 104–105
behavioural objectives 41–43, 44, 46–47
brevity (of descriptors) xxxviii–xxxix, 47
business English 84, 85, 98–100, 106–108, 189, 191, 237

categorisation of speech acts 7, 11–16, 19–20, 28–30, 33–38, 159, 227–237
categorisation of functions xxiv, xxviii, 1, 3, 7, 12–17, 19–29, 32–39, 53–54, 70–71, 79–83, 86–94, 99, 112, 117–118, 159, 170–171
circumlocution 57, 104, 234
clarity (of descriptors) xxxviii, 42–43, 47–50, 60
classification of text types 138–144, 152–154, 164
(textual) coherence 29, 99, 132–134, 142–143

collocations 95, 97–98, 104, 164
colloquialisms 29–30, 63, 112, 187, 190, 191, 194, 234, 236
communicative approach xxii–xxxvi, 7–10, 15, 18–31, 42, 51–53, 55, 63–66, 77–80, 150–152, 155–158, 161–164, 170–174
communicative language functions 1–3, 7–21, 23–30, 33–38, 52–56, 75–76, 87–93, 102, 106–109, 112–114, 117–118, 152–156, 159, 162, 164–165, 168, 170–172
comparison 88, 92–93, 106, 120
competences–general xxxii–xxxiii, xxxv
competences–communicative language xxvii–xxxiii, 1–3, 7–8, 11, 19–22, 50–54, 67, 173
competencies xxvii, xxxiv–xxxvii, 42, 50, 58–60, 75, 80–81, 150–151, 162
complexity xxii–xxiii, xxxi–xxxii, xxxviii–xxxix, 26, 30–31, 33, 35, 58, 63–64, 67, 87, 96–107, 109–113, 115–121, 127, 129, 131–134, 143, 151–152, 156, 159–161, 171, 188–202, 227, 228, 233–244
comprehension xxiii, 3, 14–16, 34–35, 48–49, 52, 54, 69, 100–102, 109–110, 112, 116, 119–121, 129, 132–136, 143–144, 151–156, 234–235
computational linguistics 119, 143
conative function 15–17, 118
conclusions 90, 92, 99, 110–111, 188, 194–196, 238, 240, 241, 243
concordances 97–98, 103
concreteness of information xxix–xxxii, xxxvi, xxxviii–xxxix, 33, 47, 60, 64, 65, 68, 98, 103, 105, 106, 109, 115, 120, 123, 134–135, 137–138, 140–142, 147, 150–151, 161, 189, 195, 197–199, 201, 202
condition (vs performance/criterion) xxxv, 42–44, 47, 49, 57–62, 75–77, 79, 81, 89, 94, 99, 103, 112–113, 148–150–158, 169–170, 172
connectives 123
connotative meaning 29–30
constraints xxxv, 24, 32, 42, 57–58, 62, 75, 77, 110, 150, 156, 169–170

(scale) constructors 148–149
contexts xxiv, xxv, xxxi, xxxiii, xxxv–xxxvi,
    2, 7–9, 11–12, 14–19, 24, 29, 31, 35,
    37, 42–43, 45, 49–50, 55–56, 58, 60–62,
    65, 67, 70–71, 80, 96, 99, 104–107, 110,
    112–113, 116–118, 120, 136, 150–151,
    157, 159–162, 169, 171–173, 227–237
conversation xxv, xxxii, 11–16, 27, 29, 32,
    36, 52–53, 55, 57–58, 60–61, 63, 80, 89,
    98, 102, 163, 171, 173, 187–189, 191,
    194, 200, 201, 221, 223, 229, 233, 236
corpora xxvii, 2, 94–97, 123–126, 154,
    165–168
corpus linguistics xxvii, 94–97, 123–126,
    161, 165–168
course (of study) xxi–xxiv, xxvii–xxviii,
    xxx, xxxiii–xxxiv, xli, 9, 22, 24, 37–38,
    53–54, 69–72, 79–86, 114, 192, 195, 196
criterial differences 89, 94–114, 116,
    122–124–144, 169
criterion (vs performance and condition)
    42–50, 57–61, 67, 75–77, 89, 148,
    151–158

(English Profile) database 71, 80–87, 89–96,
    103–104, 108, 129
definiteness (of descriptors) xxxviii–xxxix,
    47, 60
deixis 10, 18
(reading for) detail xxxii, xxxviii, 31, 49–50,
    63–64, 67, 100–102, 111, 151–152, 162,
    191–193, 241–244
dialects xxxii, 19, 20, 102, 112
dialogue xxiv, 9, 36–37
dictation xxii
discourse xxx–xxxi, xxxv, xxxix, 10, 12,
    19–20, 27–29, 32, 35–36, 42, 51, 58, 63,
    78, 87–90, 95, 101, 106, 109–111, 120,
    132–144, 152, 157, 159, 163, 173, 189,
    194, 221–222, 227–233, 244
discourse competence 19–20, 28–29, 42, 51,
    58, 109, 173
downgraders 35

education xxi–xxvi, xxix–xxxvii, xxxix,
    7–10, 19, 31, 34–38, 41–43, 69–71, 77,
    80, 82–88, 103–114, 147–154, 156, 158,
    161, 163, 169–170, 172–174
educators 3, 7–8, 43, 69–70, 79, 82, 112,
    114, 147–149, 169, 173
elaboration 60–61, 67, 70–72, 102, 115–116,
    149, 154–161
emic 12
(General) English 59, 70
English for academic purposes xxxviii, 39,
    53, 58, 63, 78, 98–107, 110, 113, 118,
    156, 228–244

English for specific purposes 35
environment (conditions for
    communication) xxvi–xxvii, 22, 36,
    101–102, 106–107, 117, 121
ethnography 14
ethnomethodology 17
etic 12
examinations xxi–xxii, xxv, xxviii, xxx–xxxi,
    2, 38, 45, 55, 59–62, 71, 79, 81, 84, 102,
    112, 114, 116–119, 122, 125, 159, 164,
    165, 197, 201
examiners xxii, xxv, 49–50, 103, 110
exegesis 28
exemplification 60–61, 67, 70–72, 81,
    102–103, 115–118, 155–158
exponents (grammatical and lexical)
    xxxi–xxxii, 9–10, 21–22, 25, 27, 30,
    32, 37–40, 43, 70, 112–114, 117–118,
    165–167, 171
exposition 22, 28, 29, 53, 90, 92, 120, 241

factual (information) xxvi–xxvii, 11–12,
    21–22, 25, 27–31, 49, 52, 64–65, 80,
    100, 106, 117–118, 203
familiar (topic) xxxviii, 14, 23, 29–31, 33,
    55, 57, 63–68, 80, 96–97, 101, 105–112,
    135–136, 151–152, 170–173, 197, 198,
    200–201, 219, 236–237
fluency xxxii, xxxviii, xxxix, 30, 39, 50–51,
    58, 112, 113
formality 24, 53, 55, 96, 171, 227–234
formulaic expressions 35–38
frameworks xxxiv–xxxvii, 1–3, 20–21,
    29–33, 41–62, 67–72, 75–79, 81–83,
    120–121, 135, 152–156, 170–174
French xxi, xxv, xxix, xxxiv, 24, 47
functions xxiv, xxvii, xxviii–xxxiii, xxxix,
    1–3, 7–25, 27–40, 44–45, 53–55, 77–83,
    86–94, 108–113, 116–119, 155–158,
    170–174

genre 27–30, 35–36, 53, 55–56, 67–68,
    95–99, 103, 105, 112. 120, 143 152, 159,
    171, 238–241, 244
German xxii, xxv, xxxix–xl, 24, 47, 71, 78,
    188, 189, 191–193, 196–202
(reading for) gist xxxii, 48–49, 102, 151–152,
    244
grades xxii, 44–46, 84–87, 106–112,
    118–119, 122–129, 133, 138–141
grammar xxi–xxvii, xxix, xxxi, xxxix–xl,
    1–2, 9–10, 12, 14, 16–20, 30, 34–35,
    39, 40, 51, 53, 60, 70–71, 75, 77, 88,
    95, 99–104, 109–116, 118, 120–132,
    135–136, 143, 149–151, 157, 161, 165,
    167–168, 171, 173, 188, 190, 194, 196,
    202, 227–235, 244

grammatical competence xxi–xxii, xxxix, 10, 19–20, 30, 51, 60, 99–100, 104, 109–110, 112, 151, 157, 168, 188, 190, 194, 196, 202, 227–235, 244

horizontal (aspect of the CEFR) xxxvi–xxxvii, 49–50, 58–59

idioms 19, 29–30, 56, 63, 95, 101–102, 104, 112–113, 153, 187, 190, 191, 192, 193 194, 196, 234
imperatives 14, 16, 26
implicature 14–15, 36–37
implicit information xxxviii, 101–103, 152, 192–193, 236, 242, 243
independence (of descriptors) xxxii–xxxviii, 29, 46–48, 60, 62
independence (of language use) xxiii, xxvi–xxvii, xxxvii–xxxviii, 24, 64, 77, 100, 103, 190, 197, 198, 201
indirectness 14, 24–27, 34–37, 168, 171
inferencing 71, 92, 95, 100, 111–112,
informality 23–24, 29, 52, 53, 56, 78, 88, 104, 106, 109, 157, 159, 219–221, 227–234, 236, 243, 244
informational content xxvi, xxxviii–xxxix, 14–17, 20–22, 28–31. 33, 49, 52, 55–56, 62, 64–66, 68, 88–93, 97–100, 106–110, 117–118, 120–121, 134–135, 147, 156, 159–160, 162, 169, 171–172, 188–194, 198–201, 203–205, 234, 236, 237, 238, 240, 242–244
input xxxviii, 2, 52, 87, 96, 102, 108, 115–143, 155–157, 161–162, 227, 228, 230, 232, 234, 238, 240
interlanguage 34–38
interpersonal xxv–xxvi, xxxi–xxxiv, 17, 20–22, 24, 29–30, 54–56, 113
interview xxii, 43–44, 50, 52, 53, 55–56, 109, 189, 201, 237
intonation xxviii, xxxi, 25–26, 157, 188, 194, 195, 227–237
instructional 98, 164
introspection 12–14
invitation 25–26, 29, 35, 217, 218
Ireland xxxiii, 83, 108
Irish 102, 109
Italian xxv

Japan 84, 87, 100
Japanese 36, 70, 86, 136
joke 11, 102, 107, 190, 193
judgement 22, 90–91

keyness 94–99, 103, 108
keywords 94–99, 103, 108, 115, 116

Lebanon 82, 84, 101, 109
lexical competence xxxix, 20–21, 30, 51, 57–58, 99, 104, 168, 236, 237, 242–244
lexicon xxxix, 2, 102, 124
lexis xxiv, xxix, 94–95, 152, 161
linguistic (competences) 20–21, 50–54, 89, 99, 104–106, 109, 112, 157–158, 173
(applied) linguistics xxiii–xxiv, 3, 19–37

macrofunctions 28–29, 99, 108, 171
mastery learning 41–43, 45–46, 69
matriculation 82–83
microfunctions 28–29, 90
modifiers 35, 37, 80, 129–131, 136–137
monologue 31, 52, 75, 108, 112, 159, 235–237
motivation xxv, xxxiii, xxxix, 173

native (speakers) xxxviii, 21, 30, 34–36, 52, 55, 63–64, 89, 104–106, 111, 172, 188–189
Netherlands xxviii
Norwegian xxxiii
notions (general & specific) xxiv, xxviii–xxxii, 10, 12, 18, 21, 27, 31–32, 34, 39–40, 43, 71, 75, 78, 81, 88, 113–114, 163, 167

objectives xxiii–xxvi, xxix–xxxiv, xxxvi–xxxvii, xxxix–xl, 2–3, 8, 21–22, 27, 39–51, 56–59, 69–71, 75, 87, 89, 94, 113, 149, 154–155, 161, 170–171
obligation 18, 26, 209, 213
occupational domain/workplace domain xxxv, 50, 120, 163
operations 18, 48–49, 62, 71, 152–154, 163–164
organisational competence xxxviii, 19, 76
organisers xxxiii, 200
outcomes xxvi, 41–44, 61, 69–70, 113–114, 147
output 99–108, 155–158

paragraphing 67–68, 76, 109–110
phonetic 102, 162
phonological 17, 20, 51
phrasal xxxix–xl, 125, 165
phrase xxxviii, 14, 21, 30, 34, 43, 66, 80, 98, 104, 105, 129–131, 136–138, 153, 164–165, 168, 187, 225, 226, 240
physiological (performance conditions) xxxv, 51–53
planning 30, 52–53
pluriculturalism xxi, xxv–xxvi, 36
plurilingualism xxi, xxv–xxvi, xxx, xxxiii, 36
politeness 15, 20, 26–27, 32, 34, 171, 215
polysemy xxvii
Portugal 60–61

positiveness (of descriptors) xxxvii–xxxviii, 40–41, 46–47
possessive 18
pragmalinguistic 34–36
pragmatic competence 1, 20, 30, 34–36, 50–53, 75, 87–88, 100–105, 112, 156–157
pragmatics xxxi, 19–20, 34–37, 120–121
praxeogram 28, 53
predictor variables 137–140
(language) processes xxxvi, 150, 161–162
production (spoken/written) xxxii, xxxv, xxxix, xli, 1–2, 15, 29–32, 35–37, 50–55, 75, 87–88, 96–99, 102, 108–113, 156–159, 173, 194–196, 234, 238, 240, 241
progression (functional/grammatical/lexical) xl–xli, 2–3, 28–53, 56–62, 75–79, 81–83, 99–112, 116–118, 165–168, 170–173, 203–226
propositions 13, 30–31, 51, 64, 90, 92, 109, 111, 116, 120, 127, 134–135, 236, 242, 244
proverbs 102
public domain/social domain xxxv, 53–55, 120, 150, 155, 161–165, 197–200
punctuation 76, 95, 100, 104, 190, 196
punning 16

qualifiers 60
quantifiers 18
questionnaires 36, 62

raising constructions 168
Rasch (measurement) 47, 62, 69
raters 44, 149, 154
ratings 44–51, 171–172
readability (formulae) 118–144
reception (spoken/written) xxxii, xxxv, 1, 51–54, 63–66, 88, 96–98, 100–103, 109–112, 116–119, 122–142, 192–194, 236–237, 242–244
register xxxi, 19–20, 32, 63, 67, 87–88, 100, 105, 111, 117, 191, 234, 242–244
regression 119
requests 12, 24, 28, 29, 33, 35–36, 53, 88, 92, 106, 117, 189, 190, 214, 215, 223, 230
rhetorical 20, 28, 105, 112, 120–121
routines xxiii, xxvii, xxxviii, 27, 31, 33, 36–37, 75, 99, 106, 107, 172

scales xxi–xxiii, xxx, xxxvii–xxxix, 2, 18, 22, 29–33, 40–62, 71, 75–77, 80, 85, 87–89, 96–113, 144, 148–153, 159–160, 164, 171

scaling xxi–xxiii, xxxvii–xxxviii, 47–48, 50–53
Scandinavian xxxiii
Scanning xxxii, 64, 100–103, 153, 162, 194
scores 36, 59, 62, 86, 124–142, 148–149
sentences xxii, xxiv, xxviii, xxxi, xxxviii–xl, 11, 16, 28, 47, 53–54, 104–105, 109–110, 118–142, 162, 168, 171, 225, 242–244
(textual) simplification 111, 120, 124–125, 132
Singapore 84, 105, 109
situational approach xxiv, 9
sociocultural xxxii, xxxix, 20–21, 25, 27, 173
sociolinguistic competence xxxii, 1, 19–20, 29, 37, 42, 50–53, 88, 99–101, 104–105, 112–113, 156–157, 171, 227–244
sociolinguistics 7, 11, 24, 37, 71, 121, 152, 159
sociopragmatics 34–36
softeners 35
speakers 11–18, 57–58, 63–67, 88–89, 112–113, 156–159, 170, 214, 226, 237
specialist (language use) 76, 78, 103, 107, 234, 240
specification xxvii–xxx, xxxix–xli, 2, 7–8, 15, 18, 21, 24–31, 42–43, 71, 77–82, 86–90, 107–108, 129, 148–149, 153, 155, 165–167, 187–202
speech xxxv, 7, 28–30, 40, 54–58, 62, 102, 109, 111–112, 170, 187, 191, 192, 194, 197, 199, 227–237
speech acts 11–16, 19, 34–38
standard setting 62, 148
standardisation 81–82
statements xxxvi–xxxix, 3, 22, 39–50, 51–53, 57–61, 67, 75–83, 86–94, 95–116, 129, 147–160, 165, 172–173
strategic competence 1, 19, 54, 99, 156
strategies xxxi–xxxii, xxxv, 15, 19, 32, 40, 50–54, 56–57, 100, 111, 150–151, 153, 156
subordination 17
summative (assessment) 44–46
Sweden 83, 109
Swedish xxxiii, 83, 109
Swiss xx, 47, 83, 96, 99, 101, 104–106, 108, 111
Switzerland xxiv, xxxiii–xxxiv, xxxvii, xl 8, 47, 83
syllabuses xxii, xxvi, xxviii, 1, 3, 9–10, 18, 22, 37–39, 79, 83–84, 86–88, 96, 104–109, 132, 165
syntax xxxviii, 35, 120, 123, 129–132, 137, 140–141, 142–143, 151–152, 171, 242, 243

Taiwanese 70

tasks xxxv–xxxvi, xxxviii, 36–50, 53–61, 67–72, 80, 81, 88, 89, 96–100, 106–108, 111, 115–116, 118, 122, 144, 147–153, 156–162, 165, 169, 171–172, 237

taxonomy xxxv–xxxvi, 13, 48

teachers xxii, xxv, xxviii–xxix, xxxiii–xxxiv, xxxviii, 3, 8, 10, 14, 38, 41–50, 53, 54, 61, 67–71, 103, 118, 152, 154, 174, 189, 193, 195, 199

teaching xxi–xxii, xxv, xxix, xxxiii–xxxvi, 1, 7–10, 16–19, 37, 41–43, 68–70, 77–82, 86, 118, 149, 161, 165, 189, 197

testers xli, 71, 79

testing xxviii, xxxiii, 36–38, 61–62, 70, 81, 120–124, 139–141, 149, 161, 195

tests xxix, xxxvi, xl–xli, 9, 36–38, 43, 45–46, 49–51, 54, 59–62, 70, 84–89, 99, 106, 110–112, 116–121, 132, 139, 144, 148, 172

texts xxii, xxvii–xxix, xxxii, xxxv–xxxvi, xxxviii, 2–3, 9, 11–17, 19, 27–28, 48–49, 51–56, 60, 62–71, 75–76, 87–90, 94–144, 147, 150–155, 157, 162–164, 171, 173, 190, 192–202, 222, 225, 227–244

textual 17, 19, 27, 29, 99, 101, 116, 124–136, 172, 190

themes xxxv, 3, 10, 59, 87–88, 94, 100, 106, 110, 114, 150, 155, 161–169, 188–202, 221, 222

tokens 123–132

tourist domain 57, 189, 192

training xxiii, xxv, xxviii, 86, 132, 148–149, 195

T–series xxii–xxxiv, xxxvii, xxxix, 2, 8, 15, 16, 18, 20–22, 24–28, 31–32, 39–40, 43, 71, 75, 82, 89–90, 165–168, 170–172

utterances xxxi–xxxii, 11–19, 25, 28, 30, 35, 53–54, 60, 162, 171, 187, 194, 225

vagueness (of language) xxxvii–xxxviii, 60, 149–150

vertical (aspect of CEFR) xxxvi–xxxvii, 49–50, 58–59

vocabulary xxii, xxvi–xxvii, xxxi, 2, 9–10, 32, 40, 51, 58, 66, 71, 78, 87–88, 99–101, 104–105, 109–112, 118, 120, 122–129, 143–144, 147, 151–152, 157, 163–166, 188, 190, 194, 196, 227–235, 242–244

word families 97–99, 126, 164–166

Speech acts and functions index

addressing 12–16, 23, 24, 52, 56–57, 99, 159, 190, 196,214 218–219. 234–235, 243–244
advising 91, 106, 117, 216
apologising 10, 26, 27, 35, 106, 212, 214
argument xxxviii, 22, 28, 29, 52, 64, 89–92, 99, 101, 106–112, 117, 118, 120, 157, 159, 171, 172, 188, 189, 193, 195–200, 227, 238–241
assertives 13, 207, 188, 189, 194, 207, 234

behabitives 13

commissives 13, 17
complaints 212, 232
concession 29, 111

declaratives 14, 168
directives 13, 14, 17, 28

excusive 54
exercitives 13
expositives 13
expressives 13–17

ideational 17–19
illocutionary 12–14, 17–20, 24, 34, 121
instructions 28, 33, 68, 117, 198, 214, 235, 237

interactional xxiv, 1,7, 17, 19, 30, 36, 51–57, 109, 110, 117, 121, 165–157, 159, 187–190, 227–233, 237–239
invitations 25–26, 29, 35, 217–218

joking 11, 101, 107, 190, 193

locutionary 12

perlocutionary 12
phatic 11, 15–17, 120

referential 15–17, 120
requesting 12, 24, 28, 29, 33, 35–36, 53, 88, 92, 106, 117, 189–190, 214–215, 223, 230

transactional xxiii, xxx–xxxi, 33, 52–55, 58, 163

suasion 20, 22, 27, 28, 32, 90, 91, 120, 214, 237
suggestions 26, 35, 91, 106, 214, 237
summarising 21, 53, 106, 109, 117–118, 197, 222

verdictives 13

Text type index

advertisements 16, 66, 197
articles 58, 64, 68, 98, 100, 107–111, 129, 144, 151, 152, 192, 192, 197, 240–244

essays 31, 52, 53, 58, 96, 98, 108, 110, 111

messages 52, 55, 66, 67, 76, 96, 162, 243–244

newspapers 65, 66, 68, 98, 107, 110–111, 143, 152, 164, 242–244

poetry 16, 96, 193
presentations 40, 95, 97, 98, 99

speeches 88, 98

textbooks xxii, xxviii–xxix, 9, 38, 43, 53, 71, 79–81, 83, 85, 98, 114, 122, 138, 197

Levels index

A1 xxxviii, xl, 30–31, 33, 48, 56–59, 66,
82, 86, 87, 122, 164, 166, 170–172,
203–204, 206, 208, 210, 212, 214, 216,
218, 220, 222, 224, 226
A2 xxxviii–xxxix, 29–33, 48, 58, 62, 65–66,
78, 82, 87, 117, 119, 122–135, 151, 166,
167, 171, 172, 203, 204, 206, 208, 210,
212, 214, 216, 218, 220, 222, 224, 226
alignment of 59, 86

B1 xxxviii–xxxix, 29–33, 48, 57–61,
64–65, 75, 76, 78, 82, 87, 108, 117, 119,
122–135, 151, 153, 166, 167, 170–172,
203, 204, 206, 208, 210, 212, 214, 216,
218, 220, 222, 224, 226
B2 xxxviii–xl, 29–33, 56, 58–60, 62–64,
76–77, 79–80, 82–83, 86–112, 116–119,
122–143, 153, 156, 159, 164, 166–167,
170, 171, 203–204, 206, 208, 210, 212,
214, 216, 218, 220, 222, 224, 226
basic user xxxvii–xxxviii
beginner xxx

C1 xxxviii–xl, 1–2, 29–33, 57–61, 63, 76–79,
82, 86, 87, 90, 94, 95, 98, 99, 101–102.
104, 106, 107, 110–112, 114–119,
122–144, 151, 153, 168, 171, 187–202
C2 xxxviii–xl, 1–2, 29–33, 49, 57, 58, 75–79,
82, 86, 90, 95, 96, 99, 101–102, 105,
108, 110–112, 114–119, 122–144, 166,
171–173, 187–191, 193, 197

effective operational proficiency 1
equivalence xxxix, 45, 86, 87

independent user xxxvii–xxxviii, 77
intermediate 43, 67, 85, 104–110, 122

mastery xxi–xxii, 1, 35, 41–43, 69, 99, 101,
102, 105, 107, 110, 112, 116, 119, 143,
187, 194

proficient user xxxvii–xxxviii, 1, 37, 77, 103,
116

Product index

Bogazici University 83
Bournemouth English Book Centre 80
Breakthrough xxxii–xxxiii, xxxvii, 2, 28, 32, 39–40, 78, 82, 148, 167–168, 170–171, 203–226

Coh–metrix 123–124, 131–134, 139, 141
Compleat Lexical Tutor 94

DIALANG 61–62, 67, 71, 75–77, 84, 152

Eiken 70, 84, 87, 106, 107
English Profile xxi, xxvii, xxxix, xl, 1–3, 10, 37–38, 40, 41, 50, 67, 69, 70, 71, 72, 75, 77, 78, 79, 81, 103, 112, 114, 115, 116, 119, 122, 125, 143, 144, 147–150, 152, 154–161, 165, 168–174
Eurocentres xxiv, xxxiv, 46
Eurybase 82
Eurydice 82

Follow Me! xxix
FREQUENCY (see RANGE)

Kontakte xxx
Kontaktschwelle xl, 24

Le Français Fondamental xxix
Linguapeace 87

Profile Deutsch xl, 70, 78, 187–202

RANGE 123–125
Rüschlikon xxiv, xxviii, xxxiii, xxxiv, 8, 11, 46

The British Council 79–80
Threshold xxi, xxvii–xxxiii, xxxvii, xxxix–xl, 2, 8, 10, 14, 15,16, 18, 20, 22–28, 31, 32, 39, 40, 71, 78, 82, 89–90, 135, 167, 203–226

Un Niveau Seuil xxix, xl, 24

Vantage xxxi–xxxii, xxxvii, xxxix, 2, 27–28, 31, 32, 40, 82, 102, 165, 167–168, 170–171, 203–226

Waystage xxx–xxxii, xxxvii, xxxix, 2, 28, 40, 82, 167, 203–226
Wordsmith Tools 123–124